Values in Sport

'2

How will sport keep pace with current scientific and biological advances? Is the possibility of the 'bionic athlete' that far away and is this notion as bad as it might first appear? Is our fascination with sport winners fascistoid? Questions such as these and many others are posed and examined by the contributors to this volume. Some are sceptical of future developments in sport and demand radical reforms to halt progress, others are more optimistic and propose that sport should adapt to new advances just as other realms of the cultural sphere have.

Some of the topics examined here, such as the genetic engineering of athletes and the significance of the public's fascination with sport winners, are being discussed for the first time, whilst others such as sex segregation, nationalism and doping are being revisited and reintroduced onto the agenda after a period of suggestive silence.

This book provides the reader with a deep insight into the moral and ethical value we place on sport in today's society. Challenging and demanding, its contributors urge us to think again about current sports practices and the future of sport as a cultural phenomenon.

Torbjörn Tännsjö is Professor of Practical Philosophy at Gothenburg University and has published extensively on moral philosophy, political philosophy and medical ethics.

Claudio Tamburrini is a Senior Researcher at the Department of Philosophy, Gothenburg University and the author of several international articles on issues of penal philosophy and sport philosophy.

Ethics and Sport

Series Editors: Jim Parry, *University of Leeds* and
Mike NcNamee, *Cheltenham and Gloucester College*

The Ethics and Sport series aims to encourage critical reflection on the practice of sport, and to stimulate professional evaluation and development. Each volume explores new work relating philosophical ethics and the social and cultural study of ethical issues. Each is different in scope, appeal, focus and treatment but a balance is sought between local and international focus, perennial and contemporary issues, level of audience, teaching and research application, and variety of practical concern.

Also available in this series:

Ethics and Sport
Edited by Mike NcNamee and Jim Parry

Fair Play in Sports Competition (forthcoming)
A Moral Norm System
Sigmund Loland

Spoilsports (forthcoming)
Understanding and Preventing Sexual Exploitation in Sport
Celia Brackenridge

Values in Sport

Elitism, nationalism, gender
equality and the scientific
manufacture of winners

Edited by Torbjörn Tännsjö
and Claudio Tamburrini

London and New York

First published 2000
by E & FN Spon
11 New Fetter Lane, London EC4P 4EE

Simultaneously published in the USA and Canada
by E & FN Spon
29 West 35th Street, New York, NY 10001

E & FN Spon is an imprint of the Taylor & Francis Group

© 2000 E & FN Spon; Chapter 11 © 1999 Kluwer Academic
Publishers

Typeset in Garamond by Taylor & Francis Books Ltd
Printed and bound in Great Britain by TJ International, Padstow,
Cornwall

British Library Cataloguing in Publication Data
A catalogue record for this book is available from the British
Library

Library of Congress Cataloging in Publication Data
Values in sport: elitism, nationalism, gender equality, and the scientific
manufacturing of winners/[edited by] Claudio Tamburrini and Torbjörn
Tännsjö.
    p.   cm. – (Ethics and sport book series)
    Includes bibliographical references and index.
    1. Sports–Moral and ethical aspects.   2. Sports–Social aspects.
    I. Tamburrini, Claudio Marcello.   II. Tännsjö, Torbjörn, 1946– .
    III. Series.
    GV706.3.V35   2000   99–40341
    796–dc21

ISBN 0–419–25360–2 (hbk)
ISBN 0–419–25370–X (pbk)

Contents

Contributors

Gunnar Breivik is Professor of Social Sciences at the Norwegian University of Sports and Physical Education in Oslo, Norway. His research interests encompass philosophy of sport, psychology of stress and risk taking, and sociology of values, and he has published contributions to journals and books in all these areas. He is former President of the Philosophic Society for the Study of Sport and is the present Rector of the Norwegian University of Sport and Physical Education.

Robert B. Butcher is Assistant Professor at Brescia College affiliated with the University of Western Ontario, Canada. He has published in the field of applied ethics, in particular sport ethics, business ethics, health/medical ethics and police ethics. His most recent publications are *Ethical Reasoning in Policing* (1998), co-authored with David R. Evans and 'Fair Play as Respect for the Game' (1998), co-authored with Angela J. Schneider for the *Journal of Philosophy of Sport*.

Nicholas Dixon is Associate Professor of Philosophy at Alma College, Michigan. He specialises in applied ethics and has published articles on such topics as handgun control, assisted suicide, abortion, civil disobedience, the adversary method, and sportsmanship.

Paul Gomberg teaches philosophy at Chicago State University. In his writing he develops Marxist criticisms of contemporary liberal moral and political philosophy.

Sigmund Loland is Professor of Sport Philosophy at the Norwegian University of Sports and Physical Education in Oslo, Norway. He has published in the fields of sport ethics, epistemological aspects of human movement, sport and the history of ideas, and alpine skiing technique. His most recent book is *Idrett, kultur, samfunn* (Sport, Culture, Society), a textbook published by Norwegian University Press in 1998.

Graham McFee is Professor of Philosophy at the University of Brighton. His major research interests include the philosophy of Wittgenstein, the problem of freewill, and aesthetics (especially the aesthetics of dance). Related interests include educational theory, especially arts education, physical education and dance education. His principal publications include 'The Surface Grammar of Dreaming' (Proceedings of the Aristotelian Society, 1994), as well as *Understanding Dance* (Routledge, 1992) and *The Concept of Dance Education* (Routledge, 1994). He is an active member of the British Society of Aesthetics and has served on its executive committee.

William J. Morgan is a Professor of Cultural Studies at the University of Tennessee. He has written extensively in the philosophy of sport and the social and political theory of sport, and his most recent book is *Leftist Theories of Sport: A Critique and Reconstruction*. He was editor of the *Journal of the Philosophy of Sport* from 1994 to 1998, and is currently a member of its editorial review board.

Christian Munthe is Associate Professor of Practical Philosophy at Gothenburg University. His research has been mainly concerned with the ethics of human reproduction, including issues about the morality of abortion, prenatal diagnosis and genetic testing. Presently, he is completing a book on the ethics of pre-implantation genetic diagnosis.

Angela J. Schneider is an Associate Professor in Kinesiology at the University of Western Ontario in London, Ontario. She is also the Assistant Dean, Ethics and Equity, for the Faculty of Health Sciences. She has numerous publications in the areas of applied philosophy and ethics in sport, including: drug use, gender equity, fair play, definitions of sport, and Olympic Studies. Her most recent publications are 'Fair Play as Respect for the Game' (1998), co-authored with Robert B. Butcher, and (1998) 'Doping-Kontrolle: eine ethische Analyse aus kanadischer Sicht', *Leistungssport* 5 (September): 38. Dr Schneider is also an Olympic silver medallist in rowing.

Berit Skirstad is an Associate Professor at the Norwegian University of Sport and Physical Education. She is a member of the Steering Group of European Women and Sport (EWS), a free-standing body created after the 1989 European Sport Conference to deal with questions related to women and sports. She has published articles, and edited books (in both English and Norwegian), on youth and sport.

Claudio Marcello Tamburrini is a Senior Researcher at the Department of Philosophy, Gothenburg University. He has published *Crime and Punishment?* (Ph.D. dissertation) and articles on penal philosophy and philosophy of sports. He has played professional soccer in Argentina.

Torbjörn Tännsjö is Professor of Practical Philosophy at Gothenburg University. He has published extensively on topics in moral philosophy, political philosophy and medical ethics. His most recent books are *Hedonistic Utilitarianism* and *Coercive Care: The Ethics of Choice in Health and Medicine*.

Series Editors' Preface

The Ethics and Sport series is the first of its kind in the world. Its main aim is to support and contribute to the development of the study of ethical issues in sport, and indeed to encourage the establishment of Sports Ethics as a legitimate discipline in its own right.

Whilst academics and devotees of sport have debated ethical issues such as cheating, violence, inequality and the nature and demands of fair play, these have rarely been explored systematically in extended discussion.

Given the logical basis of ethics at the heart of sport as a practical activity, every important and topical issue in sport has an ethical dimension – often the ethical dimension is of overwhelming significance. The series will address a variety of both perennial and contemporary issues in this rapidly expanding field, aiming to engage the community of teachers, researchers and professionals, as well as the general reader.

Philosophical ethics may be seen both as a theoretical academic discipline and as an ordinary everyday activity contributing to conversation, journalism and practical decision-making. The series aims to bridge that gap. Academic disciplines will be brought to bear on the practical issues of the day, illuminating them and exploring strategies for problem-solving. A philosophical interest in ethical issues may also be complemented and broadened by research within related disciplines, such as sociology and psychology, and some volumes aim to make these links directly.

The series aims to encourage critical reflection on the practice of sport, and to stimulate professional evaluation and development. Each volume will explore new work relating to philosophical ethics and the social and cultural study of ethical issues. Each will be different in scope, appeal, focus and treatment, but a balance will be sought within the series between local and international focus, perennial and contemporary issues, level of audience, teaching and research application and a variety of practical concerns. Each volume is complete in itself but also complements others in the series.

Sally Wride worked with us to develop the series and we gratefully acknowledge her input and enthusiasm.

Jim Parry, University of Leeds
Mike McNamee, Cheltenham and Gloucester College

Acknowledgements

This collection of articles, which comes at the beginning of a new millennium, is addressed to a wide public. The editors hope that the collection will contribute to putting the focus on relevant, but much-too-little-discussed value issues of sports practices. The variety of topics discussed, the fundamental character of the questions raised and the radically different approaches adopted by the authors are intended to deepen our understanding of the most important controversies relating to the question of whether sport will continue to exist as an important global cultural phenomenon. Taken together, the contributions provide the reader with deep insights into, and controversial views of, current sport practices and their possible (or impossible) future development. Radical arguments are given, for and against, such diverse themes as elitism, nationalism, gender distinctions, doping, and the genetic manufacturing of winners in sport.

The articles collected here are (with a few exceptions) published for the first time. They result from a conference on sports and values, held in 1998 in Gothenburg, Sweden, sponsored by the Bank of Sweden Tercentenary Foundation (which has also generously helped with the publication of this volume). The Gothenburg conference was extremely rewarding. Not only were interesting papers presented there, but many new discussions started as a result of their presentation. These discussions have been documented here in the strong conviction that this is the beginning rather than the end of such intellectual controversies.

Although most of the material for *Values in Sport* is new, some chapters develop themes of articles that have been previously published. We therefore thank the editors of the *Journal of the Philosophy of Sport* for kindly allowing us to reprint (in revised form) Chapters 1 and 2, and the editor of *Ethical Theory and Moral Practice* for allowing us to reprint Chapter 11; Sigmund Loland, 'Justice and game advantage in sporting games', *Ethical Theory and Moral Practice*, 2:2, pp. 159–78 ©1999 Kluwer Academic Publishers. We also thank the Bank of Sweden Tercentenary Foundation for the grant that made both the Gothenburg conference and this book possible.

Introduction

The stadium is crowded. The 110m hurdle race is coming to its decisive moment. The runners leave the last bend and approach the hurdles. As expected, the favourite runner leads the competition and holds a clear advantage over his closest challengers. He attacks the last obstacle, tries to jump, but miscalculates the distance and falls. Some precious tenths of a second are lost. It's too much time. The nearest opponent takes advantage of the unexpected situation, and, rapidly occupying the first position, crosses the finish line as a winner. The winning time means a new record for the discipline. The multitude is euphoric. They cheer for the winner, he raises his arms and addresses the public with the victory sign.

Most of us get involved in similar practices daily, either as active practitioners, as on-the-spot spectators, or in front of our television sets. Details apart, the scenery is always the same, whichever sport discipline we happen to watch. And we do watch sports events. Sports in general, and elite sport in particular, are cultural phenomena of great importance; both money and time are spent on them. However, to a surprising degree, these cultural phenomena seem to exist, and live their own life, beyond critical reflection. If we did reflect critically, we would realise that the future of sport as a cultural phenomenon, in a world of nationalistic and gender tensions, in a world of rapid scientific development, involving doping techniques and techniques of genetic engineering, is moot. And that the future of sport as a cultural phenomenon depends on matters of value, we would also realise. It depends on how we value sport, and it depends on the values presupposed by, or expressed in, sports events.

Sport, considered as a cultural phenomenon, is far from being morally innocent. This conviction is the common ground for the articles included in *Values in Sport*. Another common ground is a serious concern for the future of sport, both as an actual practice and as a cultural phenomenon. But that is where the agreement ends. The contributions presented here are marked by their antagonistic character. The authors' controversial views on the normative issues embedded in sport practices are difficult to reconcile, when not directly incompatible with each other.

Part I ('Elitism') begins with Torbjörn Tännsjö's highly provocative article on what actually goes on when public audiences express their admiration for the winner. What lies behind our cheers for the winner? Is our fascination for sport winners 'fascistoid'? According to Tännsjö, the enthusiasm we feel for the winner of a sports contest reflects admiration for the strongest, the winner in the genetic lottery. This fascination with strength is founded upon a value judgement. To be strong is to possess an important, though genetically determined, non-moral virtue. To lack this virtue is to be deficient from an evaluative point of view. So the other side of the medal, Tännsjö conjectures, when we cheer for the winner, is contempt for weakness, a central tenet of Nazi ideology.

Claudio Tamburrini finds in current sport practices some promising signs of a more sophisticated evaluative attitude, however. Drawing our attention to the fact that sport audiences often also express admiration for losing athletes displaying different excellences of character, he articulates a defence of professionalism and commercialism in elite sports, based on their beneficial effects on society.

Sigmund Loland sees in the perpetual demand for progress in sport a kind of impossibility theorem. Our phylogenetic potential is stable; as biological beings, our capacities for improving speed, explosivity and strength are limited. This means that elite sport is rapidly reaching its limit. Further development would presuppose medical, technological or genetic innovations and interventions. According to Loland, this is not a palpable alternative (something that is questioned in Part V). However, he says, there exists a possible solution: moderation in sports. According to Loland, in '... situations of choice, participants ought always to choose alternatives that increase the intensity and/or the complexity of the joy of sports among all parties engaged'. This is a theme taken up also by Tännsjö in Chapter 7.

Sports have since long been accused of promoting unsound nationalistic feelings – not only the physical aggression of rival fans and athletes, whose most conspicuous manifestation is the hooligan phenomenon, but even exacerbated chauvinism leading to war between countries has been charged to the account of sports. Part II of *Values in Sport* is concerned with the issue of whether sport competitions between national teams lead to this kind of deplorable nationalism. It might seem that, in a world plagued by ethnic contradictions and wars, the nationalism presupposed by, and expressed in, sports events should be problematic. But in Chapter 4 William Morgan presents an account of sports as a special kind of a people's narrative that unfolds their idiosyncratic social and moral character. His argument is that the creative character of this process, and its appropriation by new nations, has allowed emergent countries not only to 'beat colonialists at their own game', but also to transform the original emulation into a self-affirming practice.

Nicholas Dixon defends a conception of moderate patriotism that he sees as compatible with the demands of universal morality. In his view, the feeling of identification we have with our national teams, and the special concern we feel for their success on the playing field, is not only morally innocent, but can even be seen as a paradigm case of a laudable concern for people close to us.

In contradistinction to Morgan and Dixon, Paul Gomberg adopts a more skeptical stance to nationalism in his article. To the extent that sport expresses or presupposes nationalistic values, this is indeed problematic, he says, for there does not exist any innocent – let alone any positively valuable – kind of nationalism.

It is remarkable that within many sports sexual segregation is taken for granted. Does this mean that this is one of the few areas where sexual discrimination is morally acceptable or even mandatory? Or, does it mean that here we face one more prejudice to be abolished? In Part III, which discusses gender equality in sports, Torbjörn Tännsjö wants to abolish all kind of divisions in sport based on sex differences. If Sigmund Loland's ideas about moderation are adopted, he claims, this suggestion may prove quite reasonable. And, if Loland's proposal is not adopted, women ought to turn their backs on elite sports, rather than compete against each other in masculinity. He also claims that, if sex difference is upheld, there should be testing for sex (but perhaps also for other chromosomal variations such as Klinefelter's syndrome).

Gender tests is the focus of Berit Skirstad's contribution. She discusses in detail how gender tests are actually undertaken within sports, and rejects this system on the ground that it is degrading for female athletes.

Angela Schneider, who has herself practised sports on an elite level (she was an Olympic medallist in 1984), goes to some length in an attempt to see to what extent Tännsjö's radical proposal can be accepted. However, she does not follow him to his logical conclusion. Some sexual discrimination will be needed within sports, at least in the near future. The problem with Tännsjö's proposal, according to Schneider, is that it is utopian. In a world that is fair, and where there is no systematic discrimination on the basis of sex, he would be right. But we do not live in that world. 'In our world, excluding women from the publicity that comes from the highest levels of sporting achievement would merely serve to reinforce women's systemic subservience to men', Schneider concludes. But Schneider, too, is skeptical of medical gender tests within sports. Just like Skirstad, she leaves it an open question as to how sex (or gender) should be established in a competitive sports context.

Schneider's own main criticism of the gender bias within sports is somewhat differently put. She wants to prepare the ground for an account of women's sports centred on sportswomen's *own* narratives and experiences. The ideal sportsman coincides with the figure of the male warrior, she tells us, but is incompatible with the role traditionally imposed on women. And it is up to the women within sports to bring about the necessary change themselves.

Part IV is about the rules of the game and, in particular, about the appropriate role of chance and notions such as spoiling in sport. Here values internal to sport practices are being discussed. According to Sigmund Loland, there is a place for chance in sport. The idea is that the basic goal of games is the thrill and excitement of practising them; games have value in themselves. This can be called the ludic (from Latin *ludus*, 'play') position. A certain influence of chance in terms of pure procedural justice or lotteries makes games more exciting. Luck that works more or less randomly on the outcome, and outside the participants' control, adds to the unpredictability of the game. Chance or luck is not just an acceptable, but also a desirable, part of games.

Gunnar Breivik – a colleague of Loland's at the Norwegian University of Sports – argues in his turn for eliminating chance from sports competitions. In his view, the excitement of sport contests depends on the uncertainty, as distinct from the arbitrariness, of their outcome. This goal could be achieved by more even sport competitions, through the introduction of further class divisions, such as height categories in basketball.

Graham McFee suggests that, besides rules within sports, which lend themselves to a straightforward *application* by referees, there also exist something similar to what Ronald Dworkin, an American philosopher of law, has called legal 'principles'. These principles can and should inform the decisions of a referee. McFee's discussion is focused on the notion of 'spoiling' in cricket.

Part V asks about the appropriate role of science in sports; in particular, whether the ban on performance-enhancing substances is justified. Does it imply a violation of the athlete's autonomy? Is the ban required to ensure fair conditions of competition? After a thorough criticism of the traditional justifications for doping bans, Angela Schneider and Robert Butcher deliver an alternative, game-theoretical argument to support restrictions in the use of performance-enhancing substances, which are intended to strengthen athletes' decision-making power. Schneider and Butcher believe that, as rational agents unwilling to take unnecessary risks in their endeavours, athletes might be able to reach an agreement concerning which drugs should be banned from sport competitions.

In straightforward opposition to Schneider, Claudio Tamburrini proposes in Chapter 14 that doping bans should be lifted from professional, elite sports. Starting from the assumption that sports are a profession like any other, he argues strongly for the unreasonableness of submitting sport practitioners to restrictions we do not find in other areas of professional life.

But doesn't doping belong to that class of controversial issues that current technological progress will make obsolete even before they are settled, when genetic engineering is in the offing? This is the impression the reader gets from Christian Munthe's thought-provoking chapter on genetic manipulation and pre-selection of individuals in sports. After having stated what it is presently possible to do in the field, and what will probably be possible to achieve, he provides us with a thorough scrutiny of the objections to producing individuals genetically adapted to sports activities. Munthe's article would have been labelled as science-fictional only a few years ago, but today it gives us a glimpse, although obviously not a comforting one, of the direction in which sports are heading in the near future.

So, what is the future of sport? What about sport as a widespread practice, what about sport as a cultural phenomenon? Will it survive the strains exerted upon it by nationalistic and gender contradictions, or by technological advances allowing for more efficient doping techniques, and even for the genetic design of winners?

There is no unanimity on these points among the contributors to this volume. While some – including one of the editors – are skeptical, or argue that the continued existence of sports, at least as a sound cultural phenomenon of some importance, requires radical reform of current practices (allowing, for example, for more moderation), others – including the other editor – are straightforwardly optimistic. Nationalism, at least if tempered, is positive; sexual discrimination (at least in some places) is natural; and both doping and genetic engineering are substantial blessings.

It is up to the reader to decide which stance is the most reasonable to adopt.

Gothenburg, May 1999
Claudio Tamburrini and Torbjörn Tännsjö

Part I

Elitism

Chapter I

Is it fascistoid to admire sports heroes?

Torbjörn Tännsjö

Introduction

Looking forward at the beginning of a new millennium to the coming Olympic Games in Sydney, I try to recollect what happened last time, down in Atlanta. How did I react? I realise that once again I was swept away with enthusiasm and admiration for those heroic athletes, who had stretched the limits of what is physically possible for humans to achieve. Some have run faster than anyone has done before; this is true of Michael Johnson. Others have excelled and shown that, contrary to what should have been expected, they are – still – invincible. This is true of the greatest of them all, Carl Lewis. My query is this: is my enthusiasm for Johnson, Lewis and all the other athletic heroes respectable? Upon closer examination, my answer is *no*, my enthusiasm is not respectable. On the contrary, it is of a fascistoid[1] nature. So the problem is really what to do about it. The problem is pressing, for my attitude towards the Games is not exceptional: I share it with a great many other people who walk this planet. This is why the Games are so widely broadcast.

Many people have pointed out that there is something unhealthy in much of the public interest in team sports on an elite level. There was a time in many European countries when the Workers' Movement fought actively against the growing focus on sports. This concern has withered, but the rationale behind it remains relevant; in fact, team sports have often been used by nationalist governments to create a chauvinist zeal in their own populations. This zeal has rendered easier the formation of totalitarian government, the oppression of minorities at home and imperialist adventures abroad. National sports teams have become emblems of their respective nations. These facts are rather obvious. It is also plain that some of the interest that most people take in elite sports events is nourished by such nationalistic sentiments, and this interest as such reinforces the nationalism. This is indeed a vicious circle, and it is the main concern of Chapter 6, written by Paul Gomberg. But what about the public interest in the individual athletes in the Olympics? Should that be condemned because it reinforces an unhealthy nationalism?

To some extent it certainly does. Even individual athletes may become the target of these kinds of sentiments. Johnson and Lewis have reinforced US nationalist sentiments. I am, on my part, more interested when a Swede succeeds in the Olympics than when someone else does. But this cannot be the only source of my interest in the Olympic Games. For my main interest is in the achievements of people like Johnson and Lewis. So perhaps much (the main part) of my admiration for their achievements is, after all, respectable? Maybe much of the general interest taken in the Games is respectable?

If this were the case, there would be room for optimism. For it seems to be part of the received wisdom that nationalism within sports withers. When big business in the form of international enterprises enters the arena, in the manner of sponsoring, advertising, and selling and buying television rights, national governments have to go. Often, the foreign NHL professionals do not bother to play with their respective national teams. Instead of nationalism and interest, on the part of the public, in one's 'own' team, admiration comes for the achievement of the outstanding individual. Local teams turn into corporations. And these corporations are seen as places where the outstanding individual can excel. However, this interest in the achievement of the outstanding individual is really no better than our (perhaps outmoded) nationalistic interest in the fate of 'our' own team. Or, so I will argue in this chapter.

My thesis here is that our admiration for the achievements of the great sports heroes, such as the athletes who triumph at the Olympics, reflects a fascistoid ideology. While nationalism may be dangerous, and has often been associated with fascism, what is going on in our enthusiasm for individual athletic heroes is even worse. Our enthusiasm springs from the very core of fascist ideology: admiration for strength and contempt for weakness.

Note that my thesis is not that there is anything fishy about the motives of the athletes themselves. I say nothing about this. Nor do I condemn those who organise sports events, those who train young people to become members of the athletic elite, or those who profit from the Games, and so forth. In the present context, the *exclusive* target of my criticism is what goes on within the enormous worldwide public, watching sports, usually through television, taking advantage of sports as a cultural phenomenon. My interest is in the values entertained by you and me; we who tend, over and over again, to get carried away by such events as the Olympic Games.

Traditional team sports on an elitist level

Before developing my main argument, let me briefly comment on why it is a bad thing to have nationalistic values expressed and reinforced by publicly broadcast sports events, a topic discussed in Part II. Even if this is a kind of danger that is becoming less pressing, it might be interesting to reflect on what it is we are getting rid of when it withers. When we see this more clearly, we are on firmer ground in our investigation of the new kind of danger that we exchanged for the old one.

The main problem with nationalism is its orientation towards abstract symbols – the flag, the team (seen as an emblem); yes, even the abstractly conceived 'nation'. When such entities are celebrated, the individual tends to become replaceable. The nation can get strong, it can be successful, even if every one of its citizens suffers. This individual suffering need not matter in the very least to the nationalistic ideology. In a similar vein, when the team becomes a representative of the nation, *its* individual members tend to become replaceable. When our football or soccer heroes are successful, we cheer for them. When they fail 'us', we despise them.

This way of regarding our sports stars as representatives of our country, conceived of abstractly, fits with a common view of the military force. It may easily spread and permeate all the relations between people in a country. Young women are treated as potential instruments that shall safeguard the strength and survival of the nation, and young men are viewed merely as potential soldiers.

One might object that this is only a description. What is actually *wrong* with celebrating abstract symbols? Why not stress the interests of the nation rather than the interests of individual beings? Why not stress the survival of a race or species rather than the survival of the individuals that make it up?

The answer, as far as I can see, is that abstract entities as such are of no value. What matters, ultimately, from a moral point of view, is what happens to individuals, capable (at least) of feeling pleasure and pain. Only *individual* values are genuine. In order to be good, intrinsically, something must be good *for* an individual, capable of feeling (at least) pleasure and pain.

This is not to say that no positive examples of nationalism exist: the US struggle, say, for national independence, was a worthy aim. But in those times nationalism had a content. It was possible to see, over and above the flags and the marches, a point to the struggle, a point relating, in the final analysis, to respectable individual interests (in avoiding oppression, of various different kinds). Even so, the flags and the marches are dangerous things: when the struggle is over they tend to stay with us and live their own life in the form of fetishes.

I will not try to argue the point in the present context that all respectable values are individual. I have discussed it in detail in my recent book, *Hedonistic Utilitarianism* (1998). The point is simply taken for granted. This means that if someone claims that the strength of his or her nation is of value in itself, he or she makes a value mistake. This mistake is dangerous if it leads to actions where individual interests actually get sacrificed for the sake of abstract, symbolic values. And this kind of sacrifice is the rule rather than the exception when a nationalistic ideology gets a firm hold of the members of a nation – in particular if the nation in question does not face the least *threat* from any other nation.

Even if this is conceded, it could be argued that the kind of nationalism fostered by the public interest in team sports events is innocent. It might even be argued that nationalism in relation to sports is a good replacement for political nationalism, i.e. the kind of nationalism that is truly dangerous. It is better if people live out their nationalism in front of their television sets, or in the seats around the sports arenas, than if they channel their nationalism through political parties and movements, for only in the latter case does their nationalism pose a real threat to important values.

I do not believe that this argument is tenable. The nationalism fostered by our interest for our 'own' national team, and the nationalism we exhibit in the political arena, tend to reinforce each other. In particular, in periods where political nationalism is strong, what happens in the sports arenas tends to become politically important. There is only a small step from being a soccer hooligan to joining a fascist organisation modelled on the Hitler Youth. I will not develop this line of thought, however. The reason for not developing it has already been adumbrated. I think the common observation, that nationalism is becoming less and less important in relation to sports, is correct.

But why is nationalism within sports becoming less important? This has to do with commercialisation and internationalisation. The best sportsmen and the best teams earn enormous amounts of money. They can afford to allow themselves a considerable independence from political authorities and interests. They can take liberties with their own sports organisations. They rely on their own impresarios rather than on the elected authorities of the Olympic Committee. However, when the old nationalism gives way, it gives way to something no less problematic. Let me now develop this main theme of this chapter.

Contempt for weakness

Nationalism, or chauvinism, has sometimes been thought to be a defining trait of Nazism. However, in his seminal book, *Our Contempt for Weakness*, Harald Ofstad has argued, convincingly in my opinion, that the nationalism of the Nazis was only a contingent fact. Yes, Hitler did put the German nation before all other nations, and he put the so-called Aryan race before all other races. However, the hard core of Nazism was something different – a contempt for weakness. This is shown by Hitler's reaction when the Third Reich broke down. To Hitler, the defeat showed not that there was something basically wrong with the Nazi ideology, but that there was something basically wrong with the German Nation. The German Nation had proved to be weak rather than strong, so eventually Hitler came to feel contempt for it (Ofstad 1989: 24).

My thesis is this: when we give up nationalism, as a source of our interest in elite sports activities, when we give up our view of individual sportsmen and teams as representatives of 'our' nation, when we base our interest in sports on a more direct fascination for the individual winners of these events – we move from something that is only contingently associated with Nazism (nationalism) to something that is really at the core of Nazism (a contempt for weakness).

Obviously, in my argument a premise is missing. It is one thing to admire the person who wins, who shows off as the strongest, but another thing entirely to feel contempt for those who do not win (and turn out to be weak). In order to reach my conclusion, I need the premise that, in doing the one thing, we cannot help but do the other. But to me this is how things stand. When we celebrate the winner, we cannot help but feel contempt for those who do not win. Admiration of the winner and contempt for the loser are only two sides of the same Olympic medal.

This is not to say that those who win the contest feel contempt for those who do not. It is one thing to compete and to want to win, and quite a different thing to admire, as a third party, the winner. My argument relates to those who *view* sports, not to those who perform. Performers may well look upon each other as colleagues. They could well feel that they are merely doing their job. The winner may well feel respect for the loser. Or, the winner may entertain any other feelings. It is not part of my project to speculate about this. My argument does not relate to the responses of the athletes, but to *our* responses to what they are doing. We, who comprise the public *viewing* the sports events, are the ones who admire the winner and feel contempt for the loser. If we are sincere in our admiration, and we often are, we cannot *help* but feel contempt for the losers. For simple phenomenological reasons we would be *inconsistent* if we did not feel any kind of contempt for the losers, once we sincerely admire the winner.

To see why this is so we should think critically about *why* we admire those who excel in the Olympics. Our feeling is based on a value judgement: those who win the game, if the competition is fair, are *excellent*, and their excellence makes them *valuable*, which is why we admire them. Their excellence is, in an obvious manner, based on the strength they exhibit in the competition. And the strength they exhibit is 'strength' in a very literal sense of the word. And it is a kind of strength with a firm genetic basis. The winners are born winners, or, at least, they are born with a capacity for becoming winners.

But our value terms are comparative. So if we see a person as especially valuable, because of his excellence (he is a winner in the genetic lottery), and if the excellence is a manifestation of strength (in a very literal sense), then this must mean that other people, those who do not win the fair competition (i.e the losers in the genetic lottery), those who are comparatively weak, are *less* valuable. The most natural feeling associated with *this* value judgement is contempt, which is expressed in the popular saying, 'Being second is being the first of the losers.'

Contempt can take very different forms, of course, and it may be useful here to distinguish between three forms of contempt:

- Contempt can take an *aggressive* form, as was the case with the Nazis. They wanted to exterminate weakness (by exterminating those who were weak).
- Contempt can take a *negligent* form. We try not to think at all about those for whom we feel contempt. We 'think them away'. We treat them as nonexistent. We do not care about them at all.
- Contempt can assume a *paternalistic* form. We want to 'take care' of those 'poor creatures' for whom we feel contempt.

Common to all these reactions, all based on the idea that some individuals have less value than others, is a tendency not to treat those who are considered less valuable with respect. They are not treated as full persons.

The surer we are that 'we' are among the strong ones, among those who are valuable, the more prepared we are to adopt the paternalistic reaction to those whom we consider weak. And the more we fear that we might really belong to the weak ones, the stronger our inclination to treat the weak ones negligently, as nonexistent, or even aggressively, with hatred – we want to exterminate them, we want to *make* them nonexistent.

This is what is going on when enthusiastically we stay up half the night watching the athletes compete. To be sure, to some extent what takes place does so only in a symbolic way. We admire Carl Lewis for his excellence and we feel some contempt for those who fall behind. However, we know that we would never stand a chance of beating Carl Lewis. Does this mean that we realise we are among those who are weak? It means, probably, that we fear this. But many of us believe we have other skills that compensate for those Carl Lewis possesses. Even if we are not physically as strong as he is, we may excel in ways that are in our own opinions more valuable than 'strength' in the literal sense of the word.

But what if we do not? I believe that some of us may fear that we might fail on *all* relevant accounts. Those of us who do are the people who cheer loudest for people like Carl Lewis.

What respects are relevant? It is not possible to answer this question in a general manner. The Nazis had one (rather vague) notion about what kind of strength was important, but we may have a different view. In fact, each person may have his or her own opinion about this. But there is really no *need* to give a general answer to the question as to what kind of strength it is important to exhibit. As soon as we hold one opinion or another about it, we are vulnerable to the kind of argument I want to level in this chapter. A person who is eager to be strong, who is prepared to feel contempt for those who are weak, and who fears that he or she may belong to those who are weak – any person who feels that those who are 'strong' (in any sense) are better than those who are 'weak' – is open to the criticism that he or she has fallen prey to the central Nazi ideology.

The kind of betterness I am thinking of is relevant to questions of praise and blame. Person S is 'better', in the relevant sense, than Person P if, and only if, S is more praiseworthy, admirable or deserving of the good things in life than P. This notion is given a fascistoid twist when betterness is conceived of in terms of *strength*.

But must we feel contempt for those who are less successful (valuable)? Can we not just admire them less? I think not, for there are normative aspects of the notion as well. Those who are less valuable have to stand back when some goods (and evils) are to be distributed. And when resources are scarce, treating one person well is tantamount to treating another person badly. This is clearly true in a sports situation. The setting is competitive; an Olympic medal (and the money and reputation that go with them) is a scarce resource.

To make sure we do not get carried away by our admiration for winners we ought to resist the very idea of excellence and betterness. In particular, we ought to resist the idea that excellence consists of *strength*.

The idea of excellence as a matter of strength of some kind is an idea with deep roots in the history of philosophy, and played a crucial role in the ethical thinking of Aristotle. Yet an ethical theory can easily be constructed without having recourse to it. The utilitarian tradition, for example, bears witness to this.

Of course, even a utilitarian must concede that a person can be more or less virtuous, depending on whether he or she has a character conducive to general happiness in society. Such a person may very well be praised. There is a point in praising him or her, since this may encourage others to develop the same kind of character. And people who behave badly towards others may well be despised on this ground, which may teach them a lesson. There is a reason for distributing praise and blame in this manner, for doing so may make a difference, since the target of this kind of praise and blame is a moral characteristic, a characteristic that can be adopted or developed if we decide to do so. Our moral character is open to change. But there is no similar point in praising strength, since strength, in the relevant sense, is not a moral quality. The capacity for strength is genetically determined, so we cannot gain strength if we do not already have the genes for it – obviously there is no point in praising a person for his or her good genes. On the contrary, when we do – when we cheer for the winner of an Olympic contest – we approach the core of the Nazi ideology. We cannot truthfully deny that we possess the notion that strength is a proper ground for admiration, a notion that underlies our fascination for the winners of sports events, but we ought to resist such an idea.

Objection: similarities in the arts and science

Those who are prepared to admit that there is something to the argument stated above may still want to protest. They may want to argue that, even if there is something fishy about the reaction of the sports public to athletic achievements, it is unfair to single out sports for exclusive concern. After all, even within science and the arts we meet with the same phenomenon. Some people exhibit an unusual scientific or creative skill (strength). They make important contributions to science or create valuable pieces of art. They are then met with admiration. Doesn't that mean we value these persons, in a manner similar to the way we value successful athletes? And, if we do, doesn't this mean we think of those who are less successful in these areas as less valuable? Do we not exhibit contempt for weakness, when, for example, we give Nobel prizes to some 'outstanding' people?

I consider this argument sound, at least to some extent. And to the extent that it *is* sound, we ought to be ashamed of ourselves. But I think it sound only to *some* extent. For when we become enthusiastic about scientific and cultural achievements, we *need* not have scientists or artists as the focus of our attention. We can admire Wittgenstein's theories and Mozart's operas without feeling that Wittgenstein and Mozart are valuable persons. We can value the *products* of their ingenuity, but not necessarily their genius. We can say truthfully that what they produced is of the utmost value, but still retain the view that *they* are not more valuable than anyone else. They are merely *instrumental* to things of importance in themselves.

Sure, even within science and the arts there are ugly manifestations of the phenomenon I have criticised within sports. Some people tend to get carried away with their admiration for lonely, heroic 'geniuses' in the development of human science and art. Philosophy is not free of this phenomenon. There are people who speak with admiration of philosophers such as Nietzsche, Heidegger and Wittgenstein, not because of any clear thoughts they have absorbed from the writings of these philosophers, but because they feel confident that these philosophers are especially 'deep' and 'inspired' thinkers. All this, like the actual Nazi ideology, is part of the legacy of the romanticism of the nineteenth century. However, while this phenomenon within science and the arts may be seen as a kind of corruption, it belongs in a more essential way to sports.

We can and we ought to admire the *products* of skilful scientists and artists, not the persons themselves, at least not because of their skill (perhaps some of them deserve our admiration because of their moral qualities, but Wittgenstein is not among those). However, we cannot help but admire the winning athletes themselves, or else give up our interest in watching sport.

Or, can we? Why not consider the sports as simply a (very popular) part of human culture, where it is the results (products) of the individual achievements that count?

Objection: we admire results, not athletes

I believe that there may be something to the objection that sport is not very different from art. In both cases there is excitement over the results of people's strivings. However, while the results are often, and should always be, the main focus of our attention within the arts, sports are different. Certainly, there is an aesthetic aspect even to sport. Some people are met with admiration not only because of their strength, but also because of the beauty with which they perform. Juantorena ran more beautifully than anyone before him. Why not say that it is the beauty of his running we admire, rather than the man himself? We admire the beauty in his running in the same way that we admire the beauty in a Mozart piano concerto.

This line of argument is tenable to some extent, but the Juantorena example is not a very good one, for had he not also once been the fastest we would not have remembered him purely for the beautiful way in which he ran. In the final analysis, whoever breaks the tape is the person who counts. But in some team sports, such as soccer, the aesthetic dimension may be seen as more important. I believe it may be of considerable importance, particularly among skilled audience members. After a match, they can discuss endlessly the beauty in a single rush, irrespective of the outcome of the match in which it took place. However, in the final analysis even *their* interest in the aesthetics of the play tend to be secondary to the outcome of the match. During the Chinese Cultural Revolution, there was a period when soccer competitions were reviewed with no mention of the final outcome (i.e. the score). This policy met with little approval (at least, among the majority of the sports public), and soon had to be changed.

Roughly speaking, then, we may say that, though there is room in science and the arts for admiration both of scientists and artists for their skill (their metaphorical 'strength') and for their results, within sports there is room only for admiration of performers. The 'results' they produce are not genuine; they are mainly results of measurements, which are intended, first of all, to establish who won and, even more importantly, who was the best among those who competed. So winning (a fair competition) is only a means, a way to prove excellence. What we admire in sports is really the excellence shown by the winner.

To remove our admiration for the winner of the genetic lottery, who has proved his or her superiority in a big sports manifestation, and you take away most of our interest in the manifestation. This is true in particular for those of us who are not experts in the field, and who tend to get carried away only now and then, when we are informed by media that something remarkable is going on in a sports arena (the Olympic Games, for example).

But could we not argue that what we admire is not really the *excellence* of the winner, but what the winner has achieved, *given* his or her natural endowments? And wouldn't this kind of reaction on our part be morally more acceptable?

There is a grain of truth in this objection – a grain of truth explaining that there is a public interest in such things as female competition, competition between seniors, competition between handicapped persons, and so forth. When someone wins the Olympics for handicapped persons, and we admire him or her for winning, we admire the achievement (given the constraints). Despite the obstacles, this person made quite an achievement, we concede. However, the relatively weak public interest in such competitions, as compared to the interest in competitions of the absolute elite, shows that this kind of public interest in sports is of minor importance.

In fact, I suspect that there is even an element of contempt for weakness underlying many people's interest in this kind of handicap sport – but it takes a paternalistic form. We do not take those who perform in handicap competitions seriously. We encourage them to go on, but only in order that they develop into something less worthy of our contempt. In any case, if we are forced to choose, what we (most of us) really want to watch are competitions involving the *absolute* elite, not the Olympics for handicapped people.

Moreover, even if we are prepared to admire people who have worked hard, at least if they succeed in the competition (and the ability to work hard need not be anything that has to be explained with reference to genes), I believe that we will have added admiration for a person who excels *without* having worked hard. If a middle-aged member of the audience who has never exercised unexpectedly walked down from the stadium and joined the Olympic 10,000m race and, because of superior natural talent, defeated all the finalists, the success would be formidable. Our admiration for this person would be unlimited. So, basically, it is talent (which can be genetically explained), not achievement, that we admire above all else. The point of the contest is to show who has the most superior talent.

Furthermore, the training of top athletes has now reached a point where all the best athletes train in an optimal fashion (given the scientific knowledge at hand). This means that moral characteristics, such as a readiness to work hard in order to obtain excellence, is of no decisive importance. All who compete try hard to become the best. It is the genetic lottery, not their ambition, that decides who will succeed.

This elitism of ours is also revealed by the way we react to doping: we want the competition to be fair. We are not prepared to admire Ben Johnson only because he has run 100m faster than anyone before him. Why? We suspect that Carl Lewis is genetically more fit than Ben Johnson. This is why we condemn Ben Johnson. He cheated.

But how do we know that Carl Lewis did not cheat as well? Perhaps he was only more clever and got away with it. If doping were allowed, we would avoid *this* problem. We would not need to fear that the winner was not the strongest individual. If everybody were free to use whatever drugs he or she finds helpful, then the crucial test, the competition, would show who is most fit. The competition would then become fair.

For this reason, it is not at all implausible that doping – the deliberate use of drugs intended to enhance our strength – will fairly soon be permitted. At least, it is plausible to assume that drugs that do not pose any threat to the health of those who use them will be allowed. This seems only an extrapolation of a development that has already taken place. After all, there was a time when training was looked upon with suspicion. No one questions training today, and all athletes engage in it. Then came a time when *massive* training, on a professional basis, was condemned; I can vividly recollect the disdain with which swimmers from Eastern Germany were regarded by the Western media during the 1960s. These days are also gone. Today all successful athletes train on a professional and scientific basis. To the extent that all have the same resources at their disposal (an ideal we are far from having realised, of course, because of social differences and differences between nations), the competitions remain fair. But if training, even on a professional and scientific basis is acceptable, then why not accept doping as well, at least so long as the drugs used are not especially dangerous to the user?

If we were to permit such performance-enhancing drugs, we would no longer need to entertain the uneasy suspicion that the winner used prohibited drugs and managed to get away with it. We could then watch the games in a more relaxed manner.

A special problem, of course, is posed by the possibility of genetic engineering. What if those who win the Olympic Games in some not-too-distant future are not winners in a natural genetic lottery, but have been genetically *designed* to do what they do? Would we still be prepared to stay up at night to watch them perform? Would we still be prepared to admire those who make the best achievements? Would we still be prepared to cheer for the winners?

This question is discussed in Chapter 15. My conjecture, which is not shared by Christian Munthe, its author, is that we would not. Interestingly enough, then, if I am right in my conjecture, genetic engineering may come to pose a threat, not only to elitist sport but also to the fascistoid ideology that I claim underlies our interest in such sports.

Objection: contempt for weakness is human nature

A fourth objection to my thesis that our admiration for sports heroes is at its core fascistoid needs to be addressed. Is not our admiration for strength, and a corresponding contempt for weakness, simply natural? Are these feelings, moreover, not natural as well? In that case, is not a criticism of them misplaced? Since our nature is given to us by evolution, and since that nature dictates that we admire strength and feel contempt for weakness, it hardly seems fair to criticise the possession and expression of these kinds of feelings.

This objection is flawed. But it renders necessary some important distinctions. It may be true that most of us are, by nature, competitive. We compete with each other and we enjoy doing so. But there is nothing wrong in this, or, at least, this competitiveness is not the target of my criticism. The competitiveness might go to an unsound extreme in certain circumstances, of course, but I do not intend to say that our competitiveness, as such, is immoral. It engenders important achievements, and it is a source of excitement and joy. It is also, of course, a source of disappointment and dissatisfaction. However, this is only as it should be – without *some* disappointment and dissatisfaction, our lives would feel rather empty. I can readily concede this, for my criticism in the present context is not directed against competitiveness as such, nor to competitiveness in sports. I accept that scientists compete in a struggle to be the first to solve a certain problem, and I accept that athletes compete to win an important race. What I protest against is the admiration we show for the winners, be they scientists or sports heroes – and the corresponding contempt we feel for the losers. This reaction of *ours*, not the natural pride felt by *the winner himself or herself*, is immoral. And, the stronger our enthusiasm for the winner (and the stronger our corresponding contempt for the loser), the more immoral our reaction.

However, isn't this admiration for the winner, and the corresponding contempt for the loser, also only natural? Well, this may depend on what we mean by calling a disposition 'natural'. Here we need another distinction.

One way of talking about 'natural' dispositions is this. A certain disposition is 'natural' if nature (evolution) has provided a species with it in the form of a blind *instinct*. If this is how the disposition is given to the species, then there is no room for blame when individual members of the species act on it. There is no point in blaming the lion for preying on the antelope, for example. Under the circumstances, the lion can't help doing what it does; nor can it help finding itself under the circumstances.

Another way of understanding the idea that a certain disposition is 'natural' is as follows. Evolution has provided the species with the disposition, but not as a blind instinct. Individual members of the species tend to act on it, of course. And there exists a good evolutionary explanation for *why* they do. However, sometimes they do not. When they don't, we need an explanation for this fact, an explanation cast not in terms of evolutionary biology but in cultural or psychological terms.

It seems highly implausible that our admiration for strength and contempt for weakness is natural in the former sense. Human beings are not driven by instinct when they cheer for the winners of the Olympics. If people choose not to do so, then they often succeed. Some people do choose, for one reason or another, not to join in, when public hysteria is raised by main sports events. And they succeed in not joining in. So this is a possible course of action.

However, it might well be that we need to explain why they do not join in, and the explanation may have to be cast in psychological or cultural terms. For snobbish reasons, say, they do not want to go with the crowd. Be that as it may, they *can* stay out of the events and they *do*.

So it might well be that our admiration for strength and our contempt for weakness, exhibited most prominently in our reaction to sports, is natural in the sense that it has been given to us by evolution – it takes education of some kind to avoid developing it. From an evolutionary perspective, it might have been advantageous to show contempt for weak individuals. It might have been advantageous to cheer for those who are skilled in aspects that relate to human survival. To borrow a phrase, 'If you can't beat them, join them.' In particular, it might have been advantageous, alas, to despise handicapped children, not to feed them – and even to kill them – rather than to raise and nurture them.

This does not show, however, that such admiration for strength and contempt for weakness is morally acceptable. On the contrary, such kinds of contempt are *not* acceptable; they are morally evil. And, to the extent we can (through education) counteract the influence of them, we ought to do so.

This raises an important and strongly contested question. If contempt for weakness is immoral, in particular when it is directed against individuals who are 'weak' in a very literal sense of the word (people who are physically or mentally handicapped), does this mean that selective abortion (of foetuses with defected genes) is not acceptable?

No, it does not. But it does mean that some grounds for selective abortion are not respectable. It is not respectable to abort a foetus because one feels a 'natural' contempt for the kind of handicap one knows it will be born with. Instead one ought to convince oneself to accept and treat with respect individuals with this handicap. However, in rare circumstances it can be obligatory to abort a foetus selectively, because one knows that the child it will develop into, if carried to term, will lead a miserable life – one filled with pain and devoid of pleasure. But then the abortion would be carried out not because of contempt for this (possible) child but, rather, out of compassion.

There may also exist selective abortions that are morally legitimate on the ground that they save the family from unnecessary burdens or, simply, because it allows a healthy child to be born rather than a handicapped one.

However, in all these kinds of selective abortions, as has been repeatedly and correctly noted by representatives of the disabled people's movement, there is a risk that we might well be acting on an immoral contempt for weakness, rather than on a morally admirable compassion. Selective abortions provide much room for rationalisation and wishful thinking, and this is something we should always keep in mind.

Conclusion

I conclude that our enthusiasm for our sports heroes is fascistoid in nature. It is not respectable. Our admiration for strength carries with it a fascistoid contempt for weakness. There are relatively innocent (paternalistic) forms of this contempt, but there is always a risk that they might develop into more morally problematic kinds, where we choose not to acknowledge those who are weak, or to reject them as unworthy of our respect or, worse yet, to seek their extermination (as did the Nazis).

It is true that sports are not the only place where this admiration for strength and a corresponding contempt for weakness is exhibited. We see the same phenomenon in the sciences and the arts. And, when we do, what we see is no less morally depraved than what is exhibited in our enthusiasm for Olympic winners. However, there is a rough but crucial difference between sports on the one hand, and science and the arts on the other. In sports, admiration of the winner is essential. If we do not admire the winners, and admire them *qua* winners of a genetic lottery, there is no reason to watch the games at all. For the aesthetic dimension of sports, however important it might be as an additional value, commands very little interest *per se*. If our admiration for strength and contempt for weakness were somehow purged from sports, I contend that there would be little reason to watch them, and barely any point in watching sports competitions.

This is not to say, of course, that there will be little reason to take part in sports. We can all take joy in the exercise and excitement they provide, and there is always someone to compete with (if with no one else, one can always compete against oneself). But if we get rid of our unhealthy enthusiasm for strength, and corresponding contempt for weakness, no one will be able to arrange the kind of Olympic Games that we witnessed in Atlanta in 1996.

Recommendation for the future

Suppose we are now convinced that there is something wrong with being enthusiastic about sports heroes like Carl Lewis and Michael Johnson. What should we do about it?

Well, our enthusiasm for sports is much like an addiction. How do we defeat addictions? There is little help in imposing sanctions and using force. We cannot compel a person not to smoke, at least not if there remains a physical possibility for him or her to continue the habit (i.e if cigarettes are readily available). The only way to make someone give up a bad habit is to *convince* the person in question that the habit *is* bad. Then a possibility opens up that this person might overcome the habit. This may take a lot of strength, skill, time, control and cunning; however, eventually, many people succeed in giving up even deeply entrenched bad habits. I suppose that something of the kind is what we ought to do with regard to our enthusiasm for sports heroes.

In sum, we ought to realise that our enthusiasm for sports heroes is fascistoid in nature. That is why it is not an exaggeration to say, in closing, that if we are to grow as moral agents we need to cultivate a distaste for our present interest in and admiration for sports.

Note

1   My neologism 'fascistoid' should be understood alongside the word 'schizoid'. Just like something schizoid is tending to or resembling schizophrenia, something fascistoid is tending to or resembling fascism.

Chapter 2

Sports, fascism and the market

Claudio M. Tamburrini

Introduction

Sports have a grip on our lives. Either as active practitioners or as weekend athletes, as active spectators at the stadium or as passive audience at home, we all come (one way or another) into daily contact with sports. They affect society in different ways. Social attitudes and character traits are framed by the values derived from – many would even say embedded in – sports. Some of these are positively judged: self-discipline, teamwork, fair play. Others are seen as clearly negative: uncritical obedience to the team authority, a disposition to beat or even hurt rivals to secure victory, an exaggerated competitive spirit. Critics of sports tend to draw a clear distinction between mass sport activities and elite sports competitions. While they ascribe the positive traits to the former, these declared enemies of elite sports strongly underline the (some of them admittedly) negative features of the practice. This resistance to elite sports is often expressed with the help of a variety of arguments, ranging from a (more or less concealed) snobbish contempt for massive celebrations or for physical activity (or for both), to pointing out the fact that enormous resources are invested in elite sport activities (seen by these critics as completely useless) that could instead be diverted to other, more important areas of social life. And, to be honest, we should grant to those critical voices that there probably is something morally dubious about a practice whose most conspicuous element is victorious athletes being raised to the level of heroes by a cheering crowd. In a word, elite sports seem to provide an ideal forum for fruitful ethical discussion.

Torbjörn Tännsjö also belongs to the group of people who are morally troubled by the way we react to elite sports and athletes. According to him, the public's (often exaggerated) enthusiasm for sports heroes is morally dubious. As a matter of fact, he expresses his worries in far more alarming terms than that. His thesis, in his own words, is that:

> our admiration for the achievements of the great sports heroes, such as the athletes who triumph at the Olympics, reflects a fascistoid ideology.

While nationalism may be dangerous, and has often been associated with fascism, what is going on in our enthusiasm for individual athletic heroes is even worse. Our enthusiasm springs from the very core of fascist ideology: admiration for strength and contempt for weakness.

(Tännsjö this volume: 10)

Tännsjö's attack is comprehensive: it is directed against all kinds of sports – individual or in team form – carried out on an elite level. However, he is not aiming to stigmatise the motives that lead top athletes to compete. Nor is he condemning games promoters or coaches who motivate young people to become top sportsmen or women. Rather, his objections to elite sports concentrate exclusively on 'what goes on within the enormous, worldwide public, watching sports, usually through television'. The target of his criticism is 'the values entertained by you and me; we who tend, over and over again, to get carried away by such events as the Olympic Games' (p. 10). Thus, what turns elite sports into a morally problematic matter is the kind of reaction it seems to evoke in us, the spectators. These reactions can be summed up in the following manner:

- Elite sports events reinforce undesirable nationalistic sentiments in the public.
- Our – the public's – admiration for winners in elite sports competitions is an expression of our contempt for weakness (which, according to Tännsjö, is an essential element of Nazi ideology).

I intend to examine Tännsjö's arguments in that order. In doing so, I will not only aim to show that there is nothing fascistoid about our admiration for sports heroes, but will also argue that, properly supplemented by professionalisation and commercialisation, elite sports might provide us with positive social models to be used in the struggle against fascist manifestations such as racism and the discrimination of ethnic minorities.

'Sports events reinforce nationalistic sentiments in the public'

One could begin by asking why we should worry about nationalism being reinforced by competitive sports. After all, national feelings in sports do not necessarily have to lead to political chauvinism. It has even been argued that sport nationalism not only is a rather innocent sort of patriotism, but even a replacement for more dubious versions of political nationalism as well. Tännsjö is well aware of this fact, but he thinks otherwise. According to him, political and sport nationalism reinforce each other:

The nationalism fostered by our interest for our 'own' national team, and the nationalism we exhibit in the political arena, tend to reinforce each other. In particular, in periods where political nationalism is strong, what happens in the sports arenas tends to become politically important.

(Tännsjö this volume: 12)

This 'mutual reinforcement' thesis is really rather strong. However, the only support Tännsjö provides for it is the assertion that 'There is only a small step from being a soccer hooligan to joining a fascist organisation modelled on the Hitler Youth' (p. 12). The example is clearly biased. If you are a hooligan, you already are a violent person. It would then not be surprising if you are inclined to join whatever organisation is suitable to manifest your violent character. The relevant example here would show that there is a small step from being a common soccer fan to joining a (politically undesirable) nationalistic organisation. Correctly formulated, this 'mutual reinforcement' thesis seems false.

So if we have to worry about nationalism in sports, this worry would have to depend on the negative consequences of the activity, rather than on its presumed connection with less desirable expressions of national feelings. Tännsjö points out one such consequence: sport nationalism orientates people towards abstract symbols, such as 'the flag, the team (seen as an emblem); yes, even the abstractly conceived "nation"' (p. 11), and this is why we should reject it. According to him, celebrating abstract symbols is wrong because:

> entities as such are of no value. What matters, ultimately, from a moral point of view, is what happens to individuals, capable (at least) of feeling pleasure and pain … This means that if someone claims that the strength of his or her nation is of value in itself, he or she makes a value mistake.

(Tännsjö this volume: 11)

As a meta-ethical statement, this latter claim is uncontroversial. However, as an objection to our interest in sports the argument is flawed on two grounds. First, it could be asked, what does it mean to see the team 'as an emblem', or the nation or the flag, as 'abstract symbols'? In the context of sports, these symbols stand for thousands and thousands of people who share the dream of seeing their team succeed. A sports team, for instance, is in part driven to win by the encouragement provided by its supporters. Victorious teams often acknowledge this support by dedicating the victory to their supporters. A particular kind of discourse is thus established between the team members and the public. This seems to me to be the sense ascribed to the traditional ritual – indeed a popular, massive celebration – in which a crowd receives its local team in a public place after a meritorious performance abroad. And, even in those cases where the victory is offered to more abstract entities than an exhilarating crowd, the symbol thus honoured (the flag, the city hall, etc.) might reasonably be seen as representing the people who identify themselves with it. In the city of Barcelona, for instance, there is an ancient custom consisting in city teams dedicating their victories to the patron saint of the village by placing a flower arrangement depicting the coat of arms of Catalonia. Such practices might be related to the tradition of armies paying tribute to the city by dedicating a victory to it in a public ceremony. The example of Barcelona is not an isolated one. Unlike ancient communities, we no longer make soldiers the object of our admiration in our societies. Their place has been taken by athletes. The hero worship of athletes might in that sense be seen as a sign of higher culture. And we should not forget that, in the context of sports, abstract symbols do refer to people, flesh and bone.

Second, there is no reason to suppose that if a sport fan cares about the strength of his or her team/nation he or she must necessarily be considering it as being valuable in itself. He or she might reasonably see this strength as instrumental to sentiments of pride, joy or whatever pleasurable state of mind the feeling of belonging to a team or a nation might bring about.

Therefore, it seems that the problem here, if there is one, cannot be the abstractness of the entities celebrated: after all, symbols usually are implemented in real-life arrangements and affect actual people. The relevant issue here is what these symbols stand for. Being generally accepted as natural, historical symbols of a community, a flag, a city hall, even a religious figure, can hardly be said to represent in themselves fascist ideals as soon as they are advocated in the context of sports events.

Another reason why Tännsjö finds spectator orientation on abstract symbols morally problematic is due to the priority given to group interests over those of individuals. Thus, he says that when 'such entities are celebrated, the individual tends to become replaceable ... When our football or soccer heroes are successful, we cheer for them. When they fail "us", we despise them'. Thus, according to Tännsjö, when all we care about is the strength of a nation, a team or a flag, individuals are sacrificed for the sake of the collective. This ideology, he argues, accords with a view that is common in the military force: there, 'Young women are treated as potential instruments that shall safeguard the strength and survival of the nation, and young men are viewed merely as potential soldiers' (this volume: 11).

Now, it can hardly be denied that there is something, to put it mildly, morally problematic about a practice that first raises a person to the level of a hero, and then discards him or her as soon as he or she fails to fulfil our expectations of victory. Such an attitude might reasonably be said to violate the Kantian principle that we should always treat other human beings as ends in themselves, and never merely as means. So perhaps Tännsjö is right after all in exhorting us to reflect upon our attitudes towards top athletes, and the kind of values we might be expressing through them. However, his account of what's going on when we express such disappointment misses the mark.

First, Tännsjö's description of the esteem in which spectators hold top athletes is simply inaccurate. The Swedish boxer Ingemar 'Ingo' Johansson and soccer player Diego Maradona are examples of such sports heroes. Both Ingo and Maradona reached the pinnacles of athletic success and attracted adoring fans. In 1959, Johansson defeated the American boxer Floyd Paterson in a fight for the heavyweight world championship, thereby giving Sweden its first (and hitherto only) world championship title in boxing. In 1986, Maradona led the Argentinian soccer team to an outstanding victory in the World Cup in Mexico. On the way to the final game against West Germany, Maradona scored a couple of goals (in the matches against England and Belgium) of such quality that, more than ten years after, they still are shown on TV sport shows from time to time. (The goal scored against England has even been recorded with both classical music and tango tunes in the background, with the intention of emphasising the plasticity of its conception.) In both cases, however, the outstanding sports performances were followed by defeats. Ingo clearly lost two return matches against Paterson and Maradona has never again reached the top level he showed at the Mexico tournament in 1986. In Maradona's case, rather than mere sports defeats, one could even talk of disappointing the wider expectations of the public by having been sanctioned twice by FIFA's disciplinary committee for using performance-enhancing drugs. Both Ingo and Maradona, perhaps to different degrees and in different ways, can be said to have disappointed the expectations of victory of their supporters. This notwithstanding, they still enjoy the almost unconditional love and admiration of their numerous fans. Although no generally valid and definitive conclusions can be drawn from only two cases, I believe that they exemplify something typical about the relationship between sports heroes and the public. In that sense, the particular personal bond that is born between them in victory seems to be more resistant to defeat and disappointment than Tännsjö's argument assumes.

But what about ordinary athletes, those who have not been blessed (if it is a blessing) by the public's unconditional devotion? Standard performers are often strongly questioned by supporters. The recognition and admiration they might come to enjoy on favourable occasions is rapidly withdrawn in defeat. Would it not then be warranted to say that these athletes are loved and admired in victory, but criticised and slandered by the public when failing to live up to its demands? And would this not be tantamount to using those athletes simply as means to express our (rapidly changing) states of mind?

To begin with, I do not think this particular criticism affects elite sports more than it affects any other profession. In our professional life, our work is expected to satisfy certain standards. If we do not live up to these demands, we get criticised. And when we, in spite of criticism, still fail to react in an adequate manner (that is, if we do not improve our work), the trust we might have enjoyed before from employers and workmates is withdrawn, we are deprived of certain benefits and, in some cases, we get fired. From a moral point of view, this situation is no worse than that depicted for ordinary athletes who do not live up to the expectations of the public. Far from being an essential trait of elite sports, responding negatively to shortcomings in performances belongs to all kinds of professional activity.

To this it could be objected that, due to the loudness and vividness of the way in which they are rejected, the criticism experienced by athletes who are not up to the mark is much stronger than in other professional categories.

My answer to this argument is twofold. First, there is no necessary link between contempt and the loudness and vividness of a critical reaction. A person can loudly and vividly criticise his or her best friend's conduct without this having to imply that she despises her friend. And contempt can indeed be expressed in very subtle ways. Indifferent workmates, for instance, can turn out to be much more cruel and contemptuous than a hilarious crowd in the sports arena.

Second, especially in the context of sports, the vividness of the situation, the emotions experienced in a competition, yield a particularly intensive communication between the athletes and the crowd. Through it, the previous bond between performers and audience – the particular discourse that takes place between them and the public – now reaches a higher level of directness and interaction. Their bond, in other words, becomes more personalised and humanised, independent of the final result of the athletic performance.[1] A similar situation seems to occur in other emotionally laden professional activities such as the performing arts. But even when an unsatisfactory result hinders the development of such a bond, there is no reason to underestimate an athlete's capacity to handle that failure. In sports, as well as in other areas of life, we have to accept that human relationships sometimes simply do not work out in a manner we would wish. This should not bother sports supporters any more than it does, say, devotees of opera.

So, concerning ordinary athletes, I also believe that it would be an overstatement to characterise the public's reaction as one of scorn or contempt. Even when overtly showing disappointment for an athlete's performance, the interactive relation that is attained between sport audiences and the athletes contains elements of human communication that go far beyond (and are essentially different from) the expression of contempt.

'Admiration for victorious athletes expresses contempt for weakness'

According to Tännsjö, nationalism in sports is no longer a threat to society. He points out correctly (to me) that the commercialisation and internationalisation of elite sports have turned the best athletes and teams into independent, transnational social phenomena. Rather, the problem with elite sports is the admiration we – the public – feel for the winner. Tännsjö formulates his second objection to elite sports in the following terms:

> when we give up nationalism, as a source of our interest in élite sports activities, when we give up our view of individual sportsmen and teams as representatives of 'our' nation, when we base our interest in sports on a more direct fascination for the individual winners of these events – we move from something that is only contingently associated with Nazism (nationalism) to something that is really at the core of Nazism (a contempt for weakness).
>
> (this volume: 13)

Tännsjö's argument is descriptive, not normative. As such, it does not tell us how spectators should behave, but rather how they actually react towards victorious athletes. When we feel admiration for the winner of a competition, his argument runs, our feelings are based on a value judgement:

> those who win the game, if the competition is fair, are *excellent*, and their excellence makes them *valuable*, which is why we admire them. Their excellence is, in an obvious manner, based on the strength they exhibit in the competition. And the strength they exhibit is 'strength' in a very literal sense of the word.
>
> (this volume: 13, Tännsjö's emphasis)

A natural objection to this argument is that admiring the winner for his or her strength does not necessarily mean feeling contempt for the weak. The link between these two attitudes needs to be substantiated. Tännsjö's attempt to support that link goes as follows:

> ... if we see a person as especially valuable, because of his excellence (he is a winner in the genetic lottery), and if the excellence is a manifestation of strength (in a very literal sense), then this must mean that other people, those who do not win the fair competition (i.e the losers in the genetic lottery), those who are comparatively weak, are *less* valuable. The most natural feeling associated with *this* value judgement is contempt.
>
> (this volume: 13–14, Tännsjö's emphasis)

In order to question Tännsjö's position, I will first argue that our admiration for top athletes may rest on other grounds than plain fascination for their excellence, literally understood in terms of 'strength'. Hence, this argument will allow me to affirm that the supposedly necessary link is, at best, a contingent one. (Tännsjö even goes so far as to affirm that ' ... we would be *inconsistent* if we did not feel any kind of contempt for the losers, once we sincerely admire the winner'; this volume: 13, Tännsjö's emphasis.) Finally, I will also argue that, when properly implemented, the public's admiration for top athletes, far from being an alarming social manifestation, might even yield socially desirable effects.

As a kind of introduction to my counterargument, let me first briefly comment on the fact, correctly pointed out by Tännsjö, that personal admiration can even be present in such areas as science and the arts. Thus, he says:

> Sure, even within science and the arts there are ugly manifestations of the phenomenon I have criticised within sports. Some people tend to get carried away with their admiration for lonely, heroic 'geniuses' in the development of human science and art.
>
> (this volume: 16)

As talented artists and prominent scientists make important contributions to society's cultural and scientific development, they (the 'strongest', in a metaphorical sense of the word, in these areas) also become objects of our admiration.

In relation to this, Tännsjö actually wonders:

> Doesn't that mean we value these persons, in a manner similar to the way we value successful athletes? And, if we do, doesn't this mean we think of those who are less successful in these areas as less valuable? Do we not exhibit contempt for weakness, when, for example, we give Nobel prizes to some 'outstanding' people?
>
> (this volume: 16)

However, even if disposed to grant this argument at least some weight, Tännsjö rejects it on the grounds that, unlike the excitement felt by spectators for top athletes, our admiration for scientific and cultural feats does not necessarily mean that we admire the scientists or artists responsible for them. In Tännsjö's own words:

> ... when we become enthusiastic about scientific and cultural achievements, we *need* not have scientists or artists as the focus of our attention. We can admire Wittgenstein's theories and Mozart's operas without feeling that Wittgenstein and Mozart are valuable persons. We can value

the *products* of their ingenuity, but not necessarily their genius. We can say truthfully that what they produced is of the utmost value, but still retain the view that *they* are not more valuable than anyone else. They are merely *instrumental* to things of importance in themselves.

(this volume: 16, Tännsjö's emphasis)

Now, why could we not come to consider Wittgenstein or Mozart as more valuable persons than average people on grounds of their achievements? After all, the fact that some people are 'instrumental' to the achievement of intrinsically important things is not necessarily a hindrance to admiring them as persons, and sometimes even rightly so (recall Mother Teresa). Furthermore, why could we not admire Carl Lewis's or George Foreman's sporting achievements without seeing them as (more) valuable (than ordinary) persons at the same time? Tännsjö believes that, while 'We can and ought to admire the *products* of skilful scientists and artists ... we cannot help but admire the winning athletes themselves, or else give up our interest in watching sport' (p. 16, Tännsjö's emphasis). In that sense, he considers this personal admiration as essential to sports activities in a way that is not prevalent in the sciences or the arts. Unfortunately, his only support for this assertion is his rather vague characterisation of scientific and artistic products as 'things of importance in themselves', as contrasted with sports results, labelled by Tännsjö as 'not genuine' on the grounds that 'they are mainly results of measurements, which are intended, first of all, to establish who won ... So winning (a fair competition) is only a means, a way to prove excellence' (p. 17). Therefore, what we actually admire in sports, he concludes, is the excellence in terms of strength shown by the winner.[2]

This characterisation of excellence in sports strikes me as elitist and gender-biased. It is elitist because it does not even consider ranking athletic achievements culturally on a par with scientific or artistic ones. However, it seems unreasonable not to rank at least some athletic achievements on a par with some cultural and scientific ones. Outstanding sports performances demand not only personal sacrifices, strenuous efforts and courage to stand up to challenges, but also the capacity to execute an effective strategy and to realise it in practice. Provided it is deserved, an athletic victory offers, therefore, testimony of skills and excellences (both of physical and mental character) that go far beyond mere strength.

Thus, our admiration for victorious athletes might very well depend on the ascription of a wider kind of excellence to the winner, rather than on an (admittedly dubious) admiration for the strongest. On this line of reasoning, it might then be argued that what we actually admire is not necessarily the strength ('in a very literal sense') of elite athletes, but rather their achievements, as cultural expressions of excellence.

Tännsjö's characterisation is also gender-biased because it focuses exclusively on strength. It is plausible to affirm that, at least in some particular sports, qualities other than strength are celebrated by the public as tokens of excellence. In rhythmic sports such as gymnastics (a well-established sport with its own world championship), for example, women are recognised as excellent, and sometimes even superior, to their male counterparts, for skills and qualities other than strength. Ice-skating is another example. Besides, some of the most successful female gymnasts and skaters have almost reached the category of celebrities (recall, for instance, Nadia Comaneci, Olga Korbut, Katarina Witt and many others). Furthermore, even in those sports where women's performances are lower than men's, they may arouse spectators' interest precisely because they display other skills than mere strength. Take, for instance, basketball. Female basketball players are physically weaker than their male counterparts. This results in the fact that women's basketball is more of a team game than men's basketball. As such, it could be seen as displaying not lesser, but a different, excellence from the men's game. It is true that the majority of the public gets more excited by male basketball. But, once the character of the women's game is properly understood, we should not neglect the possibility that a more sophisticated audience would find as much to admire – and to get excited about – in women's basketball as in men's. It is true that the interest of the public for sports where women excel and surpass males athletes is still low compared with male-dominated ones. And women are still poorly represented in most sports. Many sports, especially 'big-time' ones, have been designed and developed to favour those abilities which characterise male musculature and body type: strength, height, speed and size.[3] This, obviously, needs to be changed. Therefore, to emphasise strength as the only aspect of a sports performance capable of arousing our enthusiasm is, indeed, a regrettable concession to the status quo, not only in elite sports, but in sports activities in general. In that sense, Tännsjö simply glosses over some positive features of sports practices that make them worthy of pursuit.

In Chapter 1, Tännsjö does not discuss the role played by gender in elite sports. But he actually has a reply to my former argument about wider excellence. He says that if top performances (and the various kinds of excellence they indicate) were the real reason for our admiration of elite athletes, then we should feel equally enthusiastic about the top performances of handicapped athletes, or those of female athletes. Some of these athletes must surmount more difficult obstacles in order to produce a top performance. But the fact is that we do not feel equally enthusiastic over their performances. In any case, Tännsjö points out, ' ... if we are forced to choose, what we (most of us) really want to watch are competitions involving the *absolute* elite, not the Olympics for handicapped people' (this volume: 18, Tännsjö's emphasis). And, according to Tännsjö, the only reasonable explanation for this asymmetry in our interest is that these sorts of athletes are not as capable as their Olympic counterparts; in other words, in our eyes, they are not as powerful and physically complete as male, top athletes. Might not Tännsjö be right after all, then?

I do not think so. In assigning excellence to an athlete, the result obtained in the contest is obviously of utmost importance. It is true that, sometimes, the public honours an athlete who, though defeated, did the best he or she could to reach the top (recall the different kinds of qualities excellence includes). And sometimes the public denies this recognition to a victorious athlete who, although he or she is a legitimate winner, lacks some of the moral qualities required by excellence (for instance, he or she did not practice 'good sportsmanship'). However, in general terms, the result achieved by an athlete is a central element in the attribution of excellence. Tännsjö is right when he points out that handicapped athletes can be equally excellent in physical and mental qualities as their elite counterparts. However, they differ in the results they attain – their performances are not as good. Granted, they have achieved top results within their class, but, however deserved their victories may have been, they have not reached a top result in absolute terms. By this I simply mean that there exists another athlete who, also deservedly (he or she has also demonstrated excellence), has achieved a better athletic result.

In my opinion, this fact allows us to explain why our interest in handicapped or female athletes is not as pronounced as the interest we feel for male elite athletes. It is true that society values excellence, in the wider sense outlined above. But it is equally true that results matter. So, it would not be surprising to see that the best results arouse most excitement. This seems to be confirmed by some sports disciplines such as women's rhythmic gymnastics. Though physically weaker than their male counterparts, female gymnasts get most attention from the public, probably due to the fact that they achieve the best results within the discipline.

I am not arguing that relative performances should not be praised or admired; they might even become the proper object of our (exaggerated) admiration. But this fact does not turn our admiration for the best performances (in absolute terms) into a morally dubious one. Granted, the reverse side of our admiration for excellence is often a lack of interest for everything that falls short of it. Yet lack of interest can hardly be ranked on the same level as contempt for the weaker. There is no inconsistency in admiring the winner and not despising the loser. We just might not be as interested in 'second bests'!

But excellence is a comparative term. And so is the notion of best results. Thus, it could be asked, how much has been gained by this argumentative move? After all, so long as a relative ranking takes place, the best will be admired and seen as more valuable than the next bests. By the very act of identifying winners, we define losers. Tännsjö's crusaders might therefore argue that next bests are nonetheless implicitly despised by us, even if not consciously. So – they will probably stress – there is, after all, some inconsistency between ranking someone as more valuable, and not expressing (in this implicit manner) contempt for next bests.

However, provided we adopt a wide characterisation of excellence, I see no difficulty in ranking an athlete as best without feeling contempt, not even implicit, for others. In Tännsjö's unidimensional ranking (where excellence is defined exclusively in terms of strength), there is no possibility for next bests to excel: only one athlete, the winner, can be celebrated as the strongest. Contrary to Tännsjö, I have argued that the ideal of excellence in sports involves a plurality of qualities. The most excellent athlete will naturally excel over others on the whole (that is, in most qualities and most of the time). But (at least some) next bests might excel in some particular quality. Or they may temporarily become the most excellent (for instance, in connection with a particular competition). As a matter of fact, next bests sometimes can even surpass the most excellent in this limited sense. Some examples might help to clarify what I have in mind here. A losing athlete may have made more sacrifices, or shown more dedication and courage, than the winner. Or, to focus on the athletic result, both the winner and the second best might have broken the former world record for the sport in question. Similar possibilities are open in team sports. Given a high level of performance, the public seldom despises a losing team. And, for instance, in a low-level soccer match, spectators usually show their discontent with both teams, not only with the losing one. The fact that next bests too can show this kind of partial excellence might, in my opinion, neutralise the implicit contempt suggested by the present objection. Once again, Tännsjö seems not to have paid sufficient attention to the fact that the admiration or disapproval of the public is evoked by a variety of qualities and circumstances.

So, if it is still to have any bite, the argument of implicit contempt must be limited to those athletes who never show any sign at all of excellence. As their performances always fail, they cannot compensate for their shortcomings by excelling in a particular quality, or by winning a contest from time to time. Perhaps it could then be said of them that they must submit to the implicit contempt that might be embedded in value rankings?

Maybe. However, no matter how contemptuous, the public's attitude towards these athletes does not seem directly related to admiring excellence. Such a complete lack of valuable qualities results in negative reactions on its own. Besides, within the realm of elite sports, we just do not see this kind of athlete. You simply cannot get to the top without excelling in some way.

I do not want to leave the subject of our admiration for the best athletes without calling attention to the role that professionalism can be said to have played, and can reasonably be expected to play in the future, in the reappraisal of ethnic minorities. Social ideals are not usually dictated by standards and prototypes belonging to ethnic minority groups. Heroes, and the corresponding ideal picture of success that youths aspire to, are commonly depicted in terms of the characteristics – racial, social, cultural and economic – of the dominant groups in society. The spread of elite sports – mainly due to professionalism and the intensified commercialisation that followed in its wake – has in my opinion undoubtedly contributed to counterbalance this trend. Unlike Tännsjö, I cannot see anything morally troublesome in our admiration for the best-skilled athletes. But, even if he were right in his negative account of athletic admiration, this should be seen in the light of other positive effects that might follow from it.

To put it crudely, when condemning the public's admiration of elite athletes, we should not neglect the fact that the winner might, for instance, be a member of an ethnic minority. This appears to me to be of the utmost relevance in the current political situation, where racist trends threaten to distort the values inculcated in society. Any serious discussion of the moral status of elite sports must pay attention to this matter.

Conclusion

Is Tännsjö right, then, when he affirms that, 'if our admiration for strength and contempt for weakness were somehow purged from sports, I contend that there would be little reason to watch them, and barely any point in watching sports competitions' (this volume: 22)? Is this admiration for strength and contempt for weakness, as he puts it, 'morally evil' (this volume: 21)? In the course of this chapter, I have tried to show that Tännsjö's arguments in Chapter 1 are flawed or, at best, not sufficiently developed to sustain his thesis.

To support my claim, I made a distinction between admiring athletic excellence (as it is shown in victory), and despising the weak. We often get excited over top performances, both within and outside of sports. Most of us feel more devoted to top sports events, because this is where the most outstanding athletic performances occur. This, however, does not mean that our lack of interest for average sport performances should be interpreted as a sign of contempt for those who do not manage to reach the top. In my view, there is no reason to assume the existence of such motives. As a matter of fact, sports promote, perhaps as no other human activity does, all kinds of excellences in the Aristotelian sense. Physical skills and strength are developed to their maximum; excellences of character (such as discipline, temperance, self-sacrifice, even righteousness – a central ingredient in 'fair play') are both a requisite for and a result of sport practices. And, finally, the capacity to plan a strategy for victory and implement it successfully requires all the intellectual skills (understanding, judgment, cleverness, etc.) that are characteristic of that excellent state of the soul which Aristotle calls practical wisdom.

Thus, provided we adopt a plural notion of excellence, I see no inconsistency in admiring the most excellent athletes without feeling contempt for the less skilled. Tännsjö has failed to show any substantial link between this admiration and contempt for next bests. That link, however, is essential to his argument.

My disagreement with Tännsjö's thesis, however, is deeper than that. I do not want to deny that, for some people, admiration for winners may have its roots in undemocratic social ideals. However, I do not think this constitutes a serious objection to elite sports events. First, such social phenomena must reasonably be seen in a wider social context. Undemocratic sports fans are surely in the minority. As I see it, elite sports can even be enlisted to combat racism in sports and in society at large. Through the influence of commercialisation on sports, members of ethnic minorities might become social prototypes for young people. In my opinion, this possible effect of elite sports would greatly outweigh the feared excesses of undemocratic sports fans.

Second, the skills and qualities included in excellence are socially valuable. Some of them (for instance, respect for competitors and 'fair play') might even be regarded as expressing a praiseworthy moral attitude. In that sense, it is perfectly understandable to admire top athletes because we know, or at least can imagine, what it takes to reach those heights in sports activities. And, even more important, this admiration is rational on a general social level as well, as it can lead to the fostering of desirable character qualities among the public.

The social rationality of the admiration for excellence extends also to one of its main components: the achievement of a top result. Individuals cannot reasonably be celebrated as excellent in their specific activity if they never succeed in implementing their strategy. This factor, in my view, explains why spectators feel more enthusiastic about top sports performances. Handicapped athletes, for instance, only achieve relative top performances. However, this does not necessarily imply that they are despised by the public. As a matter of fact, they might even be admired by the excellence they show within their class. But it is socially rational that the absolutely best performers are admired most. To sum up: the positive results of the public's admiration for sports heroes seems to outweigh the eventual negative consequences of the practice.

Finally, an objection to my arguments could be that the public does not actually embrace a plural notion of excellence. Along with Tännsjö, a critic might maintain that a majority of sports spectators admire victorious athletes on no other grounds than their strength, in the literal sense of the word. This, however, is a factual statement, and Tännsjö has not provided any support for it. Contrary to Tännsjö, I have argued for the possibility of other skills and qualities evoking our admiration for top athletes. That, it should be granted, is a speculative statement. Obviously, it would be unwarranted to affirm that all spectators, or even most of them, actually feel the way I have described them. Sports audiences are still not that educated. However, I believe my views are supported by some of the reactions of the public. In some women's sports, for instance, we see a similar admiration for their most excellent practitioners as we find in men's sports. Furthermore, next-best athletes also sometimes get the admiration and enthusiasm of the public. Maybe these are not conclusive arguments. But the ones advanced in Chapter I are not substantiated enough to justify dismissing mine. And if we are to condemn a whole range of generally accepted social practices, it seems more reasonable to me that the burden of proof be put on those who wish to reject them.

This would be enough to save elite sports from wholesale condemnation.

Notes

1 We often see the public honour a failing athlete who, though not winning, has at least 'done his or her best'.
2 Tännsjö attempts a broader interpretation of 'strength' in terms of '[natural] talent'. On page 18, he suggests that we would feel a boundless admiration for a middle-aged spectator at the Olympics who, without previous training, 'walked down from the stadium and joined the 10,000m race and, because of superior natural talent, defeated all the finalists'. My intuition is that most of us feel even more excited in front of a much less talented individual who, motivated by that event, submits himself to hard training and personal sacrifices and, four years later, joins the race and triumphs.
3 Some authors, for instance Betsy Postow (1995: 323–328), have even asked whether women should refuse to engage in sports unsuited to their physical characteristics and concentrate instead on sports where they can more easily achieve excellence (such as gymnastics, diving or ultra-marathoning).

Chapter 3

The logic of progress and the art of moderation in competitive sports

Sigmund Loland

Introduction

As with other human practices, sports express the basic norms and values of the historical and sociocultural contexts of which they are parts. According to historians and sociologists, competitive sports are typical products of what is somewhat vaguely referred to as Western culture (Guttmann 1978; Mandell 1984; Tangen 1997). The agonistic element of competition and the (Homeric) ideal of striving towards always being the best have roots in ancient Greece. Modern versions of sports bear distinctive marks of their particular background in last century's England, 'the land of sport'. Their emphasis on exact measuring, comparison, and ranking of competitors according to strict, rule-governed standards of performance is seen as a clear expression of the values of capitalist, industrialised societies.

More specifically, competitive sports can be considered as particularly strong carriers of what Nisbet calls 'the great idea of progress' (1994) that has permeated Western culture from ancient times and up to today. Whereas 'the Homeric maxim' prescribes all men to surpass all others and win, modern conceptions tell of progress in more objective, quantitative terms. There has been a gradual shift from an understanding of progress in subjective, particular ways ('Today I ran faster than you'), towards exact and inter-subjective measures and comparisons; for example as in the idea of the sport record ('This was the fastest 100m ever') (Guttmann 1978; Tangen 1997).

In this chapter I will discuss critically these two interpretations of progress in sports as philosophical possibilities. The interpretations of progress will be understood as forms of social logic. By 'forms of social logic' I mean consistent systems of norms and values that guide actions in, and are used to justify, social practices (Tranøy 1986). Consistency means that the norms and values are linked together in relationships of meaning and that they are mutually supportive, or at least that they do not contradict each other (Aarnio 1987). Typical norms in sports are 'Equality of opportunity to perform!' and 'Play fair!' Norms are justified by reference to more general norms and, ultimately, to final ends or values. For example, the two norms above can be justified by referring to sports as arenas for realisation of values like equality and justice, and ultimately as elements of what can be seen as the one final end – the good life.

In what follows, the logic of quantifiable progress and the logic of qualitative progress will be described and critically evaluated. The argument will be that the qualitative interpretation is by far the most promising of the two. In the last part of the chapter, I will sketch a series of possible ways of moderating current sports to update and better realise the norms and values of the logic of qualitative progress.

The logic of quantifiable progress

The British origins of modern sports were based on educational ideas. Sports were considered efficient means in the disciplining of unruly bodily passions and hence towards moral progress. Pierre de Coubertin, the founding father of the modern Olympic movement, saw competitive sports as the clearest symbol of the possibility of continuous physical, social and moral progress of mankind in which he so strongly believed. Inspired by his friend and collaborator, the Dominican *Père* Didon, Coubertin articulated the Olympic motto, 'Citius, altius, fortius' (Faster, higher, stronger) as the very core of the ideology of Olympism. Moreover, Coubertin referred to the idea of the record as having the same status in the ideology of Olympism as the law of gravity does in Newtonian mechanics: it was the eternal axiom (Loland 1995).

The basic norm in this interpretation is:

Quantifiable progress of performance!

This view of sports has given rise to a set of more specific norms that together seem to constitute a consistent norm system. The norms of the system can be articulated as follows:

Quantification!

The very idea of quantifiable progress depends upon the possibility for measuring performances in exact physical-mathematical entities. From the invention of the stopwatch in the 1730s, exact measurements of sports performances have increased in technological *raffinement* (Inizan 1994). Today, advanced methods and instruments measure hundreds and thousands of seconds; marginal differences that at the same time are of decisive importance in the quest for sports success. Moreover, the drive towards quantification is expansive. The interest in statistics of various kinds is overwhelming. Classic record sports like athletics, weightlifting and swimming keep official lists of their various records from the very first organised competitions right up until today. Even team sports and games in which performances are relative and where exact measurement of performance is difficult are marked by the quest for quantification. (When one of the great heroes of American baseball, Joe DiMaggio, died in early spring 1999, an obituary in *Time* magazine (22 March) was elegantly built around the magic numbers of his career: 56, 61, 16, 9, 369, 0.89, 457, 3 and 13!)

Standardisation!

Quantification is a necessary but not sufficient condition for precise evaluations of progress. To be able to compare performances across time and space, we need identical conditions, or at least as equal conditions as possible. As with quantification, standardising of facilities has developed along with advanced technology. In many sports, the technical requirements on facilities are numerous. Even an arena for the 'simple' events in track and field has to meet detailed norms on homologisation as defined by the governing body of the sport, the International Amateur Athletics Federation (IAAF). One line of development seems to be to move traditional outdoor sports indoors to avoid the uncontrollable influences of outdoor conditions. In addition, indoor facilities improve spectator comfort. This is for instance the case with speed skating, which had its first indoor Olympic competitions during the Lillehammer Games in 1994, and this might become the case with all skiing disciplines – cross country skiing, alpine skiing and ski jumping – in the future (Gilberg 1996).

Record-setting!

On the basis of quantification and standardisation, the idea of the sport record found its form. The record is the paradigmatic expression of the logic of quantifiable progress. A sport record is a performance, measured in exact mathematical-physical entities (metres, seconds, kilogrammes) within a standardised spatiotemporal framework defined by sport rules, that is better than all previous performances measured in the same way (Loland 1998b). The first sports records in this sense were officially registered at a track and field meet between Oxford and Cambridge universities in 1868 (Mandell 1984). Today, we talk of a variety of records: personal records, arena records, local, regional and world records, records linked to specific arrangements (Olympic records, European Championship records), and so on.

Specialisation!

Increased demands on quantifiable progress require continuous performance enhancement. The amount of time, energy and resources needed to meet increased demands on performance leads necessarily to concentration and specialisation. Different sports disciplines pose different physical and mental challenges on athletes, and today it is almost (biologically) impossible to perform at high levels in more than one sports discipline. Even within sport disciplines, specialisation is required. For instance, most sprinters run 100m and 200m distances only. A few athletes, like Jackie Joyner-Kersee (heptathlete) and Carl Lewis, also compete successfully in the long jump, which imposes the same requirements on speed and explosive muscle force. However, good performances in the 400m requires so much specialised training on anaerobic capacity that maximum speed will be influenced in a negative way.

Objectivity!

The logic of quantifiable progress is built on an ideal of objectivity. The aim is exact measurements of performance under controlled circumstances that can be compared across time and space. In this respect, sports seem to be dominated by a quest for objective knowledge similar to what we find in the scientific experiment. The main questions deal not with particular athletes or events but can be articulated as empirical research questions. How fast can a human being run the 100m dash? How far can a human being throw a javelin, or a discus, with a well-defined weight and shape? How fast can a human being swim 200m?

The logic of quantifiable progress has in a common-sense manner become a normative ideal in sports. For example, without new records, important events like the Olympic Games and the World Championships are considered failures both by the media and the public. This logic seems also to be an ideal for a series of current developments in sports. Through the quest for standardisation and objectivity, scientific and technological know-how is applied to control the uncontrollable, to eliminate chance, and to measure performance improvement in an increasingly more accurate way.

One might ask: 'What is the rationale for these norms. What is their core value?' This is a difficult question. The ideal of unlimited quantifiable progress has long historical roots and deep sociocultural explanations, but lacks clear and articulated statements of final ends. It is difficult to find any other value position behind the norms than that the very process of quantifiable progress, or the very transcendence in objective terms of previous performance, is considered an end in itself independent of its consequences.

Critique

The logic of quantifiable progress can be criticised from many perspectives. Marxist critics like Rigauer (1969) and Brohm (1978) see competitive sports as an extension of the repressive forces of capitalism. Athletes and teams become small insignificant pieces in the fundamental struggle over hegemony and power that characterises society in general. With their references to equality of opportunity and fair competition, international high-performance sports are nothing but carriers of false ideology that have to be fought and defeated. Other lines of critique, for example from Lasch (1979) and Gibson (1993), consider the logic of quantifiable growth to be reductionist, as it does not take seriously the internal goods of the practice of sports; their possibilities for the cultivation of moral virtues and their potential as an arena for education. In Chapter 1, Tännsjö launches an even harsher critique and claims that our fascination for competitive sports is based on fascistoid elitism and a cult of physical perfection and strength with a consequent contempt for weakness.

The critique here will be less ideological in a traditional sense, but to a larger extent will focus upon the consequences of the logic of quantifiable progress for sport itself. Record sports are paradigmatic expressions of this logic. And it is in the record sports that we most clearly see their problematic sides. The quest for records tends to reduce the potential for human progress to one narrow capacity such as the ability to run fast, jump high or long, or throw far. As biological beings, our capacities for improving what Martin *et al.* (1991) refer to as *konditionälle Fähigkeiten* (basic physical qualities) – which to a large degree depend upon genetic dispositions such as endurance, strength, speed and flexibility – are limited. It is, for example, hard to think of a 100m sprint ever taking less than five seconds. Our phylogenetic potential is stable. If performance frameworks are kept the same, sooner or later further quantifiable progress in the specialised record sports requires significant changes in human genetic potential.

To a certain extent, such manipulation seems possible even today. Biochemical manipulation of athletic performance is called doping, or 'artificial performance enhancement'. Bouchard *et al.* (1997) anticipate that within fifteen to twenty years researchers will reach a complete overview of 'the performance genes'. In Chapter 15, Christian Munthe gives a detailed overview of the possible utilisation of this knowledge in sports. It would be naive to think that these opportunities will not be taken. Georg Henrik von Wright (1991), philosopher and cultural critic, talks about 'the technological imperative': if a certain technology is available, and if it is an efficient means towards desired ends, it will be used no matter the costs.

Logically, of course, finer calibrations of performance measurements, such as thousands and millionths of a second, a metre, or a kilogramme, make it possible for even microscopic improvements to be recorded and for new records to be set again and again. Moreover, as recent records on running distances like the 400m (Michael Johnson) and the 1500m (Hicham El Guerrouj) indicate, many disciplines have probably still a long way to go before approaching human limits. But, provided that the spatiotemporal frameworks for record setting are kept the same, the human costs for every improvement will probably increase. The quest for infinite quantifiable progress will sooner or later lead towards pressing moral dilemmas that challenge our very idea of what a human being is all about.

The core problem of this logic is that it builds on the impossible demand for unlimited progress within limited systems. Enough is never enough! This logic is built on a blind quest for progress as it includes no critical reflections on ends and values. Why is objective knowledge of the physical capabilities of human beings of value to sports? The logic presents no clear idea of its own justification. The norms 'Quantification!', 'Standardisation!', 'Record-setting!', 'Specialisation!' and 'Objectivity!' seem to have no clear foundation in final ends or values, either for sports or for human life in general.

The logic of qualitative progress

The critique of the logic of quantifiable progress is serious, but may at the same time seem somewhat one-dimensional. Obviously, not all sports are vulnerable to the critique. The most popular sports in the world both in terms of numbers of participants and spectators are the great ball games, soccer, volleyball and basketball. They seem to build on a different logic. Performances are not quantifiable in exact physical-mathematical entities, and there is little or no talk of records here. Performances are relative and depend upon interplay between competitors. Every game is different and cannot easily be compared in quantitative terms. What norms and values guide practice and development here?

Game-specific advantage!

In games, performances are measured in non-accurate entities like goals, points, games and sets, and with no ideal of total correspondence between quality of performance and advantage given. In fact, tennis players can win matches in spite of losing the majority of games as long as they win the decisive points (7–6, 0–6, 0–6, 7–6, 7–6). The primary goal is, of course, that the best performer wins. The very logic of competition is based on meritocratic distribution of advantage. The number of goals and points must correspond to the quality of performance. At the same time, luck (in soccer a goal is a goal with no differentiation of the performance that lies behind it) is allowed to play a certain part. (For an elaboration of these points, see Chapter 11.)

Equal opportunity to perform!

To be able to evaluate and rank competitors according to performance, ball games as well as record sports need a framework in which all competitors are given equal opportunity to perform. A certain standardisation, such as competing according to the same rules, with the use of similar or identical equipment and under similar external conditions, is a necessity. The point, however, is that the conditions are as equal as possible within each competition, and not necessarily from game to game. We might think of two soccer games, one played on a sunny day with no wind, and one played in rain and strong wind. Although the games might take on very different character, both games can be exciting, challenging, entertaining and well played. In fact, we could argue that the norm of equality of opportunity (as opposed to standardisation) adds complexity and variation to sports and that this ought to be a weighty argument against the increasing development of indoor arenas.

Play to win!

In games, the idea of competing against objective standards of excellence becomes less important. Record-setting in the traditional sense is meaningless. Indeed, players and game enthusiasts discuss questions such as what is the best game of the season, who is the best player this year, who was the best player ever. But there are no clear possibilities of finding answers based on objective quantifiable standards. Endless series of statistical 'evidence' and arguments of various kinds support different standpoints. In fact, the impossibility of clear-cut objective standards is probably the very entertaining *raison d'être* of the discussions. What counts in ball games is the performance in each particular game. Based upon the standards of excellence given in the rules, the focus is upon winning today, winning now. The norm in games is not to set records, but to play to win!

Complex skills!

In most ball games, standards of excellence are complex and open. Basic physical qualities, such as endurance, strength, speed and flexibility provide a means only. The primary challenge is on technical and tactical skills that have to be learned through practice and experience in social interaction with others. Moreover, in team games, performance depends upon complex interaction within a team and between two teams. A team never plays better than the opposition allows. Performances are relative. There are no fixed, quantifiable standards of performance here. Emphasis on tactical aspects instead of on basic physical qualities would decrease the importance of lucky genetic dispositions and to a larger extent emphasise mental qualities and skills acquired through training and one's own efforts in social interaction with others.

Particularity!

The alternative logic of qualitative progress focuses not on objectivity but on particularity. Talk of objective, quantifiable progress in ball games makes little sense. Of course, questions like 'How fast can a human being kick a soccer ball?' or 'What is the fastest tennis serve ever?' might be of a certain interest, but they tell little of performance in the game. In the logic of qualitative progress, each game has an independent standing. There is no cult of abstract entities like the sports record or of maximum performances of the human species here. The only reasonable question concerns the particular players in this particular game: Who will win this soccer match? Who will win this tennis match?

One might ask about the rationale for these norms. What is the value upon which the norms are justified? Bernard Suits (1995) has suggested a well-known answer. According to Suits, games are built on the logic of play. The specific ends of games can only be reached through the realisation of a set of constitutive rules that prohibit the most efficient means in favour of less efficient means. In soccer, for example, the particular end of the game is to move a ball over a white line on the grass. At the same time, soccer prohibits obvious efficient means (such as using the hands) and allows only what, at least in a first stage of playing, is less efficient means (such as heading or kicking). As Suits says, 'Playing a game is the voluntary attempt to overcome unnecessary obstacles' (1995: 9).

The reason for accepting 'unnecessary obstacles' is to be found in the playful (lusory) attitude. 'Unnecessary obstacles' realise values in the very activity of the game – experiential qualities such as fun, challenge, excitement, a sense of mastery, a sense of community, a sense of rivalry. In this way, games offer a 'gratuitous logic', as Morgan (1994) calls it in his development of Suits' ideas. Competitions are about 'putting oneself on the line', to borrow an expression from Fairchild (1987). The point is not whether any records are set, nor whether performances are better than ever, but whether the competition realises experiential qualities among the parties engaged.

Strong and valuable experiential qualities in sports can be called the joy of sports. Or, to be more precise, the joy of sports consists in valuable experiences that arise in the process of measuring, comparing and finally ranking competitors according to the performance of athletic skills as defined by the constitutive rules of the game. Progress in sports, then, is progress in the joy of sports.

Progress can take the form of an increase in intensity of joy. Usually, the intensity of joy in a game increases with increased mastery of technical and tactical skills. This does not necessarily mean that the expert experiences more joy than the beginner. The first successful carving turn on alpine skis can in terms of experiential values be just as strong as the experiences of a successful final race that leads to a World Cup victory. At the same time, progress in joy can be an increase in complexity. Learning new technical and tactical skills opens possibilities for new kinds of valuable experiences and heightens the number of possible experiential values of a sport.

The norms 'Game-specific advantages!', 'Equal opportunity to perform!', 'Play to win!', 'Complex skills!' and 'Particularity!' represent a consistent logic of qualitative progress. The final end or value upon which these norms are realised is joy in sports for all parties engaged. The main norm is:

Progress in the intensity and/or complexity of joy in sports!

Joy is not possible to quantify in a strict, objective sense. Joy can progress both in terms of intensity and complexity, and there are probably as many quantities and qualitative aspects of joy as there are participants and games. No player or game is ever the same. The potential for progress in joy is infinite. The logic of qualitative progress is built on the ideal of unlimited growth in unlimited systems.

Critique

A possible critique of the logic of qualitative progress is that it is idealistic; it does not correspond to reality. In real-life sporting games, especially at high levels of performance, the logic seems marginal. Joy seems to have no guiding force at all.

For example, the norm of quantification seems to spread in games. American baseball and British cricket fans seem to love the statistics of their games. Over the last decades, coaches have become increasingly interested in the almost law-like regularities of many games. In soccer, successful play can to a certain extent be operationalised in quantitative terms. Computer analyses of team performances, like those of Olsen et al. (1994), are helpful in the critical evaluation of efficient strategies. However, there is need for a word of caution linked to what sometimes seems to be a naive belief in numbers here. The very logic of soccer, in which a goal is a goal no matter what the quality of the play behind it, allows for an element of luck and unpredictability that can never be fully operationalised, explained and predicted.

Moreover, the norms on all-round skills and on playing to win are threatened. American football has cultivated highly specialised skills. Necessary conditions to become a good defensive player are body mass and strength, a fact that has led to extensive misuse of anabolic steroids to stimulate 'artificial' muscle growth. Strong specialisation and hazardous practices like drug use must be understood against the background of the possibilities for extensive payoffs. Ball games have had commercial success as TV entertainment, and victories have become the means through which large profits can be reached. Playing to win becomes unimportant and in fact irrelevant to reach one's aims. The predominant norm seems to be to end up on top of the final ranking of competitors no matter what the costs.

The critique is to the point. However, it does not really challenge the argument. This chapter deals not with empirical claims about the views and values among athletes, coaches or spectators today. It is a philosophical argument examining in a critical and systematic way two interpretations of the social logic of these practices. The fact that an ideal is not realised in practice, or the fact that an ideal is threatened and perhaps losing its influence, is of course no decisive argument against it. Ideals are by definition not reality. They must be understood as guiding norms. And ideals might be under pressure but at the same time, from a moral point of view, represent the best alternative. I should also mention that in my opinion the logic of qualitative progress plays a more important role in competitive sports than many seem to realise. I will return to this point in the discussion of the realism of our ideals below.

Another criticism points at the problem of ranking different sport disciplines according to ethical standards. Our argument seems to indicate that the logic of qualitative progress is particularly linked to what we have called games. Does the argument really claim that athletics is morally inferior to soccer, or to tennis?

No. The claim is simply that some disciplines are more vulnerable than others to the logic of quantifiable progress and not that they are morally inferior in principle. As we have seen, record sports such as the 100m sprint are exposed to the unfortunate consequences of the logic of quantifiable progress, but it does not need to be practised accordingly. The sprint in athletics may realise just as much joy among participants and spectators as soccer does.

In other words, sports do not have any necessary social logic or essence – they are open for interpretation. As I have tried to show, competitions can be interpreted and developed according to the norms and values of both alternative interpretations given here. The main point from a critical normative view, then, is to evaluate actual forms of logic and support the logic that seems to be supported by the best reasons.

Competitive sports as games

The argument is that, due to the unfortunate consequences of the logic of quantitative progress, the logic of qualitative progress is to be preferred as the guiding set of norms and values for all sports. According to Suits, all sports can be understood as games in which participants voluntarily attempt to overcome unnecessary obstacles by the use of some kind of physical skill. I will argue in favour of this hypothesis by using one of the hardest cases available – 100m dash – which we might at first glance find to have no 'unnecessary obstacles' at all. The point is to run as fast as possible towards the finishing line. If sprint can be understood within the game logic, most other sports can as well.

Figure 3.1 shows that if we choose to follow the logic of quantifiable growth to its full consequence, there would be no clear distinction between a sprint race and a (scientific) experiment. The basic question would be to explore the maximum speed of the human species. But then there is a series of arrangements in current sprint practice that does not make sense. Why allow only two starting attempts? Why place sprinters in heats with seven other runners, with the psychological stress that follows from such arrangements? Why prohibit certain methods and biochemical products if such means can enhance performance and give better ideas of the biological limits of human running speed?

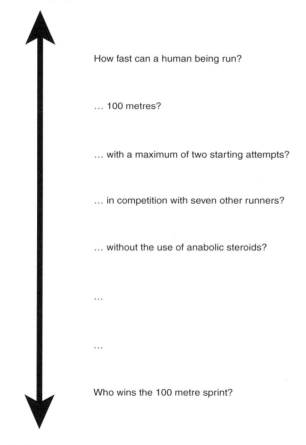

quantifiable progress

How fast can a human being run?

... 100 metres?

... with a maximum of two starting attempts?

... in competition with seven other runners?

... without the use of anabolic steroids?

...

...

Who wins the 100 metre sprint?

qualitative progress

Figure 3.1   The logics of quantifiable and qualitative progress in sport

Obviously, as Figure 3.1 indicates, if competitive sports are to be understood as something different from scientific experiments, the most promising answer seems to be in line with Suits' idea of 'unnecessary obstacles'. The rules exist because adherence to them realises an activity that is challenging, exciting, uncertain. 'Unnecessary obstacles' are introduced to give the activity value in itself. Who wins today? All basic rules in all games share this characteristic. Even the 100m can be interpreted and practised according to the logic of games. The step further, then, is to reflect upon how this logic can become the predominant logic in practice. How can it be cultivated in all sports disciplines?

Moderation of competitive sports

Below follows a brief outline with a few examples of how the norms of the logic of qualitative progress can be used to moderate sports. The basic norm for moderation is: 'Progress in the intensity and/or complexity of joy in sports!' Again, we follow the principle of testing the possibilities on the hardest cases. Practical examples are taken from the sports in which the logic of quantifiable progress seems to hold its firmest grip, most notably record sports such as running.

Game-specific advantage!

How can exact quantification of performances be transformed to less exact game-specific measurements? In sprint in athletics, for example, one could simply stop timing and record-keeping in the events and instead count and give points for wins and losses in a series of sprints. This norm is already followed in Grand Prix events, in which wins and losses are accumulated in a series of competitions. A win can give five points; coming second, three points; and third place gives one point. When the season is over, it will be possible to distinguish the best overall sprinter during the whole season. This would give new dimensions to sprint and it would provide more possibilities for success. For instance, it is possible that one season a sprinter wins who has not actually won a single race, but has shown a remarkable stability and come second and third in all competitions. Quantifiable results in terms of timing would become less important. The whole point in each race would be to cross the finishing line first. Similar moderation could be suggested in all record sports.

Equal opportunity to perform!

A certain standardisation of external conditions, such as playing according to the same rules and under the same external conditions, is a necessity for sports competitions to be realised in a meaningful way. However, equal opportunity is a basic principle in each particular competition and should not be understood as a norm on identical conditions across time and space. Record sports can learn from disciplines with non-standardised arenas, like the marathon and cross-country skiing. A sprint run can take place on different surfaces and under different weather conditions. Each arena could have its own particular surface, its own particular track profile and its particular characteristics. In Africa, runners could compete on the famous red soil, in Florida one could run barefoot on the white sands of Miami Beach, and in Oslo one could run in the wintertime on hard-packed snow. This would enhance the diversity and thrill of competing and soften the quest for quantifiable results in favour of the norm 'Play to win!'

Play to win!

If the norms above are followed, we have a system in which the result of each single competition is primary. In sprint, for instance, record-setting would become impossible. Based on the model from parallel slalom, one could instead cultivate to its full extent the duel principle. Through a series of heats, two sprinters will end up facing each other in the final race. The whole competition should be arranged to take place within one day with no idea of restitution in order to set any kind of record in the final other than to win it. This norm was tested in real life, in fact, in the 150m duel between Michael Johnson and Donovan Bailey (champions of the 200m and 100m respectively) in 1997. The principle of duels could be followed in longer running distances as well. What counts is to run to win a particular race.

Complex skills!

How is it possible to change sprint or running in athletics according to the norm of complex skills? How can the norm of specialisation be softened? As suggested above, the external framework of the skill test can encourage more complex skill development by (in running, for instance) varying the surfaces on which athletes would have to run. In addition, the distances could be subject to variation. The short sprint could be between 80m and 400m; middle distance, between 400m and 3000m; and long distance, from 3000m and up. To accumulate points as indicated above, runners would have to compete over distances ranging from the shortest to the longest alternative within their range of running, and on different surfaces and under different climatic conditions.

More generally, a good principle for avoiding narrow specialisation is to include significant technical and/or tactical skills that have to be learned in social interaction with others. Recent moderation of speed skating provides a good example. In traditional competitions, skaters compete against each other and against time under standardised conditions. Records – personal, local, regional, national and of the world – play an important part. The main tactical challenge is to utilise one's basic physical qualities – endurance and strength – in the best way possible during the race. In the relatively new sport of short-track skating, the point is to cross the finishing line first. Skaters compete in heats with many participants, and the challenge is to pick the right line and attack at the right time. Short-track skating requires more complex skills and is therefore a less vulnerable sport.

Particularity!

If the norms above are followed, the focus will to a larger extent be on the qualities of each competition and each individual athlete instead of an objective focus on human performance. The focus would be on particular athletes, teams and competitions, and not on records. This strengthens each particular athlete's position in the sports system. Complex technical and tactical skill challenges make the manipulation of performance more difficult. One can enhance endurance and strength with pills and injections, but no biomedical cure or no system of genetic engineering can create technical finesse and tactical understanding. Technical and tactical performance has to be learned through experience, first and foremost in social interaction with others. Hence, to a larger extent than within the logic of quantifiable progress, results are products of the talents, efforts and good luck of individual athletes and teams. Athletes and teams stand forward with primary responsibility for their own performances.

Moderation – a realistic ideal?

How do the norms for moderation stand in relation to current developments in competitive sports? Are our views realistic at all?

In the postwar period up to the early 1970s, competitive sports were still in many ways in their innocent childhood. Indeed, the logic of quantifiable progress was predominant. Records held a strong fascination among athletes and the public. However, the problematic consequences of this logic were not well-known. Most athletes were still amateurs, with no strong financial, scientific or technological systems to support them. The logic of quantifiable progress was rooted in an amateur ethos with an emphasis on morality. Investment of extensive resources, professionalism and extensive use of sports medicine were unusual.

The amateur ethos is still to be found, even at high levels of performance, especially in non-commercialised sports like international orienteering and canoeing. Over the last two decades, other record disciplines, such as track and field, and cycling, have experienced considerable commercial success and are among the more popular products on an international entertainment market. Possibilities for large payoffs in terms of fame and fortune have increased. Hence, an increasing number of talented and well-trained athletes take part. Gradually, performance enhancement has become an end towards which any means seems justifiable. High-performance sports have gone through what Heinilä (1982) calls a totalising process: the competition now is between total systems of material, human, economic, technological and scientific resources. Reports like the one from the hearings on the use of drugs in Canadian (and international) sports (Dubin 1990), and the EPO scandals in professional cycling, provide vivid examples of some of the problems that ensue.

On the other hand, it is too simple to view commercialisation and entertainment as the root of all evil in sports. Great public attention has led to interesting, alternative developments. MacAloon (1984a) describes from an anthropological point of view the transformation of Olympic events from rituals with firm frameworks, obligatory participation and no clear distinctions between participants and spectators, to spectacles with a clear distinction between the two. What counts in a spectacle is strong and varied experiential values: drama, intensity, joy and extreme performances. To a certain extent, entertainment represents the logic of qualitative, and not quantitative, progress. Entertainment products have to offer their consumers valuable experiences of many kinds. It does not matter how fast a speed skater is on the 10,000m if the staging and the visual image of the sport is boring. The race has to produce joy.

This does not mean that the logic of qualitative progress coheres with the forces of commercialism. The logic of commercial entertainment is profit. Commercial payoff depends upon marketing potential, which again depends upon high ratings in terms of high numbers of (television) spectators. The primary criterion for quality assessment in the media is public joy and not the joy of the athletes themselves. This can be problematic indeed.

The so-called 'fair weather spectator' has no loyalties or feelings for any particular athletes or sport disciplines, but goes to where the action is. The extreme variant is the sports-interested 'TV channel surfer'. He (it is more often a he than a she) changes sport interest with the latest fashion, and identifies with, and cheers on, athletes according to who is currently winning. 'Fair weather spectators' are not genuinely engaged. They invest no personal engagement, no personal risk, no existential value. They do not put themselves 'on the line'. The means used by athletes and their consequences are uninteresting so long as the products are competitions with drama, excitement and spectacular performances. The underlying ideology is the production of pleasure for profit. The focus is on immediate consumption of pleasure, not on the joy of sports. Understood in these ways, the logic of entertainment is destructive.

But, as newer anthropological research has shown, sports spectators are of a great variety (Archetti 1992). An alternative version is the serious supporter who invests identity and meaning in his or her sport interest. Supporters follow loyally their favourite sports, athletes and teams, and they seem to be genuinely and playfully engaged. They know their game, its history, its traditions, and they participate in the struggle against hegemonic interpretations in the present. A striking example is the devoted Chelsea fan Sut Jhally. In 1997 he reacted when seeing the logo of the beer brewer Coors – known in the US for its support of the political Right – on the chest of Chelsea manager and star player Ruud Gullit. To Jhally, this kind of cooperation was against the values of soccer and the club he loved. In an emotional comment, Jhally (1998: 224) compared the situation to '... if Jesse Owens had been forced to wear Hitler's swastika'. The guiding norms of the devoted fan seem to come close to the logic of qualitative progress. The joy of sports for the supporter becomes similar to the participant's perspective as discussed above.

There is a final trend in competitive sports that indicates that the logic of qualitative progress may be more promising than it might initially appear to be. An emerging youth culture with focus on identity construction through leisure and technological innovation has provided the basis for a series of new sports activities over the last decades: windsurfing, off-road biking and the so-called board sports, surfing, skateboarding, snowboarding. In fact, at the Winter Olympic Games at Nagano in 1998 snowboarding was part of the official programme for the very first time. These sports are by no means typical expressions of the logic of quantifiable progress. They have their commercial aspects and are influenced by strong business interests aiming for profit at the immense youth markets. But their origins and, at least up to now, their guiding norms, are different from those in traditional entertainment sports. In their relatively loose measurements of performance, their moderate standardisation, and their focus on each particular athlete and each particular event, they are expressions of youthful opposition, of rebellion against quantification and objectification in favour of playfulness and joy (Humphreys 1997).

The art of moderation

New sports based on alternative lines of logic have appeared on the scene. More sports of this kind will probably develop as leisure time and the resources put into leisure seem to increase. However, established sports can, and to a certain extent ought to, be moderated as well. The key, then, is mastery of the art of moderation: in Goethe's words, 'In der Begrenzung zeigt sich der Meister' (Mastery is expressed through moderation).

Every sport discipline has its own history, its traditions, its customs, and ideals that ought to be respected. There are lessons to be learned here. Sports disciplines can be understood as social practices in the MacIntyrean sense of the word; as practices with internal goods that can only be realised in the process of following the established standards of excellence as participants in the practice (McNamee 1995). But one should respect these traditions, customs and ideals, but not follow them uncritically.

Traditions and ideals in competitive sports do not always have good explanations or a sound rationale. Why, for example, do we count points in a tennis game in the strange way of 15–30–40–game? The counting is a result of a historical particularity. This particularity is unproblematic and in fact enjoyable, and makes tennis a game with originality. Some particularities and local traditions in games ought to be cultivated and strengthened.

Other arrangements and traditions can be of a more questionable kind. For example, as Tännsjö points out in Chapter 7, the rationale behind placing men and women in different competition classes can indeed be questioned. An example linked to the discussion here can depart from the fact that standardisation in athletics is different from standardisation in cross-country skiing. This is, of course, in part due to external, climatic conditions. Whereas a sprint arena can be standardised quite easily, snow surfaces are constantly changing and never identical, not even during the same race. However, as we have seen, less standardisation on the 100m would make it a less specialised and thereby a less vulnerable sport. The important thing is not standardisation over time and space but equality of opportunity in each particular competition. The 100m ought to go, as suggested above, in the direction of ski racing, and not vice versa.

The art of moderation lies in the balancing in a given sport of its traditions, customs and ideals as a social practice, and critical and systematic reflection based on the logic of qualitative progress. In situations of choice, we ought always to choose alternatives that increase the intensity and/or the complexity of the joy of sports among all parties engaged. The fundamental strength of the logic of qualitative progress is its infinite potential for progress.

Competitive sports will not change overnight. But one should demand from its participants, coaches and leaders a certain reflective and constructive attitude to the cultivation of joy and thereby its flourishing in the future.

Concluding comments

The logic of quantitative progress tends to narrow the possibilities for human progress to one or a few special qualities that are vulnerable to manipulation by outside expertise – medical, technological, scientific. The main problem is that there is no clear reference to final ends here, or that the final end, for example 'the perfect human being', is of a morally problematic nature. This logic seems to imply a search for objective knowledge, such as an answer to the question: How fast can a human being run the 100m? But why are such answers of value to sports at all? The result can be what

Hoberman (1996) calls a 'dehumanisation of sports' based on the impossible quest for unlimited progress in (biologically) limited systems.

The logic of qualitative progress has as its main norm progress in intensity and/or complexity of joy in sports. Game-specific advantages and non-standardised arenas make strict comparison of results that are independent of time and place quite meaningless. Complex skills cannot easily be manipulated by outside influence but have to be learned through experience and social interaction. Particular athletes and teams stand forward with responsibility for their own performance and attempt to play to win each particular competition. We deal here with the fascinating quest for unlimited growth in unlimited systems.

I have argued that the logic of qualitative progress is the normative ideal that ought to guide future development of competitive sports. The most fundamental justification of this logic can be found in its connections to final ends. The exploration of joy by particular athletes in particular games has an important existential dimension. In competitive sports, we put ourselves 'on the line'. In the joy of sports, we touch upon basic, existential questions that are meaningful for most of us. Who am I? To whom do I belong? What can I achieve alone or together with others? What are my/our possibilities in time and space? In this way, competitive sports can provide meaning and value in people's lives, and become important elements of what is often referred to as the final end for us all, 'the good life'.

Part II

Nationalism

Chapter 4

Sports as the moral discourse of nations

William J. Morgan

Introduction

Appiah writes that 'nations matter morally, when they do ... for the same reason that football and opera matter – as things desired by autonomous agents, whose autonomous desires we ought to acknowledge ... even if we cannot always accede to them' (Appiah 1996: 28). I understand Appiah to be saying here that if love of country, patriotism for short, figures in our moral reflections at all, it does so principally in sentimental ways registering our desire to identify with our community and compatriots, to acknowledge and nurture our emotional bond with them.[1] It is but a small step from this sentimental understanding of patriotism to sports, since sports are nothing if not sentimental vehicles, capable, for instance, of whipping people into an emotional frenzy over the victory of their national team. Indeed, David Miller, in his fine new book *On Nationality*, makes the connection explicit when he recounts a remark of a friend that 'he was quite unaware how much importance he attached to being Dutch until a night in June 1988, when the Dutch football team defeated the German team in the European Cup, provoking a mass celebration on the streets of Amsterdam' (Miller 1995: 14). Miller is of the view that it is emotionally charged events such as these that are necessary to arouse our national sentiments and allegiances.

What I find of interest about Appiah's thesis and Miller's anecdote is that it sets up a moral connection between sports and nationalism that is of central interest to this chapter. However, since I believe Appiah's thesis is mistaken, I also believe that the moral connection it implicitly draws between sports and nations is the wrong one. But since I also believe that Appiah's mistake is an instructive one, I think a more persuasive account of the moral relation between sports and nationalism can be made by showing in what sense his account goes awry.

What is mistaken about his thesis is that it gets the moral import of nations exactly backward; for when nations morally matter it is not our mere desiring them that confers their moral significance but the fact that they are normative of our desires. That is to say, nations morally matter, when they do, because they belong to the class of what Charles Taylor calls strongly valued goods, and it is the mark of such goods that they:

> are not seen as constituted as good by the fact that we desire them, but rather … are seen as goods which we ought to desire, even if we do not, goods such that we show ourselves as inferior or bad by our not desiring them.[2]

(Taylor 1985: 120)

Appiah's moral picture of patriotism is skewed, then, because in reducing patriotism to the desires and preferences of its members it fails to see how a strongly valued good patriotism belongs rather to the evaluative frameworks by which we assess the moral worth of our desires, not to mention make sense of our moral lives.[3] The patriotic refrain that runs something to the effect of 'that's not the way "we" do things around here' is, therefore, at bottom a moral one, and what makes it so is that it stakes out where 'we' as a people stand with regard to the good – registering those desires, actions, forms of life which are worthy of 'us' as a people and those which are unworthy.[4] That is why, when love of country and the communal sense of belonging that it inspires assume moral significance for 'us', they become so much a part of who 'we' are, of our conception of ourselves as moral beings, that, as Larmore aptly puts it, 'to imagine them as objects of choice would be to imagine ourselves as without a guiding sense of morality – and so not only ill-equipped to actually choose them, but also lacking the right sort of identification to them' (Larmore 1996: 130).

To mistake the strongly valued good of nationalism for a weakly valued desire to identify with our larger community is, therefore, to miss the moral force of nationalism, of what constitutes it as a moral ideal. It is also to miss the moral connection that yokes sport to this moral ideal. For it is character-istic of strongly valued goods like nationalism, Taylor tells us, that they 'only exist for us through some articulation', only 'become available for the people of a given culture through being given expression in some manner' (Taylor 1989: 91). Sports, I want to argue, are one important, perhaps even paradigmatic, form in which that expression takes place. Their expressive capacity in this regard is not to be confused with their, perhaps, better-known ability to forge sentimental attachments to country, which explains their political but not their moral salience, and so why the State and its political operatives are often disposed to manipulate sports to suit their own sectarian interests. Rather, the expressive qualities of sports have to do with their storytelling capacity, with the narratives they churn out. And I will maintain that one of the chief narrative roles sports play in the contemporary age – a role enshrined, for example, in such global sporting events as the Olympic Games, the Commonwealth Games, and the World Cup – is to show how the unfolding stories of the lives of individual people are woven into the unfolding stories of the different nations and cultures to which they claim allegiance, thereby imparting to those lives a social and moral sense of purpose and meaning they might otherwise not have. If I am not off the mark, then a close reading of sporting narratives promises to shed important light on disclosing what nationalism comes to as a moral ideal, on what evaluative frameworks it has to offer us to sort out the moral point of our lives. I should say that in pushing this moral line I am not denying that at least some of the appeal nationalism commands today is sentimental in nature. Nor do I wish to deny that sports are powerful purveyors of such national sentiments. Archbishop Croke's lament regarding the encroachment of English sports on the traditional sports of his homeland (Ireland) in the late nineteenth century is a case in point: 'If we continue travelling … in the same direction that we have taken for some time', he insists:

> condemning the sports that were practised by our forefathers, effacing our national features, as though we were ashamed of them, and putting on, with England's stuff and broadcloths, her mashier habits and other effeminate follies as she may recommend, we had better at once and in public abjure our nationality, clap hands for joy at the sight of the Union Jack and place 'England's bloody red' exultantly above the green.
>
> (Bairner 1997: 4–5)

What I am denying, however, is that when nations and sports tug on the emotions and sentiments of people in this fashion they do so in what can reasonably be described as moral ways.

I realise, of course, that in taking this moral line I am opening myself up to certain and instant rebuke. For nationalism is more known and instanced today for its blood-letting excesses than for any moral uplift it may have provided ascendant nations in the past, is providing existing nations presently, or might yet provide aspiring ones in the future. Barbara Ehrenreich's (1997) sweeping claim that the modern nation requires the blood of other nations to sustain and nurture itself is only the latest in a long line of critical put-downs of nationalism. This does not bode well for my effort to portray sporting narratives as forms of nationalist self-expression, which, in this inhospitable climate, is likely to be construed by many rather as a smear on sports than a comment on their moral possibilities.

But while some, if not much, of this nay-saying is deserved (that part of it, at any rate, that is focused on the particular actions of particular nations), I think blanket condemnations of nationalism are not. For those who go in for such wholesale criticism, who are inclined to hatred and rejection of all things nationalistic, are not dissimilar in their outlook and bearing from those who disdain and write off argument, and those who disdain and write off their fellow human beings. As Plato long ago observed:

Misology and misanthropy arise in just the same way. Misanthropy is induced by believing in somebody quite uncritically. You assume that a person is ... truthful and sincere and reliable, and a little later you find that he is shoddy and unreliable... After repeated disappointments ... constant irritation ends by making you dislike everybody and suppose that there is no sincerity to be found.

(Plato 1969: 89d)

Nationalism has similarly leavened our social hopes, most recently in Eastern Europe, only to dash them. But, for the very reason Plato suggests, we should resist the temptation to expunge it altogether from our moral vocabularies. And while my attempt to trace the narrative lines that lead from sports to national self-expression rules out any full-scale defence of nationalism against its critics, what I have to say regarding the sophisticated ways in which such national self-images are fashioned will, I hope, help to dispel the idea that nationalism is a morally pernicious notion, that loving one's country is somehow incompatible with criticising and feeling shame for its shortcomings and for giving other countries the respect owed them.

A forceful objection

My claim that sports are a morally rich language of nationalism, where language is broadly understood to include not just the words we speak and write but the various modes of expression (gestures, movements, actions, symbols) we use to convey meanings and values that are important to us,[5] is admittedly a controversial claim. As such, it is open to challenge on a number of fronts. For the purposes of the present chapter, however, I want to consider one especially powerful challenge that argues that the main story lines generated by global sporting events like the Olympics are just too coarse and enmeshed in stereotypical tales of cultural superiority to do any real moral work. I will argue that, while this objection is not groundless, it is not persuasive either, and therefore should be rejected.

This objection focuses on the hard-to-miss statistical bent of sports, what Brown aptly calls their capacity to produce 'numerically translatable events' (1992: 55), and their penchant for larding their narratives with these numerical translations. It is this feature of sports that explains why so much of the storytelling that goes on in sports is shot through with numerical accounts of their actions and results. In the case of the international sports featured here, this numerical reckoning is centred on the awarding of medals and/or points for individual or team athletic performances, which are then tabulated and assigned to their respective nations. While this sort of statistical evocation of nation-ness makes for handy referencing and easy comparison, one which allows us to rank nations on a global athletic scale according to their athletic prowess – much as they are ranked on a global

economic scale according to their GNP, the argument is that it does not make for strong, morally robust stories, since it limits what sports are able to tell us to what can be plotted on this scale. Numbers loom large here not just because they are the language in which comparisons between nations are made, but also because they mould and shape the narratives that are trotted out to explain the comparisons, to account for why a given nation is located where it is on this scale.

The upshot of this argument, then, is that international sports prove to be more fitted for culture-bashing than moral edification because of their fetish for numbering, for telling stories based on numerical transcriptions of athletic performances that make for – better, invite – invidious comparison. This athletic trafficking in numbers is alleged to have this baleful effect because it precludes any meaningful dialogue between nations that might call into question the stereotypes that circulate in their midst. That is because, as Taylor argues, whereas names are forms of address that call people into a conversation, a 'web of interlocution', numbers are forms of 'easy reference' that are meant to keep people out of the conversation, to block their entrance into any meaningful 'web of interlocution' (Taylor 1989: 525). Tagging people as referents is, therefore, merely a pretext for denying them a space in the conversation, for divesting them of any conversational standing that would make it possible for them to make known their desires and wishes to others. In worst-case scenarios, this kind of divestment is intended to strip people of any identity at all. This explains the perverse logic behind the meticulous numbering of members of nations singled out for genocide, the kind of numbering we witnessed, for example, in the concentration camps of World War II, and the kind of numbering that was recently discovered in the back rooms of the Tuol Sleng torture chambers of the Khmer Rouge, in which hapless victims were both numbered and photographed before they were slaughtered (14,000 in Tuol Sleng alone). For those steeped in the logical calculus of this genocidal numbering, whose purpose, once again, was to destroy the identity of the persons targeted, it was, apparently, a small step from this nominalist obliteration of people to their physical obliteration – from depriving people of their good name to murdering them.

Of course, the numbering that international sports go in for does not completely deprive people of their name and identity, although it very often does deprive many of them of their good name – I should think it goes without saying that it is does not harbour any aim, secret or otherwise, to deprive them of their physical person. Part of the reason why it does not have this wholesale identity-cancelling effect is that numbers are only affixed to names, not substituted for them and, moreover, affixed to *all* names not just a select few. Still, although the monological effects of these numbering schemes are certainly benign by comparison, and surely less debilitating and seemingly more egalitarian than other such schemes, their

effects are real enough and, as it turns out, hardly as egalitarian as they seem.

They are real in the sense that they constitute a clear obstacle to genuine conversation, since those nations marked as referents will get talked about but will not themselves get the chance to talk, and thus will have things said about them that they will be unable to challenge and, if necessary, debunk. The monological effects of athletic numbering are real in the further sense that when nations are merely referenced in this fashion they are turned largely into foils for addressee nations, such that addressee nations are not only able to describe themselves contrastively by playing themselves off against these nations, but are able to deploy these contrastive descriptions in ways that make their own members look good by making the members of these other nations look bad. This is, for example, precisely how the 'American' game of baseball – a game whose 'statisticity', Brown rightly argues, rather than its 'pastorality', accounts for its 'timelessly American' character – has been portrayed since the late nineteenth century, in which it was claimed that only Americans were able to play the game in the 'manly' manner in which it was intended to be played, thereby opening other nations who chose – dared – to play baseball to invidious comparison (Brown 1992: 55).[6] And since this way of referencing others requires no dialogical interaction with them, there is little to prevent dominant nations from availing themselves of the numerical grid that sports provide to demean dominated ones as they see fit, to tar them with one depreciatory story after another.

The effects of this athletic numbering are also, as I insinuated, not nearly as egalitarian as they might seem at first blush. For although all nations are numbered in international sports, some are numbered in ways that do not compromise their dialogical status while others are numbered in ways that clearly do compromise their dialogical status. The reason for this is that the numbering schemes of international sports rank nations not just in terms of their athletic prowess but also according to their economic, social and political clout. This fact skews, or so the argument suggests, the entire ranking system in ways that privilege the rich and powerful nations of the West; for it is these nations that hold an ideological monopoly over international sports. Indeed, the complicity of the prosperous West in this regard is almost total: the sports that make up the 'official' slate of international sports are with very few exceptions Western inventions;[7] these same sports are also played, organised and financed in characteristically Western ways; the fascination with numbers and records that are a trademark of these sports are as well a Western contrivance – as is, finally, the very idea of using sports as markers of national identity.

It is this ideological advantage enjoyed by the dominant nations of the West in international sports, therefore, that explains the otherwise hard-to-explain fact of why the non-dominant countries of the West and the East

are often not accorded the respect and recognition owed them by their athletic triumphs. For when such nations come out on top in these sporting competitions, which is increasingly the case these days, that success is typically explained away – to be exact, demeaned – by stereotypically laden stories. Thus it was that Finland's astonishing successes in the 1924 summer Olympic Games were greeted by a flood of stories in the mainstream Western press that attributed their accomplishments to, among other things, their diet, their Mongolian racial heritage, the harshness of their environment and their fondness for saunas (Guttmann 1994b: 42–43). And thus it is today that the remarkable athletic successes of African nations are similarly explained away by stereotypical (bordering on overtly racist) stories that unashamedly invoke the image of 'uninhibited natural athletes' and their forbidding environment, and that harp on the primitivism and lack of cultural sophistication that are alleged to be their national features.

Rejoinder

As I said earlier, this is a forceful objection but not a persuasive one. It is not persuasive because its central thesis, that the numerically friendly narratives of international athletic games give the rich and dominant nations of the West free rein to say whatever humiliating things they like about poor, dominated nations, does not hold up. The reason why, I argue, is because the numbers that adorn these stories very often have the opposite effect, helping to pry open a space of interlocution in which national stereotypes can be hashed out and contested. More strongly, I argue further, international sports are actually structured in such a way that this opposite, stereotypical-busting effect is the more likely narrative outcome.

The argument I want to press here is an adaptation of an argument made by Allen Guttmann to good effect in his discussion of how dominated nations were able to reverse the 'ludic' monopoly of the dominant West by becoming so accomplished at the 'master's' sports that they were, and still are, regularly able to 'beat them at their own game' (Guttmann 1994a: 179). It is this feature of 'beating them at their own game' that I want to pick up on and explore further in terms of our discussion of the narrative promise of international sports. For it provides subordinate nations with an opportunity not just to win at games not of their own making but, more importantly, an opportunity to win a place for themselves in the conversations they touch off. It is in this sense that we can understand the numerical predilections of sports as an aid rather than a hindrance to their storytelling capacities. That is because the numbers and rankings in this case actually do double duty, both referencing the accomplishments of said nations and, in carving out a name for them as nations to be reckoned with in the world of sports, reserving a place for them in the conversations that ensue. Indeed, referencing and naming go hand in hand here, since the numbers themselves in

such instances help secure the dominated nations in question with the recognition and legitimacy they must have if they are to be interlocutors at all – a recognition, I might add, summarily denied them in most other spheres of life.

Of course, while recognition is better than non-recognition, it is no antidote for misrecognition. Indeed, with recognition comes the possibility of misrecognition. So my argument that the numerical bent of sporting narratives abets rather than deters dialogue, managing the difficult feat of referencing and addressing nations at one and the same time, does not claim that this in any way indemnifies them against stereotypical distortions, distortions of precisely the sort the Western press circulated to explain away and demean the successes of Finnish and African athletes (see page 65). What it does claim, however, is that just as dominated nations are able to turn the tables on dominant ones by defeating them at their own game, they are also able to turn the tables on dominant nations in narrative terms by parlaying their athletic successes, specifically the name recognition they bring them, into conversational ones. Sure, this in no way seals the fate of stereotypes in the narratives of sports, but it does seal their monological fate by giving dominated nations a say, an opportunity to confront them headlong and to launch counternarratives that send the conversation off in new directions. MacAloon, I believe, had something like this in mind when he argued that the 'Olympics are a kind of hyperstructure in which categories and stereotypes are condensed, exaggerated, and dramatised, rescued from the "taken for granted", and made objects of explicit and lively awareness' (MacAloon 1991: 274–275). It is this release from the 'taken for granted', where stereotypes do their best nasty work, I am arguing, that gives these sporting narratives their dialogical purchase. And since the numerical features that are, evidently, an integral part of those narratives help establish rather than undermine the identity of dominated nations in these cases, etching their names (so to speak) in the pantheon of international sports, they open up a talking point, a story line, from which such nations can spin out their own counter-stories.

If what I am arguing above has any credence at all, then we should be able to cite instance after instance in which subordinate nations willingly and readily avail themselves of the narrative credentials of sports, numbers and all, to bolster their own national self-images and to loosen the grip, in effect, on their collective psyche of the bad things that have repeatedly been written and said about them. And that is apparently what we do find when we trouble to look at the historical record. A few prominent examples should make the point.

Expatriates and former colonists, both white and black, of England, Perkins tells us, made much of their ability to beat the mother country at her native sports, cricket and soccer. They even went so far as to regard such athletic triumphs as a kind of 'rite of passage', one that proved their 'fitness

for home rule' (1989: 151). Similarly, when young Japanese schoolboys first took up the game of baseball in the late nineteenth century, they did so mindful of their tarnished national image. Playing baseball, Roden notes, was for them a way to repair this image. They were also of the view that if they could play baseball not just on a par with Americans but better than them, they could 'compel Westerners to reconsider fictitious stereotypes' (1980: 529), stereotypes that the West had long held over their head with pernicious effect. And in this they proved prescient, for their successes over American teams gradually, if begrudgingly, won the respect of American players and spectators, who, as Roden tells us further, were increasingly willing to shake the hands of and cheer the performances of their Japanese rivals (1980: 529).

The case of Africa is perhaps even more noteworthy in this regard. Following decolonisation in the 1960s, many African nations were racked by internecine strife, attributable no doubt to the fact that opposition to colonial rule was the main social glue that held them together. As a consequence, new sources of national identity had to be discovered and/or invented. Sports were quickly mobilised in this effort, and as early as the 1970s became an important vehicle of national pride and solidarity. The remarkable achievements by African athletes that soon followed in international sports, including the Olympics, put sports at the forefront of such nationalist campaigns; and with good reason, for they presented a very different picture of the African continent to an incredulous West. As Baker nicely put it, 'what cultural ambassadors and African representatives to the United Nations attempted, athletes achieved with apparent ease: publicising an image of strength and success rather than poverty and instability' (1987: 273). What makes this counternarrative of a healthy, vibrant Africa a significant one, and not, take your pick, a pathetic smoke screen or pipe dream, is that it flies in the face of a stubborn Western insistence that Africa is, with the possible exception of South Africa, a hopeless, lost cause – to wit, consider a 1997 cover of *The New Republic*, which featured a photograph of an emaciated, and apparently terrified, African mother and daughter bearing the caption 'Africa is dying'. The point here is not that the nations of Africa are, in fact, prospering rather than faltering, for they clearly are facing trying (and in some cases certainly desperate) times. Rather, the point is that the West seems interested only in their calamities, in addressing them almost exclusively as nations under siege in need of some form of paternalistic oversight – which might explain why it can think of precious little to say about these countries that cast them in a more positive light. Sports, I contend, are an important and telling exception.

I could, of course, have just as easily cited Cuba's triumphs over the United States in baseball, or Brazil's victories in the World Cup, or West Indian successes in cricket. For this 'beating them at their own game' phenomenon, and the vertiginous narrative outpouring it induces, is a widespread one indeed, and, at least with respect to the dominated nations involved, a dialogical coup of sorts. If anything, the numbers that are part of this outpouring add an authenticating and readily understood touch to this athletic reversal of fortunes.

But the other point not to lose sight of here is that the narratives of sports – again, numbers and all – spur dialogue, not only by enlarging the conversational space of dominated nations but by shrinking the conversational space of dominant ones. For much of the space freed up for subordinate nations to narrate their stories of athletic ascendancy was formerly taken up by dominant nations, which is just another way of saying that the latter nations controlled those conversations by controlling the space of interlocution – which accounts for their monological character. My point that sports reclaim a portion of this conversational space for dominated nations to unfold their own stories is anticipated in Perkins' argument that losing at sports helped pave the way for the relatively smooth dismantling of the British empire and its replacement by a Commonwealth of Nations. As Perkins avers:

> Losing at organised sports and games prepared the British ... just as winning prepared the colonials, for decolonisation and for mutual respect and independence on both sides, and just as winning and losing prepared the British themselves, working class professionals triumphing over gentleman amateurs, for a more egalitarian ... society.
>
> (Perkins 1989: 153)

I would like to argue that this apparent new-found respect for marginalised nations to which Perkins draws our attention here is attributable to the fact that athletic tales of this 'beat them at their own game' genre help to break the one-sided character of the conversations that normally occur between dominant and dominated nations by altering the moral psychology of each of the conversational parties. For, just as the athletic successes of dominated nations give them cause to take themselves more seriously, to take moral stock of themselves in ways that bolster their self-worth and moral horizons, those same athletic successes give dominant nations reason to take themselves less seriously, to take moral stock of themselves in ways that deflate their self-importance and moral horizons. This process of moral deflation and inflation can obviously go too far. On the deflationary side, it has at times undermined the moral confidence of the West in, for example, its traditions of social justice, traditions that, though more often than not observed in the breach, it should be rightly proud of and ready to defend, and, more to the point, be prepared to deploy against itself as the occasion arises. On the inflationary side, it has at times prompted 'new' nations to take themselves too seriously, thereby inspiring an indifference, if not bellicosity, towards other nations that is not only unwarranted but dangerous.

But, since my focus in this chapter is the enabling effects of this process, I have chosen not to dwell on these problematic features in my text. That does not mean that I am unaware of them and their pernicious influence; only that I do not think that they cancel out the positive moral benefits I discuss here.

A reasonable process of moral deflation and inflation helps to disarm the complacent and smug outlook of dominant nations that moral discourse begins and ends where their own moral concerns begin and end at the same time that it emboldens dominated nations to think of themselves as the moral equals of dominant ones in conversational terms. By 'moral and conversational equals', I do not mean that all nations and cultures are of equal worth and must be judged accordingly, a demand which, as Taylor rightly notes, rests on an 'act of breathtaking condescension' (1989: 70) since it requires that such judgments be made without even studying the nations and cultures in question. Rather, I mean that all nations are of sufficient worth so as to be the conversational equals of every other nation when it comes to narrating their own life stories, a claim (rather than a pre-emptory demand) that rests on the different and, I believe, reasonable presumption 'that all human cultures that have animated whole societies over some considerable stretch of time have something important to say to all human beings' (Taylor 1989: 66). Sports, or so I have been arguing, help us to see lumpen nations in the light of this latter presumption, which would explain in part the self-confident and self-conscious manner in which many such marginalised nations and groups now present themselves to others. As MacAloon avers, 'No group, no matter where they are located or how peripheral to Northern Hemisphere centres of power they might be, any longer need outsiders ... to inform them they have a distinctive culture worth representing and preserving' (1991: 42).

But if the narratives of athletic triumph give dominated nations a conversational edge they would not otherwise have, in what sense (as I also claimed earlier) do the narrative structures of sports themselves – apart, that is, from how they are put to use by specific groups – encourage this favourable dialogical result? The answer, oddly enough, lies with what Guttmann refers to as the 'standardised universality of modern sports', a universality that makes it possible, he further notes, for 'everyone to play the game – whatever game it is' (1994a: 188) – and one, I should further add, that lends the numbering and ranking schemes of international sports their credibility. I say 'oddly enough' because in calling attention to this universal feature of modern sports I seem to be reintroducing the notion of an ideologically advantaged West, a notion that I have been trying very hard to dispel. Let me explain.

The 'standardised universality' of modern sports was achieved, like almost everything else in the modern period, at the expense of traditional forms of sporting life and the background social forms of life that sustained them.

It was thus part of a larger paradigm shift in sports that marked the triumph of distinctly Western notions of sports, replete with their formal rules and passion for records and all manner of quantification, over non-Western ones. What is more, as an important player in this paradigm shift, it was directly implicated in the net loss of what Guttmann aptly referred to as 'the bewildering variety of traditional sports' (1994a: 188); that is, the homespun sports and games played mostly by non-Western peoples. So laying claim to the 'standardised universality of sports' as a prominent reason for the dialogical successes of disenfranchised nations seems problematic at best, since the significance and value of those successes rests to a large extent on their promise of greater diversity, on their bringing to an increasingly homogeneous, uniform world *more* cultural variety and difference, not less.

I believe, however, that these worries over Western ideological dominion and lost pluralism are largely unfounded. To begin with, the idea of standardising the conditions in which sports are played, while indeed a Western one, has nonetheless worked to the advantage of non-Western peoples in just the 'beat them at their own game' ways I have indicated. There is just too much empirical evidence for these athletic turnabouts and the greater dialogical leverage they afford such nations not to take them seriously. Moreover, while it is also true that the 'standardised universality' of modern sports did result in a net loss of diversity in terms of the sheer numbers and kinds of sports played, the same cannot be said for the meanings generated by these modern sports, which increased dramatically in both number and kind as a direct result of the greater variety of people who were able to play them. In other words, what we have with the advent of modern sport and its remarkably successful diffusion is not a simple loss of pluralism, but rather a replacement of one kind of pluralism with another. What was lost was the pluralism of 'sheer' numbers and varieties of sports represented by traditional, indigenous sports, a pluralism founded on the monological premise that 'the world [is] richly multicultural ... largely because many people within it are not' (Gutmann 1993: 184). What was gained was the pluralism of meanings churned out by modern sports, a pluralism founded on the dialogical premise that the world is richly multicultural largely because many of the people within it are likewise. So the diversity and cultural differences modern sports ushered in were precisely the sort of diversity and cultural differences one would expect to find when pluralism is no longer estimated by the isolation of nations and their social practices from one another, but by their relations with one another and the constant intercultural interaction their shared social practices make possible.

Conclusion

I have argued that the numbers with which international sports suffuse their narratives of athletic exploit more often than not bolster the moral effect of the stories they tell and the intercultural comparisons they turn out. That is not to say, as I noted earlier, that they indemnify these stories against nation-bashing and stereotypical distortion, but only that they provide a readily understandable (if abstract) discourse in which such bashing and distortion can be challenged and even, on occasion, reversed. I have argued further that sports are almost alone in this respect, and have given dominated nations a voice denied them practically everywhere else.

But it might well be rejoined at this point that I have made far too much of this narrative upside of sports, especially of the moral significance of its recognition-garnering capacity. It might be so rejoined because, while the achievement of national recognition does not count for nothing, morally speaking, it hardly ranks up there with such morally weighty fare as distributive justice (with the equitable distribution of income and property, and equal access to paid work, health care, education and leisure). To make matters worse, it is not just that the achievement of recognition is not to be confused with the achievement of distributive justice, but that the former seems to have nothing much to do with the latter. For, as the recognition of previously unrecognised and misrecognised nations has proceeded apace, thanks in no small measure to international sports, the gross inequities that separate these newly recognised nations from the prosperous West have narrowed hardly at all, and in some cases have actually grown larger. This makes it doubly difficult to regard the narrative successes that sports have racked up in getting peoples the national recognition they seek as anything more than hollow moral triumphs.

It would be foolish to take issue with this criticism if it means conflating recognition with distributive justice. These two are obviously not the same and, in arguing that sports are morally rich languages of nationalism, I meant only to underscore their contributions to recognition not to distributive justice. But it would be equally foolish, I hasten to add, to deny the moral importance of national recognition of this kind for at least two reasons – one of which does at least have implications for distributive justice.

First, the achievement of national recognition is an important moral accomplishment in its own right. I believe that the view that it is not is a prejudice of the dominant West, whose members can afford to take their national standing as well as the cultural security it provides them for granted, not to mention the salience it carries with the rest of the world. But the subaltern peoples of which we have been primarily speaking cannot be so complacent, since their national standing has not only seldom been acknowledged, but repeatedly denied. That is why national recognition is for them a very big deal indeed. And that is why it figures prominently in Frantz Fanon's famous claim, penned in his widely acclaimed book *The Wretched of the Earth*, that the chief weapon the colonisers wielded against the colonised was not the Gatling gun, but rather the imposition of their depreciatory images of the colonised over these subjugated peoples (Taylor 1989: 65).

The drive for recognition is crucial to Fanon's point because it is spurred by the desire to get out from under such debilitating impositions, because impositions of this imperial sort only work if non-recognition and misrecognition prevail over recognition. So it appears that gains in recognition are not the hollow moral victories they might seem to be, and therefore that the narrative contributions of sports in this regard must be accounted as morally noteworthy ones.

The second reason why we should not give short shrift to the moral importance of national recognition and the narrative capacity of sports to deliver it is that, while the achievement of such recognition is not to be confused with the achievement of distributive justice, it can and does, after all, serve the cause of distributive justice. For, if the historical record tells us anything it tells us this: if there is ever to be anything like distributive justice on a world scale, those peoples that have not been (and presently are not) on its receiving end will have to be able to stand up for themselves, to press and articulate their own moral case as to why they should be the rightful beneficiaries of the resources and opportunities that are the mark of such justice and, therefore, why their exclusion from them constitutes a grievous moral offence. Relying on the altruism of the dominant West in this regard, on the Western democracies to speak for them, will not work for the same reason that it has not worked in the past. But the point is that if subaltern nations are going to be able to exercise their moral agency in this forthright manner, they must first be recognised as legitimate moral claimants; that is to say, they must be seen as the conversational partners of the West rather than as their monological foils. The conferral of nationhood upon them is, I submit, indispensable in this regard.

I have been arguing that this is where sports of the international kind do their best and most effective work. MacAloon's claim, that 'To be a nation recognised by others ... a people must march in the Olympic Games opening ceremonies' (MacAloon 1991: 42), is therefore no idle boast. But it is also, rightly understood, a clue to the moral efficacy of sports and their story lines. For the extent those sports and the tales they spin have helped the cause of subaltern nations in forging a name and carving out a place for themselves in the conversations that occur between nations, is the extent to which we should view the narrative work they do as legitimate and important moral work.

Notes

1   While I reject Appiah's moral rendering of patriotism, I think his moral rendering of the State is on the mark. As he writes, 'States ... matter morally ... because they regulate our lives through forms of coercion that will always require moral justification' (1996: 28). I find this persuasive because states are foremost regulatory institutions that govern the lives of the people who inhabit them by claiming a monopoly of the 'legitimate' force that may be exercised

within their borders. Since, however, my present concern is with the moral character of nations, I will have nothing further to say about the moral character of states, notwithstanding the complex moral, cultural, social and political relations that often hold between them.

2   My heavy debt to Charles Taylor will become increasingly evident as my argument unfolds.

3   I have used the notions of nationalism and patriotism interchangeably. I have done so because I regard patriotism (love of, and devotion to, the best traditions of one's country) to be one important strand of nationalism. Efforts to distinguish these two notions, such as the commonplace 'patriotism stands for love of country and nationalism for hatred of others', strike me as stipulative at best, and therefore as subject to the usual reproof of factual incorrectness.

4   Whether the moral standing of patriotism is compromised by its avowed ethnocentrism is another question and, no doubt, another paper.

5   Once again, I follow Taylor's (1989: 33) lead here.

6   This was the gist of Spaulding's bold claim that baseball was an American game through and through, a game, therefore, that featured 'all the attributes of American origin [and] character'. Among those attributes claimed to be expressed through baseball, Spaulding included (all of which he capitalised to drive home his point), 'American Courage, Confidence, Combativeness; American Dash, Discipline, Determination; American Energy, Eagerness, Enthusiasm; ... American Vim, Vigor, Virility' (1911: 3–4).

7   Judo is the lone exception among Olympic sports, and it counts only as a partial exception, since the manner in which it is presently engaged and organised in and outside Olympic circles is distinctly Western.

Chapter 5

A justification of moderate patriotism in sport

Nicholas Dixon

Both participants in, and followers of, international sport are often motivated by patriotism. Players are often proud to 'represent' their country and especially eager to acquit themselves well. The pride supporters take in their national team's successes is at first sight curious: how can they be proud of something that they had, in all probability, no role in achieving? The answer seems to be that fans believe that they share, albeit indirectly, in the credit that a successful national team merits. A national team's success reflects well on a country, and fans may feel that they, in turn, are augmented by an increase in the worth of the country to which they belong. This is similar to the pride that we sometimes feel when friends or relatives enjoy triumphs in any field, even though we likely contributed little or nothing towards them. Key elements in the patriotism that both participants and followers feel are an identification with their country and a concern for its success on the playing field.[1]

This type of patriotism in sport is widespread and appears to be morally innocuous. Indeed, the sight of athletes giving their all when representing their country while being willed on by their adoring compatriots seems to be not only an exemplar of the virtues that sport makes possible, but also a paradigm case of healthy, morally justifiable patriotism. Nonetheless, patriotism in general has been subjected to serious moral criticism, and this chapter is an examination of how these criticisms apply in particular to patriotism in sport. I will defend a 'moderate patriotism' in sport, based on Stephen Nathanson's general defence of patriotism (Nathanson 1989).

Patriotism, sport and jingoism

Patriotism can easily spill over into 'the exclusive desire for the wellbeing of one's own people'.[2] When this happens, laudable feelings of goodwill toward our own country may be accompanied by hostility towards other countries. And this hostility may manifest itself in mistreatment of foreigners, the worst instance of which is waging war. Now patriotism in sport will rarely result in wars or any kind of general mistreatment of citizens of the rival country. When it does turn ugly, its victims are usually confined to the rival team, coaches, fans and officials. However, we can easily find examples when patriotism among members or supporters of a national team has indeed gone hand in hand with indefensible negative attitudes and behaviours towards athletes and other people from rival nations.

A tiny minority of English soccer fans sometimes rampages through foreign cities where the national team is playing, destroying property and attacking opposing fans. Even when no physical violence occurs, racial and ethnic abuse of players for rival national teams is an all-too-common excess of nationalism. And chauvinistic fans can deliberately or inadvertently interfere with the performance of athletes from other countries, for instance by yelling as a player is about to serve a tennis ball or hit a putt, or – as happened during the 1996 Olympics held in Atlanta – inappropriately chanting support for the United States' team during the routines of foreign gymnasts. Sometimes the guilty parties are neither fans nor players. Politicians and members of the media have wrongly portrayed some international sporting contests as a test of national supremacy. For instance, the 1998 World Cup soccer game between Iran and the United States was marred by some ugly, jingoistic rhetoric by non-participants before the game. The players of both teams, to their great credit, rose above the rhetoric and conducted themselves throughout in exemplary, sporting fashion, making clear that they were participating in a sporting event, not a battle between rival world-views. Finally, the patriotic fervour of athletes and their coaches may lead them to overstep acceptable boundaries in their pursuit of victory. The widespread use of illegal drugs in international athletics tournaments, often fully sanctioned in private by coaches, is a familiar example. What all of these instances of inappropriate, excessive patriotism have in common is a simple lack of moral regard for athletes, coaches and other people from rival countries.

When coaches encourage or coerce their athletes to take performance-enhancing drugs, another set of victims of jingoism in sport emerges: athletes from our own country, who can become mere pawns for achieving national glory, regardless of the probability of harm to their long-term health. A similar disregard for the welfare of our own country's athletes was displayed in another infamous case from the 1996 Olympic Games, when the coach insisted that a severely injured American gymnast make one final attempt at the vault in order to ensure that her team won the gold medal. While the fairy-tale ending delighted the host nation's fans, grave questions remain about the propriety of urging a young athlete to perform a vault that could easily have resulted in permanent, debilitating injuries. Patriotism in sport, then, can result not only in a jingoistic lack of moral regard for people from other countries but also in a callous disregard of the welfare of our own athletes.

Moderate patriotism in sport

If patriotism in sport inevitably involves such abuses, then we should roundly condemn it. However, none of the offensive, jingoistic attitudes and behaviours described in the previous paragraph are essential to patriotism. To see why this is so, we need to return to the general concept of patriotism. Both in sport and in other contexts, patriotism can indeed degenerate into a lack of moral respect for people from other nations. But patriotism itself – an identification with, and a special concern for, the wellbeing of our own country and our compatriots – implies no negative attitudes towards foreigners. The fact that we favour our compatriots over foreigners does not mean that we regard foreigners as having no moral standing whatsoever (Nathanson 1989: 537–539). As *moderate patriots*, we temper our preference for our own country by refusing to act immorally in furthering its interests. For example, while annexing a small, peaceful neighbouring country in order to appropriate its rich mineral deposits would undoubtedly be in their country's best interests, moderate patriots would not dream of proposing such a blatant violation of the neighbouring nation's rights. Only when it degenerates into an exclusive concern for compatriots, unbound by any moral regard for outsiders, is patriotism objectionable. But this is jingoism, and it does not impugn patriotism *per se*, any more than courage is impugned by the fact that, when displayed excessively and imprudently, it can degenerate into recklessness.

However, even if we allow that patriotism need not involve negative attitudes towards outsiders, a deeper objection remains, based on the principle that morality demands impartiality. Impartiality is central to all non-egoistic normative ethical theories. For instance, utilitarianism demands that each person's interests be given equal weight alongside those of everyone else in our moral deliberations. The correct action results from the summing up of rival utilities, without giving preference to our own or to those of any particular group of people we may happen to favour. And Kant's universalisability principle requires that we refrain from acting on maxims on which we would not will others to act – in other words, that we refrain from exempting ourselves from moral restrictions that we would impose on others. The problem is that patriotism appears to do precisely what impartiality rules out: it involves giving special treatment to a favoured group of people.

The best way to respond to the objection that patriotism violates impartiality is to give a more precise analysis of the moral demands of impartiality. It is, strictly speaking, a restraint on our behaviour that prevents us from harming people who are not part of our 'in group'. While it is legitimate for us to pursue our own interests and those of our allies – family members, friends, compatriots, etc. – we may not trample on the interests of outsiders in doing so. Impartiality demands that we respect the negative rights of all people, whether or not they belong to our favoured group. However, if I choose to donate money to a particular cause, other causes have no right to complain that I have wronged them by not supporting them. The only time when such an action would be wrong is when my making a donation would prevent me from fulfilling a pre-existing duty of justice to a particular person or people, such as repaying a debt or supporting my children. When it comes to benefits that I choose to bestow on a person or group of people, I am morally free to follow my whim, as long as the cause that I support is not itself immoral. In most cases, we do not *owe* such favours to anyone. Similarly, the undoubted preference that we give to our friends and family members in extending extra help and performing favours that we do not do for strangers in no way violates any moral duty of impartiality. And the same applies to patriotism, which is simply a more diffuse form of favouritism, in that it involves our giving special preference to a wider group of people.

We may use the expression 'conditional altruism' to refer to the attitude that is displayed by our acts of generosity towards family members, friends and compatriots. Like all exercises of altruism, it is a prima facie good. Its goodness is not diminished by the fact that we do not extend it to all people.[3] As long as conditional altruism is accompanied by no negative attitudes towards outsiders, or violations of their rights, it is positively virtuous. Indeed, a failure to give priority to people who are close to us – for example, our family members and friends – may be morally negligent. Suppose that a parent who is unduly responsive to the demands of impartiality decides that starving children in a war-torn African country are in more urgent need of her money than her own children. The money she sends to famine relief organisations may indeed save the lives of dozens of starving children, but if her own children become sick and die as a result of her diversion of funds to African children, we would regard her as a moral fanatic who has abjectly failed in her basic duties towards her own children. Giving preference to our own children is, therefore, not only morally permissible, but in some cases also morally required.

Showing that we also have special duties to other family members and friends requires further argument, since in these cases we cannot refer to the voluntary act of bringing a child in the world, which carries with it the obligation to raise the child until he or she becomes self-sufficient. However, such an argument is not hard to find. For instance, in the case of parents with whom we enjoy a friendship in our adult years and our close friends, we have voluntarily entered into a caring, loving relationship. And such relationships surely do generate duties of friendship, which demand that we perform duties towards friends and parents that we do not owe to strangers.[4] Nor are these duties a mere matter of repayment for past services rendered to us by our parents and friends. Duties of friendship are based on the extent of our friends' needs and our ability to help them, not on the amount of help they have given us.

That we have duties to help friends and family members that we do not have regarding strangers is also supported by a utilitarian approach. We can use our largesse more efficiently if we direct it towards people whom we know well, since we are more aware of their specific needs than those of strangers. And the extra empathy that we feel towards people who are close to us will likely act as a greater motivator for our acts of beneficence than if the people we are helping are strangers. Overall utility will therefore be maximised if we all confine our efforts to helping friends and family members. The argument in this paragraph concerns only people's individual efforts to help others, and in no way precludes governments from having obligations to provide for the basic needs of all their citizens.

Whether patriotism is ever obligatory is even more controversial than whether we have special duties to our family members and friends based on our particular relationships with them. Our relationship with our country and compatriots is far more distant than our ties with family members and friends. Rejecting any Lockean argument about tacit consent, a key difference between this case and our duties to our family members and friends is that we normally have no meaningful *choice* in being a citizen of our country. Consequently, our duties to our country are weaker than those that we have towards children whom we choose to bring into the world, and parents and friends with whom we choose to have an ongoing loving relationship. Nonetheless, we can think of situations where a failure to give preference to compatriots over foreigners would be morally questionable. Parallel to the parent who allows her children to starve so that she can send her money to even more needy children overseas, the person who makes large donations to overseas charities despite the equally urgent need for famine relief in her own country demonstrates a striking lack of loyalty to her country. Whether this absence of loyalty is blameworthy will depend on many factors, including the extent to which a person has benefited from his or her country, whether it is a democracy in whose decisions he or she has a meaningful say, and whether the government conducts itself at home and abroad in a way that is worthy of loyalty.

Given that part of patriotism is identification with one's country and a special love for it, the only duties that seem to be involved are conditional ones; i.e., *if* a person has the identification with and love for country that are part of patriotism, then he or she does indeed have certain duties of loyalty that require giving preference to that country. But we do not appear to have a duty to *be* patriotic in the first place, any more than we have a duty to form any particular friendship. Fortunately, we can safely leave open the question of whether patriotism is ever mandatory. All that matters for the purposes of this chapter is that patriotism is sometimes morally permissible. And the arguments presented earlier in this section demonstrate that moderate patriotism, which is unaccompanied by negative attitudes towards and mistreatment of foreigners, is indeed permissible.

Returning to the specific case of patriotism in sport, we have seen in this section that, while it has sometimes been associated with reprehensible, chauvinistic attitudes and actions, they are extrinsic to patriotism. All that is essential to moderate patriotism in sport is a special concern for the success of athletes from our own country. And this special concern is no more problematic than any other act of conditional altruism, in which we confer special benefits on a selected group of people, be they relatives, friends, beneficiaries of charities or, as in this case, compatriots.

Critiques of moderate patriotism

However, defending moderate patriotism is not as easy as the previous section would indicate. Opponents have attacked it from two completely different viewpoints. First, Alasdair MacIntyre has argued that moderate patriotism is so qualified by respect for foreigners as not to qualify as patriotism at all (MacIntyre 1984). Second, and in complete contrast, Paul Gomberg has condemned it on the ground that it is indistinguishable from jingoism (Gomberg 1990a). Neither objection, however, gives good reasons for abandoning moderate patriotism in sport.

Is moderate patriotism sufficiently patriotic?

Nathanson gives a detailed discussion of several of MacIntyre's arguments (1989: 540–551). What they have in common is the claim that moderate patriots are so concerned to keep their actions within the limits set by universal (i.e., impartial) morality that their alleged patriotism 'amounts to no more than a set of practically empty slogans'. First, zero-sum conflict situations arise in which we simply have to take sides when our country and a rival nation are competing for scarce resources. Unlike the acts of beneficence described in the previous section – whether for family, friends or country – favouring our country in these conflict situations does indeed involve harming other nations. In such cases, the only way to be patriotic is to stand by our nation. But since doing so would violate universal morality, this is precisely what moderate patriotism forbids. Moreover, genuine patriotism requires that we act on our own society's conception of the good life, even if, as in MacIntyre's own extreme illustration, it regards raiding and pillaging other nations as an acceptable practice. One might conclude 'so much the worse for MacIntyre's conception of patriotism', and think that this very consideration is itself an effective reductio ad absurdum of his view. But he would bite the bullet and deny the intuition that underlies this reductio; namely, that any meaningful external moral vantage point exists from which a community's moral standards may be criticised.

In response to MacIntyre, Nathanson argues that his position with regard to conflict situations is genuinely patriotic. A moderate patriot who is concerned to respect the rights and interests of people of other nations will go out of her way to find compromises that avoid zero-sum conflicts. However, when no such accommodations are possible, she will regretfully take her own country's side against other nations. So when push comes to shove, and contrary to MacIntyre's objection, the moderate patriot does stand by her nation. The superiority of the moderate patriot's approach consists in the fact that she is painfully aware of the moral remainders[5] caused by her own country's violation of the interests of other nations – in contrast to MacIntyre's extreme patriot, for whom no moral dilemma occurs at all, since only her own country counts morally (Nathanson 1989: 540–542).

With regard to a community in which raiding and pillaging its neighbours is regarded as an essential ingredient of the good life, the moderate patriot would clearly disapprove, since such actions violate universal moral principles. In response to MacIntyre's argument that such moral criticism of our own country's practices is unpatriotic, Nathanson claims that patriotism does not require uncritical acceptance of our country's actions. If it did, then abolitionists were unpatriotic when they criticised slavery – hardly an appealing consequence for MacIntyre's concept of patriotism (1989: 544). However, as we have seen, MacIntyre can deflect such reductio ad absurdum arguments by rejecting the distinction that they presuppose between a community's values and practices and, on the other hand, morality *per se*. The debate appears to have boiled down to a conflict between two fundamentally opposed rival paradigms: Nathanson's moral realism and MacIntyre's moral relativism.

In order to show that we can make a meaningful distinction between morality and the prevailing norms in our society, Nathanson points out that moral debate often arises precisely because the demands made by our community standards are either unclear or contradictory (1989: 548). Moreover, even if MacIntyre is right that morality is essentially based on the prevailing norms of a given social group, this still does not entail a form of nationalism that conflicts with universal morality. The community in which our moral code is grounded could be a subgroup within a nation: e.g. a village or family. Indeed, patriotism may even contain the seeds of universal morality. Patriotism is a relatively recent phenomenon that required an evolution from more primitive moral codes that accorded standing only to members of our family, village or some such small social unit. Since nationalism already represents a considerable widening of the moral circle from these primitive origins, the further widening of this circle to include all people of all nations – i.e., the largest social group of all – seems to be the logical consequence of this progression (1989: 549). Consequently, no irreconcilable conflict exists between patriotism and universal morality, and MacIntyre's criticisms of moderate patriotism are unfounded.

MacIntyre's view is especially unpalatable when applied to sport. It would seem to tolerate a Machiavellian win-at-all-costs mentality in international athletic contests in any country in which such practices are generally accepted. Thus we would have no moral perspective from which we would be permitted to criticise the use of illegal substances in giving the athletes of a certain country an unfair advantage in contests. Worse yet, the refusal to use such means to ensure victory might even be considered unpatriotic, at least in countries in which these practices are encouraged. However, the acceptability of MacIntyre's view as it applies to moderate patriotism in sport may well be a moot point, in that his general critique of moderate patriotism – which we have in any event seen good reasons to reject – applies primarily to emergency situations in which the very survival of our nation is at stake, and this is clearly not the case in international sporting events.

Can we distinguish patriotism from jingoism?

The force of MacIntyre's critique was that moderate patriotism is so luke-warm a form of loyalty to one's nation that it is not really patriotism at all. The next objection is similar to MacIntyre's in that Gomberg, too, contends that we have to choose between patriotism and universal morality: there is no 'genuine third alternative between chauvinistic patriotism and unpatriotic universalism' (Gomberg 1990a:145). However, whereas MacIntyre concluded from this alleged incompatibility that universal morality sometimes has to take a back seat to our national loyalties, Gomberg concludes that we must simply reject patriotism, including Nathanson's moderate version.

Gomberg argues that even moderate patriotism is indistinguishable from racism. We can easily see the immorality of favouring a certain racial group – such as white people – within our society, for instance by giving them priority in hiring. Even if our only intention is to help people we like, such as family members, friends and acquaintances, and we have absolutely no negative attitudes against members of excluded racial groups, the de facto harmful effects of our policy, especially on ethnic groups that have long suffered disadvantages, is enough to make it wrong. Gomberg points out that a parallel argument condemns the practice, which moderate patriotism would permit, of giving preference in famine relief to poor people in this country over even more needy starving people in especially impoverished developing nations. Our 'charity begins at home' policy, while its only motive is to help our needy compatriots, has the effect of widening international inequities (1990a: 147–148).

Now, moderate patriotism as defended above (see pages 76–77) distinguishes between harming outsiders (which it forbids) and, on the other hand, bestowing benefits on our compatriots that we do not extend to outsiders (which it allows). The effect of Gomberg's argument is to challenge the moral relevance of the distinction between acts and omissions that underlies this position. Both racial minorities in our society and poor people in other countries can be harmed by our omission when we choose not to help them. Universal morality requires that we help those who are most in need, regardless of whether they are members of our 'in group'.[6] Gomberg concludes that the only way to reconcile patriotism with the universal morality that condemns racism is an 'indirect universalism': the questionable empirical belief that the most efficient means of maximising wellbeing and respect for persons throughout the world is for everyone to focus their efforts on the people who are closest to them, including their compatriots (Gomberg 1990a: 149–150).

Gomberg has raised a serious question about patriotism as a criterion for the allocation of economic benefits, for instance the policy of 'charity begins at home' in famine relief. In particular, he has shown that we must qualify the claim made above (see page 77) that impartiality in no way prevents us from conferring positive benefits on whomever we please. If our beneficence towards our compatriots, however free of jingoistic motives it may be, has the effect of exacerbating the suffering of millions of people in poverty-stricken countries, then it is problematic from the viewpoint of universal morality. But Gomberg's argument has no force as an objection to moderate patriotism in sport, because athletes' attempts to win and fans' preference for their own country's athletes in international sporting contests inflict no significant harm on people in other countries. Whereas people in poorer countries can starve to death as a result of 'charity begins at home' economic policies in more affluent countries, athletic losses by foreign competitors normally result only in disappointment and a possible reduction of individual athletes' career earnings. Indeed, a central theme of William Morgan's contribution to this volume (see Chapter 4) is that international sport can be positively beneficial for disadvantaged nations by giving them an arena in which they can outshine more affluent nations.[7]

Furthermore, patriotism in supporting national athletic teams – unlike favouring my compatriots in my charitable donations – is only in a very limited sense a zero-sum situation. Granted, when my country plays a rival, my patriotism only permits me to support my own team. However, whereas a donation made to Country A is by definition one not made to Country B, I can easily support several countries' national teams at the same time. Whether because of personal attachments to another country, or admiration for the style of play of its national team, I may wish for its sporting success on all occasions when it is not competing against my own country's team.

Gomberg presents his view as a general critique of moderate patriotism. However, a charitable interpretation of his view that makes it more plausible would construe it more narrowly as a restriction on when – if ever – patriotism is permissible in the distribution of economic benefits. Indeed, the very harmlessness of moderate patriotism in sport – fans' and athletes' desire for the success of their nation in the sporting arena, but strictly within the rules of the game and without harming or disrespecting foreign opponents – provides a striking reductio ad absurdum of a blanket condemnation of moderate patriotism. If moderate patriotism is inappropriate even in the world of sport, then athletes should not try their best to win events for their countries, and fans should not cheer for them and wish for their success. Instead, they should work together to try to bring about victory by the most needy athletes from the most needy countries. Sport in which athletes conspired – with fans' support – to ensure victories by the athletes who would most benefit from winning would be a self-defeating mockery. If need, instead of athletic excellence, became the criterion for victory, it would lose all interest for fans and athletes. The very victories that are engineered for less fortunate athletes would be hollow, since everyone involved would realise that they do not reflect any athletic superiority. We do indeed go out of our way to ensure that athletes compete under conditions of equality in order to maximise the probability that the best athlete will win – this is why we have, for example, strict rules governing performance-enhancing chemicals. This meritocratic spirit may even require that sporting organisations in affluent countries provide funds to support the development of promising athletes in poorer countries. But in no way does it entail making sport a vehicle for correcting inequalities in *other* areas of life, by simply allowing athletes from disadvantaged countries to win international events in order to compensate for the hardships they face. Once the contest has begun, athletic excellence should be the sole determinant of victory.

This is not to say that athletes and fans should be oblivious to the non-sport-related hardships suffered by athletes from other countries. An excellent example of just such an awareness was the inspiring welcome that the French public gave the athletes from war-torn Bosnia at the opening ceremony of the 1992 Winter Olympics at Albertville. However, once the games began, athletes quite appropriately did their utmost to secure victory for their countries, cheered on by their own fans. The fact that athletes and fans were able to commit themselves wholeheartedly to their own countries' success, while still showing considerable compassion for the tragedy that their Bosnian rivals were enduring in their own country, is evidence that moderate patriotism is indeed possible in sport.

Moderate patriotism in sport is one of several benign instances of patriotism in which love of, or a desire for, the success of our country is unobjectionable and even desirable. In these cases, no pernicious attitudes or harmful, unjust actions towards foreigners are involved. The goodwill that we feel towards our country is, just like our special concern for the welfare of our friends and family members, an intrinsic good. Other benign exercises of moderate patriotism include a love of one's own country's cuisine, scenery, literature, music, or any other aspect of its culture. Neither in sport nor in any of these other areas does moderate patriotism preclude our simultaneously bearing good will towards the athletes and culture of other countries. Gomberg has given us reason to qualify the permissibility of moderate patriotism as a principle for the distribution of significant economic benefits, such as resources for famine relief. However, moderate patriotism in such areas as sport and culture is immune to his criticisms. It is separable from jingoism and racism and is intrinsically desirable.

Is patriotism in sport contingently linked to jingoism?

The reply just given to Gomberg reinforces the argument given earlier (see pages 76–79) that moderate patriotism in sport is not inherently jingoistic, and that any jingoism that arises is a *corruption* of patriotism and not part of its nature. However, if jingoism routinely accompanies patriotism in sport, then knowing that it is inessential to patriotism is cold comfort. An attitude that frequently leads to immoral actions is morally questionable, no matter how pure it may be in itself. And we saw at the start of this chapter a list of ways in which patriotism in sport has indeed spilled over into reprehensible attitudes and actions towards people from other countries.

An important reality check is to remember that this rogues' gallery of infamous incidents and practices in international sport is notable precisely because it refers to exceptional cases. Fighting between rival fans, attempts to injure rivals, racist abuse of players by fans, disrespectful chanting by fans during overseas gymnasts' performances, the use of international contests for propaganda purposes and risking serious injuries to our own athletes in the pursuit of victory are all aberrations that make headline news whenever they happen. The only dubious practice in the list that is widespread is the use of illegal performance-enhancing drugs, and even this is largely confined to certain sports, such as athletics and cycling. And even when illegal drugs are used, the motivation usually appears to be personal gain from the commercial endorsements that will follow from success on the international playing field. We may lay the blame at the door of patriotism only when national coaches and even governments instruct their teams to cheat in order to bring glory on the country by winning.

Against these aberrations, we have to weigh the routine sight of closely but fairly contested international sporting events in which players show the utmost respect for their overseas rivals. This respect is symbolised by the almost universal practice of post-game handshakes and especially by the practice in international soccer of exchanging shirts after the game. International sporting events – which would have little appeal if rival athletes and fans were not motivated by the patriotic desire to participate in or observe a win for their country – are one of the most common forms of interaction between people from different countries. Fair and respectful competition in sport is an excellent way to remind people from different countries of their common humanity and draw them closer together. This was particularly well illustrated in the 1998 World Cup soccer game between the United States and Iran mentioned earlier. Despite some intemperate pre-game comments by some politicians and members of the media, both players and fans epitomised the positive influence of sport on international relations. Both teams conducted themselves admirably during the game, the United States' players deserve special praise for their gracious acceptance of defeat after the game, and Iranian and American fans interacted in a friendly and peaceful manner.

Furthermore, even partisan fans of their national team are able to recognise and applaud skilful play by foreign opponents, and this too helps even potentially jingoistic supporters to recognise foreign opponents as people who deserve respect and admiration. For instance, British people have not always been renowned for warmly embracing people from other countries. But when legendary soccer player Johann Cruyff left the field during his final game for his Dutch club on English soil in the 1970s, he was given a standing ovation by the home fans. This process of seeing foreign players as human beings rather than faceless enemies has been facilitated in the 1990s by the huge influx of foreign players into England's Premier League, where local fans regard them as allies and even as heroes.

International sport, which would scarcely be possible unless players and fans were motivated by patriotism, thus has many beneficial effects. These positive effects are at least sufficient to balance the negative effects of the jingoism into which patriotism in sport sometimes degenerates. As a result, we cannot reject moderate patriotism in sport on consequentialist grounds. Since we have already seen in this chapter that moderate patriotism in sport is intrinsically innocuous and even admirable, my defence is now complete.

While jingoism is neither an essential component nor a likely result of patriotism in sport, any instances of excessive nationalism are regrettable. The best way to ensure that patriotism in sport remains moderate and does not degenerate into jingoism is for both athletes and fans to temper their enthusiasm for their country's success with the spirit of modesty.[8] Modest athletes realise that, no matter how superior they may be to their rivals, this does not make them better qua human beings. And modest athletes and fans realise that superior athletic performances by themselves or their compatriots do not grant them the status of a superior race. A modest attitude towards our country's athletic achievements is facilitated by bearing in mind certain reality checks. For instance, however dominant we may be in one sport, other countries will far surpass us in others. Moreover, however dominant we might be in sport in general, every country has unique qualities in other areas that will surpass ours. Keeping our nation's athletic triumphs in this perspective will go a long way towards guaranteeing that moderate patriotism in sport will *remain* moderate.

Notes

1   For an explanation of the fact that we can be proud, not only of things that belong to us, but also of things to which we in some sense belong, see G. Taylor (1985: 30–32).
2   This is the definition that Leo Tolstoy uses in his critique of patriotism (Tolstoy 1968: 106–107).
3   For a defence of friendship as a morally desirable exercise of conditional altruism, see Lawrence Blum (1980: chapter 4).
4   For a defence of the view that a robust duty to help our parents can be generated by reference to our friendship with them, see English (1979) and Dixon (1995).
5   For more detail on moral remainders – the feeling of regret that can remain even when we are convinced that we have done the right thing in a situation of moral conflict – see Williams (1973).
6   Cf. Peter Singer's argument for regarding the duty of those of us in affluent countries to send famine relief to people who are starving in developing countries as obligatory, not supererogatory (1993: chapter 8).
7   A representative sample of the benefits that Morgan sees in international sport for disadvantaged nations is that, 'just as the athletic successes of dominated nations give them cause to take themselves more seriously, to inflate their self-worth and moral horizons, those same athletic successes give dominant nations reason to take themselves less seriously, to deflate their self-importance and moral horizons' (this volume: 59–73).
8   My comments on modesty are based on a modified version of the analysis given by Aaron Ben-Ze'ev (1993).

Chapter 6

Patriotism in sports and in war

Paul Gomberg

The modern Olympic Games began in 1896. This culminated more than a century of the development of modern nation-states across Europe and preceded a century containing the most destructive wars in the history of humanity. Does nationalism in sports, epitomised in the nationalism at Olympic Games, contribute to the mobilisation of mass populations for popular wars and genocide? I will argue that it does. In doing so I am replying to the moderate patriotism of Nicholas Dixon, who argues in Chapter 5 that there is an unobjectionable patriotism in sports which consists in favouring one's national team without disrespecting the teams of other nations.[1] He surely seems right in this: it seems that we can moderate our patriotism, thus making it innocuous. Nevertheless, I will argue that in the current economic and political context, with sharpening rivalries between competing imperial powers leading to small and bigger wars, being moderately patriotic is like being a little bit pregnant.

Some background

Nationalism and patriotism were little discussed in recent English-language moral and political philosophy until around the mid-1980s. The omission of this discussion may seem odd; it would seem that patriotic sentiment and behaviour could conflict with the universalist moralities, descended from Kant and Mill, that dominated the academy. These moralities insist on equal moral regard for each individual. Yet, for a while, the possibility of a contradiction was invisible. Why? Perhaps this was a legacy of World War II: the Western Allies seemed to represent the interests of humanity against fascism, particularly Nazi fascism. So for citizens of these nations there might not seem to be a contradiction between being patriotic and conforming to universal morality.

The problem became more visible with the publication in 1984 of Alasdair MacIntyre's lecture 'Is Patriotism a Virtue?'. MacIntyre's essay defended a Hegelian conception of morality as situated in the social life of a people (what Hegel called a people's *Sittlichkeit*) and implied a view of history where wars between nation-states would continue and where nationals would have to defend 'their nations'. Thus, MacIntyre argued, patriotism is a virtue, one in conflict with universal liberal morality, and so much the worse for moral universalism.

Of course, this criticism did not sit well with moral universalists: Stephen Nathanson replied that there was a *moderate patriotism* that was compatible with moral universalism, a patriotism that embraced preference for compatriots without violating the moral rights of others (Nathanson 1989). He argued that there is a middle ground between a universalism impartial between nations and a chauvinism that disregarded the moral status of the citizens of other nations. In conflicts between nations, moderate patriots, unlike chauvinists, seek a just compromise between the interests of these nations. But, unlike the impartialists, when 'either/or' choices must be made and conflict is unavoidable, moderate patriots support their own nations.

In 'Patriotism is Like Racism' (hereafter 'PLR') I expressed doubt whether Nathanson had successfully defended a moderate patriotism that was neither chauvinist nor impartialist, and whether he had shown that preference for compatriots was compatible with universal morality (Gomberg 1990b). I discussed preference for compatriots in hiring, in philanthropic donations to the hungry, and in consumer purchases. In the cases of hiring and donations to the hungry, I suggested that favouritism (by those in relatively wealthy countries) for compatriots was like racism, helping a relatively advantaged group in preference to a group that was already disadvantaged, adding to their disadvantage.

The argument resumes with Nicholas Dixon's chapter in this volume, which occasions my reply.[2] Whatever objections there may be to favouring one's compatriots in hiring or philanthropic donations cannot apply to favouring their victory in sporting contests. Surely, it seems, Dixon is right if we look at sports competition outside of its context of the concomitant development of capitalist economy, political nation-states, competitions between national teams in sports, and wars between capitalist nations. But what happens if we put these issues in that context?

On method

It is very easy for us to argue at cross-purposes on these issues, and I will try to avoid this. This means acknowledging that Dixon is right about much of what he writes in the way in which he intends it – specifically, that there is much partisanship for a national sports team that does no direct and immediate harm and provides psychological satisfaction for national partisans.

In PLR I expressed scepticism that Nathanson had sketched a *general* moderate patriotism that was based on some coherent principles, that avoided chauvinism, that did not extend the disadvantage of those who were already disadvantaged (in this way making it like racism), that did not make war between nations more likely, and that was compatible with moral universalism. Dixon undertakes a more modest task: to specify a moderate patriotism in sports. Here internationally recognised principles of fair competition provide a fairly clear framework of limits on patriotism. While wars between nations are sometimes limited by international conventions governing war, athletic competitions (unlike wars) do not typically involve direct harm to others and hence seem unobjectionable from the usual universalist moral perspectives. So, in the sense in which he intends his arguments, Dixon seems to succeed in showing that there is a 'morally innocuous' moderate patriotism in sports.

Yet there are broader issues of the political context of sporting contests between nations, and these will be the focus of my speculations and argument. I am shifting the ground – in fairness to Dixon's argument, it is important to acknowledge this. The differences in our approaches might be characterised as differences between philosophical and political methods of argument.

Dixon isolates partisanship in sporting contests from assessments of the current political situations and movements affecting them. He mentions the thuggery of some British soccer fans without connecting these fans to racist, anti-immigrant movements in Britain. He mentions the good sportsmanship at the soccer match between the United States and Iran at the 1998 World Cup without connecting this with the political rapprochement being attempted between elements of the ruling classes of these two countries.

More important, Dixon considers sporting contests in relative isolation from the broader history of the rise of nationalism and nation-states. He does not consider how patriotism in sports may be part of a national identity that leads to mass participation in patriotic wars. The consequences of patriotism in sports are assessed very narrowly, considering only the direct effects in the arena and in the immediate social context of the contest.

Dixon is concerned with what is *essential* to patriotism and argues that patriotism need not imply a disregard for the moral status of those who are not compatriots. He is concerned with what is *morally permissible* and argues that it is morally permissible to have a special regard for those with whom one has a special relationship, and that being compatriots can be such a special relationship. Thus his arguments are typically philosophical in their abstractness; they are less concerned with what *will* happen than with what *must* or *can* happen. Questions of what to do and how to live can, to a large extent, be settled by abstract argument.

In contrast, I am not interested in abstract issues of what is essential to patriotism or what is 'morally permissible' (nor do I know what 'morally permissible' means in this context). What practical issues are raised by patriotism? To determine the effects of creating partisan patriotic identities and reinforcing them through international sports competitions; and to assess the alternatives to being patriotic and how these affect the development of wars between nations, racism, poverty and capitalist exploitation generally. The practical issues, for me, are specific, historical and political. In Friedrich Engels' terminology, the contrast of methods is between the metaphysical and the dialectical, methods that look at phenomena in isolation and those that look at phenomena in their concrete historical interconnections (Engels 1976/1894).

Laying out my view

'Patriotism is Like Racism' was written as a reply to Nathanson, and its tenor was 'you did not demonstrate what you said you demonstrated'. So, for example, I did not assert that there is no 'genuine third alternative between chauvinistic patriotism and unpatriotic universalism' (as Dixon says I did) but only that Nathanson had not shown that there is such an alternative, particularly in relation to issues of war. Nor do I think that Dixon's summary of Nathanson's discussion of how, in war, the moderate patriot will differ from the chauvinistic patriot is very satisfactory – he acknowledges no difference in practice between the two, only that the moderate patriot acts 'regretfully' and 'is painfully aware of the moral remainders'. This would be little comfort, I am sure, to the Vietnamese whose homes were bombed, or the Iraqis whose children died because water treatment plants were bombed by moderately patriotic bomber pilots, or to residents of the Chorillo neighbourhood in Panama City whose homes were destroyed and relatives killed by moderately patriotic soldiers in the United States' invasion of December 1989. As I argued against Nathanson, what is so moderate about this patriotism (Gomberg 1990b: 145–146)?

In PLR I acknowledged that there seemed to be a possible moderate patriotism compatible with some versions of universalism, but that it was not clear how such moderate patriotism was different from a moderate racism that respected certain fundamental universal rights yet exacerbated the disadvantage of disadvantaged groups. Alternatively, I argued that other forms of moderate patriotism, such as 'Buy America!' campaigns, seemed to intensify nationalist sentiment and action and thus laid the basis for military conflict.

I acknowledged that some forms of moderate patriotism might seem compatible with some indirect universalisms (where patriotism was part of a set of institutions devised to advance human wellbeing or recognise the dignity of each person), but questioned whether such patriotism in fact represented an adequate institutional safeguard of universal wellbeing or universal human dignity. While I assessed whether Nathanson had demonstrated the compatibility between patriotism and various forms of universalism, I never endorsed universalism.

In fact I am not a universalist and have raised problems elsewhere about how universalism is to be justified against more parochial moralities (Gomberg

1994). While I believe that there are problems about the compatibility of universalism with patriotism, my objections to patriotism are not grounded in morality or in universalism (and morality does not have to be universalist, nor does universalism have to be understood as a morality). Instead my objections are grounded in my understanding of Marxism's elevation of the political over the moral. The present reply thus gives me an opportunity to set out my views a little more systematically and to sketch some connections between what I will say here and what I have written elsewhere.

I understand human moralities as systems of decentralised social control that operate in the social life of particular social groups. Decentralised control was sufficient for social order when human societies sustained norms of redistribution from wealthier to poorer members according to need, but with the rise of the State economic inequality works to the disadvantage of the least well-off. These inequalities create alienation among the dispossessed and political contests, particularly between classes, over the terms of social cooperation, sometimes breaking out into violent conflict requiring the intervention of state power. A, if not the, central project of political philosophy as it arises in these class societies is to argue that we share an interest in norms creating these inequalities (Gomberg 1997). Ultimately, I believe, these projects are bound to fail: it is impossible to reduce alienation by these arguments because it is impossible to persuade people that they are better off with inequality than they would be following communist norms of sharing according to need.[3]

But the struggle for a communist future is bound to meet such fierce and violent resistance that it cannot be grounded in universal morality; it needs a partisanship that requires us to think of those who oppose us as monsters and beasts (much as Locke understood those who put themselves into a state of war against us) (Gomberg 1990a). This was Marx's profound insight that politics transcends morality (an understanding that he shared with Hegel). Yet, he thought, workers can act in concert based on an understanding of their common interests. He developed a social and economic theory to ground political activism (Gomberg 1989).

My criticisms of patriotism in general, and of patriotism in sports in particular, are best understood in this context. When large populations share patriotic feeling and identification, how does this affect the ability of capitalist governments to mobilise their populations for war? How does it affect the ability of those who would resist capitalism in general, and its wars in particular, to make their resistance effective?

Patriotism and war

Dixon defines patriotism as 'an identification with, and a special concern for, the wellbeing of our own country and our compatriots'. The definition has the virtue of displaying one of the characteristics it uses to define patriotism:

in using the phrases 'our own' and 'our', Dixon displays the characteristically patriotic identification. While identities are learned, they operate at deep levels so that it is often difficult for people to see the political assumptions that lie behind the ways they use 'we' and 'our', 'them' and 'their'. In fact, as I will try to show shortly, breaking the hold of a national identity is a profound shift in our understanding of who we are; mere rational argument about the political implications of the identity is unlikely to shake its hold.

The nation and the idea of shared nationality is the central ideological construct of capitalism through which it has organised state power. In earlier state-level social organisation, empires were typically multiethnic and did not attempt to combine our idea of nationality with the State as the locus of political power. Even the early nation-states of France and England, before the idea of nationality had been popularised, mobilised their populations for war on a much more limited basis; hence their wars were less destructive. Only as capitalism came to dominate European society did the new ruling bourgeoisie encourage and develop popular consciousness of nationhood as a way of organising the political loyalty of all classes to its rule.

Frequently, but not always, the rise of national identity has been associated with the rise of some sort of popular democracy or a facsimile – the possible candidates here range from representative democracies on the English model to the mass participation in revolutionary action of the French Revolution and subsequent regimes, including the Napoleonic to the Nazi Reich in Germany, brought to power by the old ruling class but thereafter mobilising massive popular support. When people feel that the government is 'their own', either because they have participated in elections leading to it or because they have participated in popular demonstrations that affirm some of its political principles, there is a reservoir of national sentiment that can be mobilised for other purposes. People feel deeply part of a nation and identify with their compatriots as such.

The popularisation of nationhood and of patriotic identities was accomplished through most of Europe in the late eighteenth and nineteenth centuries. Similarly, in the United States a strong popular national identity was forged in the mid-nineteenth century and consolidated in the aftermath of the Civil War. But precisely this popularisation of national identity has made it possible for capitalist governments to mobilise their populations for the most brutal wars of imperialist conquest – and mobilise them unthinkingly as their patriotic duty. Thus we get the unprecedented brutality and mass slaughter of the two world wars of the twentieth century and the incredible brutality of smaller acts of genocide in Bosnia or Rwanda. The scale of these brutalities has depended on the mobilisation of entire populations for war, and this mobilisation, in turn, has frequently been accomplished through national identities and patriotism.

When soldiers march off to war to defend the French Revolution, to defend the Fatherland, or the Stars and Stripes, they are not thinking critically about the meaning of the military combat in which they are engaging. They are acting on a patriotic identity, and it is precisely because such identities operate on such a deep and unconscious level that they are hard to shake by rational argument.[4]

Disrupting patriotic identities

These identities are hard to shake but not impossible. Let me start with two anecdotes from my teaching experience, which illustrate some of the possible relationships people may take to national identities. For the past thirteen years I have taught at a commuter college whose students are from economically disadvantaged backgrounds (on average) and are identified in American society as 'black' or, as is now in vogue, 'African-American'. In recent classes I have taught the history of the rise of slavery and anti-black racism in English-American society and the United States. I argue for the view that the characteristically American distinction between the races and the idea of racial inferiority supposedly grounded in the sciences are consolidated in the American Revolution and its aftermath. The distinction and idea are particularly clearly articulated by Thomas Jefferson in his *Notes on the State of Virginia*. Thus, I argue, the United States is founded on anti-black racism, and has maintained some such form of racism throughout its national existence, a racism that is as American as apple pie. But agreeing with such arguments does not disrupt American identity or a belief that one has a duty to vote. American identity and related beliefs are entrenched in my students' social relationships with family and friends that form the context of daily life (their *Sittlichkeit*), and mere argument is not likely to disrupt them.

This experience contrasts with another of ten years ago (a significantly different population of students). In that class I had planned a lesson based on the assumption of exploring their patriotic loyalties. I met a resistance I could not comprehend, for no one would acknowledge patriotism. I said, 'Come on, you were all raised to be patriotic, just as I was. How many of you were brought up to be patriotic?' The lone white student in the class raised his hand. I said I did not believe them. Then a young woman raised her hand, saying something to the effect of 'I was raised to hate the United States and its government. My father served in Vietnam. He told me that the government just used him, lied to him, and then discarded him when it had no more use for him.' As she said this, other students were nodding and murmuring in agreement. So I learned there is nothing automatic about patriotic identity, particularly among people who have been abused and alienated.

I am suggesting, then, that our moralities, the ways we think it right to act, are grounded in our identities, who we think we are, and in the conduct implicit in those identities. So for those who think themselves Americans and for whom such an identity is central to self-conception, there will be an associated conception of what it means to be an American, what sort of conduct is implied, typically, 'a patriotic American defends his country in war'. These moral conceptions (part of our *Sittlichkeit*) will be deeply ingrained in our moral character and in our most important social relationships. They will not be easily disrupted by argument. But where people have been raised differently, different non-patriotic identities and conceptions of proper conduct will prevail.

Disruption of patriotic identities is also possible. I *was* brought up to be patriotic but am no more. Like my student's father, I am of a generation where many of us learned better and tried to teach our children likewise. The experiences of racism and the Vietnam War were turning points for many of us. In 1967 I was at a party when it was announced over the radio that Muhammad Ali had refused the draft, saying that no Vietcong had ever called him 'nigger'. My fellow graduate students and I rejoiced: someone had taken a stand against the US government. That experience was part of a process where I and others unlearned to call ourselves Americans; not, I think, out of thoughtless rebellion, but out of a serious reflection about who 'our' people were.

We came to see that the question 'Who are our people?' was political. The United States government was napalming villages, forcing Vietnam's rural population into concentration camps (Strategic Hamlets). Whose side were we on? Many came to identify with the Vietnamese people and their revolution rather than 'their own' government. The campuses were filled with chants of 'US out of Southeast Asia!' and 'Victory to the Vietcong!' This shift of loyalty happened not just on the campuses but in the military as well, particularly among black soldiers but also among many white soldiers; many refused to fight, deserted to the other side, at least for a time, or used violence to intimidate or kill their officers. And many who were not active protesters said, 'Rich man's war, poor man's fight', implicitly rejecting the patriotic assumptions that we had to fight for 'our country'.

While the protest has died, the grounds for it have not diminished. The atrocities committed by the United States military in Panama were small in scale compared with Vietnam, but for the people of Panama City they were just as real. And in the brief Operation Desert Storm of 1990–1991 the United States dropped bombs with unprecedented intensity. This has had a devastating effect on the lives of the people of Iraq: while it is difficult to come by reliable numbers, it is reasonable to assume that the bombing and the sanctions have each killed roughly a million people. There are, then, serious arguments that embracing patriotism has had terrible effects and that we have good reason to reject identification with 'our governments' and 'our nations'.

Patriotism and our prospects

Still, arguments about the past will not settle whether patriotic identities are desirable now. We need an estimate of the period ahead; and my estimate is grounded in the classic arguments of Marx and Lenin. What are the prospects of war, including global war? What are our choices?

One hundred and fifty years ago Karl Marx and Friedrich Engels wrote that overproduction of commodities was a consequence of the anarchy of production, with competitors scrambling to control as much of the market as possible. This analysis is still valid. In 1997 an economic crisis spread across much of Asia, as the much-touted 'Asian Tigers' were hit by collapse of their currencies and precipitous declines in the values of stocks on their exchanges. All of this was part of a massive withdrawal of capital from this region. The International Monetary Fund (IMF) rescue plans for these economies, particularly that of South Korea, involve greatly increasing hardship for workers. In August 1998 the Russian rouble underwent a similar collapse in its value, deepening the poverty of many more in that country. In early 1999 the Brazilian real was devalued; legislation was approved to slash pensions and government employment. These actions have temporarily averted a similar crisis there. Much has been made by George Soros, Michel Chossudovsky and William Greider of the manipulations of currency speculators such as Soros, but only Greider also emphasises the overproduction of unsold commodities and global overcapacity in basic industry (what Greider calls the 'supply problem') (Greider 1997, Chossudovsky 1998). The disaster in the Asian economies is a consequence of overproduction; the Asian, Russian and Brazilian economies are the weakest in a world system whose markets cannot absorb all that it produces.

But even with a huge withdrawal of capital from Asia there is a worldwide overcapacity of 25–30 per cent in the automobile industry, with more capacity scheduled to be on line soon (*Chicago Tribune*, 8 May 1998). As I write, US steelmakers complain of the dumping of Japanese and Brazilian steel in US markets. Meanwhile, US agriculture has been dumping grain over the world for years – yet the oversupply is now worse than ever.

Some recent Left thought adheres to a super-imperialism model (often under the rubric 'globalisation' or 'world-systems'), where the advanced industrial powers as a group exploit the less industrial countries. The implication of this model is that competition in contemporary capitalism has been or can be moderated. With the moderation of competition comes a lessening of the prospects of war. Alternatively, some (such as Greider) acknowledge the intensity of competition but de-emphasise the importance of nation-states as the political loci of power of the various capitalist groups.

I am suggesting that capitalism is more competitive, not less; that the competition is out of control and cannot be brought under control by the capitalists, despite their efforts. Moreover, capitalists control regions and economies through the power of the various nation-states. The bipolar competition of the US–Soviet period is now replaced by multipolar anarchy. (This should not be taken to imply that the bipolar organisation of the world's powers would not have led to war had the Soviet Union not disintegrated.) Lenin's *Imperialism*, written over eighty years ago, argued that the competition to control markets, labour and raw materials inevitably leads to war among the competing powers (Lenin 1970/1916: especially chapter 9).

Lenin's argument is still valid. The centre of competition is oil, particularly in the Middle East. This oil is the lever that can be used by a militarily stronger power such as the United States to maintain hegemony over other powers (Europe, Japan, Russia, China) that may be economically stronger or potentially so. I project that the United States will go to war over oil, probably in Iraq, sometime in the next few years; that this will be a land war involving permanent military occupation; and that it will eventually be matched by military power to drive the United States from the region, perhaps sponsored partly by a rejuvenated Russia.

As this volume goes into production, the United States and NATO have completed an air war against Yugoslavia and, together with Russia, an occupation of the Yugoslav province of Kosovo. This is in addition to continued US and British air raids aimed at Iraqi oil refineries and pipelines. The background of this war is a nationalist/secessionist conflict between the Serb-dominated Yugoslav government and the Kosovo Liberation Army. But what is the United States' interest in this? I discount the moral rhetoric that invariably is used to justify these brutalities (an all sides). More to the point, US Secretary of State Madeleine Albright has noted:

> This region is a major artery between Europe and Asia and the Middle East ... Today, this region is the critical missing piece in the puzzle of a Europe whole and free. That vision of a united and democratic Europe is critical to our own security.
>
> (Albright 1999)

There are several plans to build pipelines across the Balkan peninsula to carry oil from the Caspian Basin. One proposed pipeline would cut through Macedonia and terminate in the Albanian port of Vlore. If we put Albright's remark in the context of the issues raised in the previous paragraph about control of oil, we may conclude that war over oil has already begun. Time will tell.

So wars, including world wars, are far from being at an end. To wage these wars the belligerents will rely on religious and moral appeals, but ultimately on patriotism. Patriotism makes its adherents easily controlled; as soldiers and civilians, they will be used in these contests among the capitalists.

Should we go to war against citizens of other nations, mostly workers, in wars fought under the banners of the capitalist ruling classes? Lenin, both in his writings and in his practice, represents the tradition of non-patriotic internationalist opposition to wars among imperial-capitalist powers. While other socialist parties during World War I (with the exception of the Italian one, to some extent) turned patriotic, Lenin and the Bolsheviks called for 'revolutionary defeatism', the revolutionary overthrow of 'their own' government in the war. Bolshevik soldiers at the front fraternised with their German counterparts and agitated among Russian soldiers to turn their guns against the government and make revolution. If Lenin is right, and I believe he is, we should not fight for 'our' capitalist governments in patriotic wars.

The growing rivalry between capitalists will lead to both small and global wars in the period ahead. These wars will leave us with the same two choices that Lenin and the others faced in World War I: to support the war effort or to organise for the defeat of 'our own' governments. Patriotism, even in its moderate form, will lead us to make the wrong choice.

Sports and patriotism – the danger of being 'a little bit pregnant'

Dixon may be correct in his estimate that sports patriotism is innocuous, provided that the political context is relatively stable and that sports patriotism does not lay the basis for mass participation in war. But if I am right, that the period ahead will be one of many wars that are likely to affect most of us, then we need to assess not only whether we should support those wars (as I attempted briefly earlier; see pages 96–97) but also the contribution of 'innocuous' sports patriotism to war.

Dixon rightly points out the connection between sports patriotism and patriotism generally, the identification with one's country and special duties entailed by that identification. Central among those duties is the duty of patriotic service in wartime. So the connection is clear between patriotism, even in its moderate form, and support for 'our countries' in any wars that may lie ahead. Because sports patriotism reinforces patriotic identities and such identities abet mass support for war, sports patriotism contributes to the mobilisation of populations for war, when they occur.

We can see some of this process at work in recent events in the former Yugoslavia and in Rwanda. (Here we are dealing with national identities that did not correspond to a polity, but the point would be the same about patriotism.) Groups retained separate group identities, despite decades of living side by side in harmony and intermarrying; their group loyalties were very 'moderate'. (Bosnia was the republic of Yugoslavia where peaceful relations and intermarriage between Croats, Serbs and Muslims was most extensive.) Yet economic crisis led to destabilisation of the old political order; elites mobilised people around group identities. This process led to intergroup conflict and the most brutal atrocities. National identities made these atrocities possible as out-group hostility and dehumanisation took hold of the masses.

Similarly, patriotic identity makes possible wartime brutalities against citizens of another state. Dixon is wrong to think that moderate patriotism is innocuous. He does not recognise that moderate patriotism, even as cultivated in sports, gives way in these situations to the most barbaric, fascist attacks on others, all in the service of the capitalist ruling groups who initiate this process. Awareness of 'the moral remainders' will not moderate anyone's conduct. Only the defeat of patriotic consciousness can do that. As in pregnancy, a little patriotism leads to a lot.

Notes

1　Many readers are aware that 'patriotism' and 'nationalism' are not exact synonyms. One difference is that patriotism is loyalty directed toward a state and towards fellow citizens of the same state (compatriots), while co-nationals may not share a state but perhaps only some other characteristic of a nationality such as language or religion. The development of the modern nation-states often involved the development of fictive nationality as part of creating the political basis for a struggle for a state. And pre-existing states may invent a common nationality to create an ideological ground of loyalty to the State.

2　See Chapter 5 in this volume.

3　The most common argument, that we all benefit from inequality, is the one derived from 'the functional theory of stratification' and assumed uncritically in Rawls' statement of the difference principle. I attack this argument in Gomberg (1995).

4　Here the research of the late Henri Tajfel and his associates is very useful. What Tajfel showed was that the mere acceptance of group categories led to ingroup favouritism and discrimination against the outgroup (see Tajfel 1981: especially part 4). Tajfel's research is very disturbing, because it shows that group loyalty need not be founded in rational shared group interests; thus it goes much further than earlier research by Muzafer Sherif, which showed that groups could be made to fight if they competed for the same goods (see Sherif et al. 1988). The experiment described there was carried out in the 1940s.

Part III

Gender equality

Chapter 7

Against sexual discrimination in sports

Torbjörn Tännsjö

Introduction

Sexual discrimination is a widespread and recalcitrant phenomenon. However, in Western societies, explicit sexual discrimination, when exposed, is seldom defended straightforwardly. There is one remarkable exception to this, however. Within sports sexual discrimination is taken for granted. It is assumed that, in many sports contexts, it is appropriate to discriminate (distinguish) between women and men and to have men competing exclusively with men, and women competing exclusively with women.[1] Even by radical feminists this kind of sexual discrimination has rarely been questioned. This is strange. If sexual discrimination is objectionable in most other areas of our lives, why should it be acceptable within sports?

The thesis of this chapter is that it is not. Even within sports, sexual discrimination is morally objectionable. No sexual discrimination should take place within sports. At least, the International Olympic Committee (IOC) and the leading national sports organisations should give it up.

The reasons for giving up sexual discrimination within sports, and for allowing individuals of both sexes to compete with each other, is simple. In sports it is crucial that the best person wins. Then sexual differences are simply irrelevant. If a female athlete can perform better than a male athlete, this female athlete should be allowed to compete with, and beat, the male athlete. If she cannot beat a certain male athlete, so be it. If the competition was fair, she should be able to face the fact that he was more talented. It is really as simple as that. Sexual discrimination within sports does not have any better rationale than sexual discrimination in any other fields of our lives.

However, arguments against giving up sexual discrimination within sports are not hard to come by, and in this chapter I will focus on such arguments. My thrust here is that, in various different ways, these arguments against abolition of sexual discrimination within sports are flawed. However, I will not restrict my argumentation to a discussion of arguments for sexual discrimination. One important argument against sexual discrimination, apart from the general observation that, from the point of view of sports itself it is irrelevant, will also be developed.

These are the main arguments *for* sexual discrimination within sports – some of them, no doubt, striking an indistinguishable (yet false) chord of special concern for women:

- Sexual discrimination within sports is no different from the use of, say, different weight classes in certain sports, intended to make the result less predictable. We use sexual discrimination because we seek, to use Warren Fraleigh's term, 'the sweet tension of uncertainty of outcome'.
- If women and men compete, and women defeat men, then this will cause violent responses from men. So we had better retain the discrimination.
- If we give up sexual discrimination in sports, then probably all women will find (because on average they perform poorly in comparison with men) that they are always defeated by some men. This will be discouraging for women in general and for female athletes in particular.
- Female sports are different from male sports. They represent a unique value, and if we gave up discrimination this unique value would be foregone. A similar argument can be devised with reference to male sports, of course.

I will discuss these arguments in order. After having done so I will give my positive argument in defence of giving up sexual discrimination, which is that the rationale behind sexual discrimination is simply too good. If we consistently hold on to it, we are led to all sorts of discrimination which, upon closer examination, we do not want to accept. So a kind of reductio ad absurdum leads us to the conclusion that sexual discrimination within sports should be given up.

I conclude the chapter by summing up the main tenets of my argument and by proposing, constructively, that sport as a phenomenon should not be conceived of as static. A development of various different sports takes place, and has to take place. We should consciously mould the phenomenon of sports in a certain desirable direction. We should mould sports in a direction of more moderation (in ways indicated by Sigmund Loland in Chapter 3). If we do, then we will be able to abolish sexual discrimination altogether within sports, thereby gaining a great deal from the point of view of gender equality and fairness, without having to pay any price at all for this timely reform.

If sexual discrimination within sports is abolished, this will not only be an advance from the point of view of feminism and the women's rights movement, I conclude, but from the point of view of sport itself. For the abolishment of sexual discrimination may render natural a development of sport in a direction which is, even if we put the matter of sexual discrimination to one side, of the utmost importance for sport itself, conceived of broadly as a cultural phenomenon. It may well be the case that, unless some sports develop in a direction where women and men *can* compete safely on equal terms, then there will be no future for these sports at all – or so I will argue, at any rate.

Sexual discrimination as no different to the use of weight classes?

When I have proposed that sexual discrimination within sports should be abolished, I have sometimes met the objection that sexual discrimination in some sports is no different to the use of weight classes in, say, boxing. We have such weight classes in order to ascertain that the outcome of a competition is not too easily predictable. This (evasive) argumentative strategy is completely misplaced, however. I have no objection to weight classes in boxing and some other sports. As a matter of fact, I think we should develop this kind of system even within other sports. There should be weight classes even in running, and heightclasses in basketball, and so forth. Such classes are constructed with reference to crucial characteristics of the individual athlete, characteristics with relevance for the capacity to perform well in the sport in question, and they are created in the interest of making the outcome of the competitions less predictable. It is crucial that the classes are constructed on the grounds of characteristics actually exhibited by the people who get sorted with reference to the characteristics in question, and that these characteristics are of *immediate* relevance to the capacity to perform well within the sport in question.

Sexual discrimination is different: it takes place on the ground that, *on average*, women perform less well than men in certain sports. This is objectionable. First of all, this putative fact, that women perform less well than men, is hard to ascertain beyond reasonable doubt. Perhaps this is a mere statistical accident. Perhaps it is due to socially constructed gender differences rather than biological sexual differences and, hence, could be abolished. And even if the statistical correlation is due to biological sexual differences (more below about sexual differences, and how to define them), and even if it has a law-like character, it is still only a *statistical* difference. It is only indirectly, then, that sex is relevant to the outcome of a fair competition. It is relevant in the sense that it predisposes, statistically, for more or less of a certain characteristic, crucial to performing well in a certain sport. But then, if we should discriminate at all, we should discriminate in terms of this characteristic itself and not in terms of sex.

This means that some women, who are not (statistically speaking) 'typical', perform better than many (most) men do. They do so because to a considerable degree they possess the characteristics that are crucial to winning, and possess more of these characteristics than do most men. Consequently, there are some rare women who perform better than most men in the sport in question.

It is 'discrimination', then, not only in a factual sense (in the way the term is used in this chapter), when a competent woman, who can and wants to defeat a certain man, is prohibited from doing so, on the ground that women in general do not perform as well as men in general. But it is also 'discrimination' in a *moral* sense, and such discrimination is morally reprehensible.

So while there is nothing objectionable in having weight classes in boxing (a sport in which weight is of direct relevance to winning), it *is* objectionable to have sexual classes (sex is only indirectly and statistically relevant to winning in boxing).

If boxing should be allowed at all, it should be allowed in a form where individuals of both sexes can compete safely with each other. To render this possible we would have to retain weight classes, of course. We may also have to make some other improvements of this noble art of self-defence, but I will not elaborate on this point in the present context. However, I conjecture that, unless boxing can be performed in a manner where men and women can compete safely against each other, there will (and should) not be any such thing as boxing in the future.

Sexual discrimination because of male aggressiveness?

What I have just said connects with a second argument against abolishing sexual discrimination within sports. Not only boxing, but also many other sports, are aggressive and involve a considerable amount of physical contact and encounter between competing athletes. Now, if women and men are allowed to compete against each other, and if some women defeat some men, then this would trigger violent responses from these men, or so the argument goes. In order to protect women against such outbursts of male aggressiveness, we had better let women and men compete apart from each other.

Is this a good argument? I admit that there is something to it, and it points at a real danger. However, it would be wrong to surrender to the argument, for there is another way of responding to the phenomenon of male aggressiveness against women. I am thinking here of the possibility of rendering impossible the aggressive response. This could be done if the rules of the game in question were changed. Aggressive assault on competitors could be punished much more severely than it is in many sports currently. One physical assault could mean a red card – and the aggressive male competitor would be out.

The rules of the game could be modified in other ways as well, so that the assault would be made more difficult to perform in the first place. Then there would be little need for punishment. And the sports could be modified, to render aggressiveness within the sports, even within the limits that are permitted, less rewarding and also never decisive.

Take tennis as an example. In modern tennis, the service is of enormous importance: an efficient service presupposes a lot of physical strength from the server. At the same time, an effective service tends to render the sport rather boring: it kills the game by taking the elegance out of it. An obvious solution to this problem would be to introduce a rule saying that a service is not successful unless the receiver has successfully returned it. Until it has been successfully returned, the server is granted a new opportunity. This would certainly reintroduce certain desirable qualities in tennis, and at the same time such a change in the rules of the game would mean better possibilities for women to compete successfully with men. Men would not defeat women merely by virtue of their superior strength and aggressiveness.

Were all this to be accomplished, I think we could make great strides in the general aim for sexual equality in society. *Some* women can defeat *most* men who perform any sport. Because of sexual prejudices, this is a hard lesson for a man to learn. It is hard even for me, a middle-aged man who regularly goes jogging, to be defeated now and then by a female jogger. As a matter of fact, I hate the defeat, and I go to considerable lengths to avoid it – but I sometimes fail. When I do, I get angry. I am enlightened enough to realise, however, when I do get defeated by a female jogger, that this teaches me a lesson. It is good for my mental development to be defeated by female runners: it teaches me to control my anger and it shows me something about the relation between the sexes. Some sexual stereotypes and (my) prejudices get exposed in the most efficient manner.

If this is correct, then we have good reasons not to surrender to this male aggressiveness argument regarding sexual discrimination within sports. We should allow women to defeat men in sports, and we should render it impossible for men physically to punish the women who do defeat them.

If we do so, in the long run certain sexual prejudices will hopefully wither.

Women will be discouraged?

The response to the argument relating to male aggressiveness may be considered overly optimistic. It is true that in most sports there are some women who can beat most men, but it is also true that in many sports some men can beat all women. So, even if it is a good thing from the point of view of sexual equality when a woman beats a man, is it not a bad thing, from the same point of view, when the best women in certain sports find that they cannot compete with the best men? Wouldn't this fact be disappointing for these women?

Well, I suppose this depends on whether (due to sexual differences) it is *impossible* for these women to defeat the best man, or whether there is something that can be done about this fact (the problem lies not in the sexual differences themselves but in socially constructed gender differences, which could be abolished). If there is something that can be done about it, if the problem is socially constructed gender differences rather than sexual differences, then these women may view the fact that they get defeated as a challenge. And they may take it as their mission to abolish the gender bias within sports.

This is basically the case in many other fields of society. There are men within certain sciences and arts, such as mathematics and musical composition, who perform better than all women (there is no female Gödel or Bach, for example). Should this be disappointing for women? I think not. I think rather it should be considered a real challenge, for we do not believe that it is because of their biological sex that no women solved logical problems like Gödel or composed like Bach. Typically, the lack of outstanding female logicians and composers is due to socially constructed gender differences, not to biological sexual differences as such.

There are reasons why women do not perform as well as some men do in these fields, of course, and these reasons, which are to do with gender rather than sexual differences, should come under close scrutiny; Angela Schneider describes many of the obstacles that meet female athletes in Chapter 9. Such obstacles, when identified and publicly recognised, should come under severe attack. Schneider has correctly observed that these obstacles are the outcome of a deeply entrenched ideal, according to which, from inception, 'the ancient and modern Olympic Games, and the ideal Olympic athlete, applied specifically and exclusively to men'. This is how she describes this ideal:

> From Pausanias' references to dropping women from the side of a cliff if they even observed the ancient Olympic Games, to de Coubertin's ideal that the goals that were to be achieved by the athletes through participation in the Olympic Games were not appropriate for women (de Coubertin 1912), one can easily see that the place of women in sport has been, for the most part, foreign at best. It is this basic idea, the idea that sport (or sometimes even physical activity), particularly high-level competitive sport, is somehow incompatible with what women are, or what they should be, that must dominate any discussion of the unique issues for women in sport. Philosophies of ideal sport, and ideal women, lie behind discussions of permitting women to compete, of choosing the types of sport in which women can compete, in developing judging standards for adjudicated (as opposed to refereed) sports – contrast gymnastics and basketball – in attitudes to aggression, and competition, and indeed to the very existence of women's sport as a separate entity at all.

(this volume: 123)

I believe that, if such obstacles are eliminated, if new weight and length classes are introduced in many sports, if the rules are changed so as to render it impossible for aggressive athletes to punish their competitors, and if severe punishments are introduced for violations of the rules, then women can actually compete successfully and safely with men in many sports. In fact, they do so today in some sports, such as some shooting events, all the equestrian sports, parachuting, and so forth, and the list of these sports is growing all the time – and is likely to continue to get longer in the future.

But what if this belief is not borne out by realities? What if there are some sports where the elite is made up of men exclusively – would this be disappointing to women?

Yes, of course it would. But, for all that, this seems to me to be a kind of disappointment that should be acceptable as a natural part of life. Sexual distinctions are genetic in origin, and so are racial distinctions. After all, there may be all kinds of genetic distinctions of importance for how on average people of various different kinds perform in sports, and one of these is race. Perhaps black Africans perform better on average than Caucasians in some sports. This is disappointing to white people, of course, but is no reason to introduce racial discrimination within sports. But if this is not a reason to introduce racial discrimination in sports, then we should not retain sexual discrimination either.

To elaborate this point, allow me to return to the comparison with the sciences and the arts and take my own subject, philosophy, as an example. Women are poorly represented, not only among logicians and composers, but also within the philosophical world in general. Most people believe that the reason for this is to do with gender rather than with sex, and this is what I happen to believe. It is because women have been met with the wrong expectations, when they have taken up philosophy, it is because they have not been given proper credit for their achievements, and so forth, that they have had difficulties in performing well within philosophy. However, what if it turned out that, even after this kind of gender bias had been successfully abolished, women were still poorly represented within (a certain field of, say) philosophy, would this be disappointing for women?

Perhaps it would be (to some women), but then I think it should be possible for them to live with this kind of disappointment. It would be absurd, for this reason, to have sexual discrimination within philosophy and to have female positions and special journals for women in these fields of philosophy – specially designed for them because they do not perform well enough to hold standard positions or to publish in ordinary journals within (these fields of) philosophy.

Maybe it would not be at all disappointing to (other) women, however, if it turned out that a kind of philosophy exists that is just poorly suited to the female brain or heart. Another reaction from women (and many men) upon finding this out could be the following. If this philosophy is essentially without appeal to one of the sexes, if it does not fit women, then this indicates not that there is anything wrong with women but that there is something wrong with this kind of philosophy.

We could adopt the same stance towards the more plausible putative fact that there are some sports that simply suit (on average) men better than women; that is, we could say of these sports, 'So much worse for them!'

One of my colleagues, who likes to go to further extremes than I do,[2] has objected to my argument in the following way. If we should abolish sexual discrimination within sports, he asks, why not abolish species discrimination as well? Why not have men competing with animals? Why not have Carl Lewis running over 100m against a hunting leopard?

Well, the reason not to arrange such competitions is not only (or mainly) that it would be a difficult task to arrange them, or that such competitions are hardly likely to be rewarding to animals. Perhaps the difficulties could be overcome and perhaps some animals would take some pleasure in competing with men. The main reason for not arranging such competitions is that *no* man can beat *any* (healthy) hunting leopard. This is not merely a matter of a statistical generalisation. If there were a system similar to weight classes for running, then people and hunting leopards would have to compete in different classes.

However, if the differences between men and hunting leopards were merely statistical, so that some men could beat some hunting leopards, then I am not sure that competitions between men and beasts would seem so outlandish; after all, they used to have such competitions during antiquity. It is a delicate question for the animal liberation movement, of course, whether they should promote (because of an interest in abolishing species discrimination) such competitions or oppose them (because they may fear that the animals would not take pleasure in them).

To return to the human case. It is hard to assess finally how important the statistical genetic differences are between human beings within sports. And the assessment should not be made in any simplistic manner, where gender gets conflated with sex, nor should it be taken for granted that sport is a static phenomenon. The sports evolve, to some extent in a natural way, and to some extent as the result of our active and intentional intervention. If we do not like the fact that statistical genetic differences, such as sexual or racial differences, are decisive within sports, there is a lot we can do about it.

This leads to the next argument.

Female sports represent a unique value

It may seem that female sports are different from male sports, and so they represent a unique value. To give up sexual discrimination would therefore be like giving up valuable existing sports. It would be like giving up soccer or baseball, or basketball or hurdles in running.

How should we assess this argument? The answer to it is that, largely speaking, it is false and, to the extent that there is a grain of truth in it, this grain of truth does not warrant the conclusion that we should retain sexual discrimination in sports. Rather, it does warrant the conclusion that many aspects of sports need to be reformed, so that 'female' qualities are added to them or, even, so that 'female' qualities are exchanged for 'male' ones.

Let me first comment on the major aspect of this objection – the mere falsity of it. In many ways, female sports are no different from male sports.

Angela Schneider has eloquently elaborated on the falsity of the objection (see Chapter 9). To a considerable and frightening extent, in many sports the male is simply the ideal. The good athlete is the hunter, the warrior, the man. And the conception of the masculine warrior is a narrow and simplistic one. In most athletic sports, Achilles could easily beat Ulysses. The cunning of the latter counts for nothing, whereas the superior strength of the former is decisive. This is also true when women take up these sports, and this is why women have to compete against each other and not against men. To put it drastically, therefore, I think it is fair to say that, in many sports, women compete against each other in masculinity, narrowly conceived. It is hard to find any special feminine qualities in *such* competitions.

What is the appropriate reaction to this obvious but little-publicised fact? Of course, this is hard to say. Some may find it unobjectionable. For my own part, I have to admit that I don't: I find the fact simply degrading, to both women and men. I also find that, if some women do want to compete in masculinity, why should they restrict themselves to a competition against each other? Why not compete also with men? After all, the best among them are capable of defeating most men even in masculinity. So why not do so?

I suppose that when Schneider describes how, in many sports, the male is the ideal, she intends this as a criticism. However, her criticism does not strike me as thorough enough. She seems to believe that the fact she describes in so many words is due mainly to gender aspects of sports, i.e. to aspects relating not with biological sex but to socially constructed roles and expectations. However, it is not far-fetched to believe that, even if we *were* to do away with all kinds of gender bias within sports, in many sports a genuine sexual bias would remain. Statistically, men *are* better than women in many existing sports. I will return to this fact below and to the question of what to do about it.

However, there may still be a grain of truth in the saying that women's sports in some aspects have unique qualities. I think, then, of qualities that are less to do with mere physical strength and more to do with inventiveness, sensibility, cooperation, strategy, playfulness, wit, and so forth. There may be more room for these qualities in women's competitions. And, to the extent that this is true, I think we are dealing with genuine and unique (female) qualities. However, there exists an obvious and better way of retaining these qualities than to retain sexual discrimination within sports. These qualities should be introduced in *all* sorts of sport, and they should not only be added to existing qualities but, in many cases, be exchanged for existing qualities.

It may be fruitful to speak of these unique qualities, which I suspect are more frequent in women's sport than in men's sport, as qualities of – to use Sigmund Loland's term – 'moderation' (see Chapter 3). Moderation in terms of what, though? Here I would like to be a bit more specific, in terms of gender, than Loland is himself. The object of the moderation, that which ought to be moderated, is arrogant outbursts of (male) aggressiveness and (mere) strength. These phenomena need not go away altogether, to be sure, but simplistic expressions of them should be countered. They should be moderated in the direction of values such as inventiveness, sensitivity, cooperation, playfulness and wit.

I think we are facing a happy coincidence here. Moderation is of great and growing importance within sports, not only as a means of rendering possible the abolition of sexual discrimination, but also as a means of saving sports as such, as a cultural phenomenon, from the most obvious threat to its continued existence (genetic engineering, discussed in Chapter 15).

The observation that moderation and sexual equality should go together is in accordance with a suggestion put forward in Jane English's much-discussed article, 'Sex Equality in Sports', even though (eventually) English reaches the conclusion that sexual discrimination within sports is necessary. She suggests that we develop a variety of sports in which an array of physical types can expect to excel:

> We tend to think of the possible sports as a somewhat fixed group of those currently available. Yet even basketball and football are of very recent invention. Since women have been virtually excluded from all sports until the last century, it is appropriate that some sports using women's specific traits are not developing, such as synchronised swimming.
>
> (English 1995: 287)

A similar view has been put forward by Iris Marion Young, with reference to Mary E. Duquin. Young describes Duquin's position eloquently as follows:

> Androgyny in sport means for her the incorporation of virtues typically associated with women into the symbols and practices of sport – such as expressiveness and grace – along with a corresponding decline in the present overly aggressive and instrumentalist aspects of sport which are typically associated with masculinity.
>
> (Young 1995: 266)

Sports without moderation means competition in aspects such as mere strength. The problem with this is not that there is no public interest in competitions in strength; I think there is too *much* interest in such competitions. The problem with our fascination with strength is that it has a 'fascistoid' value basis, I have described in detail in Chapter 1. A further problem, of importance in the present context, is that mere strength, or the disposition for it, is a very simple and congenital quality, so mere strength is what we could call a *non*-moral virtue: either you have it or you don't. Moreover, there is every reason to believe that, not only is the disposition for strength congenital, but it has a rather simple *genetic explanation*. If this conjecture is borne out by realities, this means trouble for sports. For, certainly, once we can identify the genes for strength, which are really genes for winning in many existing sports, then it becomes possible genetically, not only to pre-select the winners, something that may seem frightening as such, but (in ways discussed by Christian Munthe in Chapter 15) to *design* them. And, considering the enormous amounts of money and prestige that are invested in winning in sport, once the genetic design of winners becomes possible, it will take place. However, if we do design the winners genetically, then the public interest in sports competitions is likely to wither, or so I believe.

Genetic engineering, once it becomes possible, will be just as inevitable in sports as doping – unless we can render its application to sports impossible. And a way of rendering the genetic design of winners impossible is to change sports and to allow *moral* virtues to become crucial, for there are hardly any genes for inventiveness, sensitivity, cooperation, playfulness and wit in sports. All these virtues are true moral virtues: they can be learned (through training, to follow Aristotle) and, since there is a use for them outside the sports arenas as well, there is a point in learning them. To a considerable extent it is fair to say that these moral virtues, in contradistinction to the non-moral ones in sports, are typically 'female' (in the sense that there exist more of them in female sports than in male sports). So, at the same time, when we introduce more moderation into sports, in order to save sports from going extinct, we abolish the rationale behind sexual discrimination in sports, and we deepen the inherent value of sports as a cultural phenomenon.

All this means that, when we admire the winners of reformed (moderated) sports, our fascination for the winners will no longer bear a similarity to fascism, which is certainly an additional gain to be made.

Once we have reformed sports, by introducing more moderation into existing branches, and by adding new games to (and subtracting old ones from) the IOC list, we may safely give up sexual discrimination within sports and allow men and women to compete against each other on equal terms.

A reductio ad absurdum of sexual discrimination

We have seen that the standard arguments in defence of sexual discrimination within sports are weak. Let me just add one more positive argument in defence of abolishing sexual discrimination; an argument that is a reductio ad absurdum of the rationale behind sexual discrimination.

What are we to test for, when we test whether a certain athlete qualifies as female or male? Three options are open to us. We could test for genitalia, for gender, or for chromosomal constitution.

There are obvious difficulties with all three options. However, we need to stick to some of them, otherwise we will not be able to guard ourselves against athletes who want to cheat – against athletes who are really men, but prefer to compete with women under the false pretext that they *are* women. Moreover, if we have a system of sexual discrimination, and do not perform tests, there is a positive risk that women who excel in sports are being mistakenly suspected of really being men rather than women. These excellent women need the chance to reject, once and for all, these kinds of rumours and false allegations, and only efficient tests can accomplish this task.

There are many problems connected with testing for genitalia. First of all, the criterion is vague. We are operating here with a continuum. After all, even if rare, there are examples of hermaphroditism. Second, it is not clear that the test for genitalia is a valid one. In what sense are genitalia relevant? In what sports *could* genitalia be relevant? I blush when I seek an answer to that question. Finally, genitalia can easily be manipulated with: such tests are bound to be inefficient when it comes to people who (in an attempt to cheat) are prepared to undergo surgery.

The problems associated with testing for gender are even more obvious. First of all, this criterion is extremely vague. Perhaps the test should be the subjective sexual identification of the person in question, but this identification may be indeterminate. Furthermore, it may change over time. And then, once again, it is difficult to see any validity of such a test. In what sense does gender matter within sports? Finally, like a test for the appropriate genitalia, a test for appropriate gender would be only too easily fiddled with.

What, then, about chromosomal tests? These tests are what we rely on today (see Berit Skirstad's discussion of them in the Chapter 8), and I suppose that, *pace* Skirstad's opposition to gender tests as such, if we want to retain a system of sexual discrimination within sports, then chromosomal tests are what we have to rely on even in the future. The problem with chromosomal tests is not that they are vague or that they are easily manipulated with. They rate high on measurements of specificity and sensitivity, if conducted in a meticulous way. They are also fairly easily conducted, they are not very invasive and, from the point of personal integrity, they are certainly less intrusive than tests for the appropriate genitalia.

Are chromosomal tests valid? Well, if we want to find variables that, statistically speaking, correlate with sports performances, chromosomal tests may well be valid in some sports. I have argued that we should not discriminate on these grounds but, for the sake of the argument (for the sake of our reductio ad absurdum) let us assume that we should. Then a problem with our sex chromosomes is that, even if most people conform to a typical male constitution (they have the genotype XY) or a typical female constitution (they have the genotype XX), not everyone does. There are individuals with only one X chromosome (they have the genotype X0; that is, they suffer from what has been called Turner's syndrome), and there are individuals with two X chromosomes and one Y chromosome (they have the genotype XXY; that is, they suffer from what has been called Klinefelter's syndrome). Even these aberrations are of interest here. For it is natural to believe that, statistically speaking, people (women?) suffering from Turner's syndrome perform, in many sports, less efficiently than do 'ordinary' women, and it is also likely that, statistically speaking, people (men?) suffering from Klinefelter's syndrome perform less efficiently than do 'ordinary' men in many sports. There may also be sports where some of these groups have, statistically speaking, a slight advantage. This may have been true of a well-known Polish sprinter, Ewa Klobukowska, who turned out to have the chromosomal pattern XXY (again, see Chapter 8). This person may well have had an advantage in certain sports over most people with the XX chromosomal pattern because of her extra Y chromosome (she held the world record for the women's 100m).

All this means that, if we want to be consistent, and if we want to be true to the rationale behind sexual discrimination, we should go a step further and even introduce new discrimination categories (people suffering from Turner's syndrome and Klinefelter's syndrome, and people exhibiting other aberrations such as XYY, to mention just three examples). And, as was alluded to above, we may even have to introduce other kinds of genetic discrimination, such as racial discrimination, within sports, for different human races may on average perform more or less efficiently in certain sports.

However, this may strike most of us as downright absurd. But if it does, it means that we must give up the premise that led us to this conclusion. We must give up the very rationale behind the idea of sexual discrimination within sports. We must drop the assumption we adopted, for the sake of the argument – that it is appropriate to discriminate on grounds of genetic characteristics that, statistically speaking, favour or disfavour certain kinds of individuals in a certain sport.

We could add an even simpler argument to this. If we have sexual discrimination in sports, then (in order to avoid cheating and fraud) we need to have tests for sex. (I cannot see that either Schneider or Skirstad, in Chapters 9 and 8, succeeds in meeting this simple argument from justice.) We have seen that these tests need to be chromosomal tests. However, it runs counter to a highly plausible idea of genetic integrity that information about a person's genetic constitution should ever be forced upon him or her (Schneider and Skirstad both seem to agree about this). We have a right *not* to know our genetic makeup, if we do not *want* to know it. Compulsory chromosomal tests for athletes violate this right.[3]

Conclusion

I have argued that, if we reform sports in the direction indicated by Sigmund Loland (see Chapter 3), and introduce more moderation into all kinds of sports, then we may safely give up sexual discrimination within sports. This is something that the IOC and the national sports organisations should do. And even if moderation in sports will prove to be utopian, I think we should give up sexual discrimination. But then the appropriate reaction from women may be to turn their backs on those kinds of elitist sports where males (on average and for simple genetic reasons) have the upper hand.

Certainly, this abolition of sexual discrimination is consistent with there remaining a possibility for those who like to arrange sports competitions for one sex exclusively, just as there exists a possibility for arranging special sports competitions for certain races, political beliefs or sexual orientations. However, in more official settings there should exist a strict ban on *all* such sorts of (from the point of view of sports itself) irrelevant discriminations. It should be incumbent upon the sports organisations themselves to make sure that such a ban becomes a reality. And it should also be a condition of obtaining public funding that a sport organisation does not discriminate between women and men.

The reform of sports indicated here does not guarantee that there are no branches where, statistically speaking, men will perform better than women (just as there may exist sports where, say, black people perform better than Caucasians), but this does not warrant that we retain a system of sexual discrimination, nor that we introduce racial discrimination within sports. We should all be perfectly capable of living with the truth that such differences exist – and freely allow them to surface in sports competitions. Yes, there are also likely to exist examples of sports where the order is reversed. This is certainly true of some equestrian sports, such as dressage. There has been only one male Olympic winner in dressage since 1968 but surely this is no reason to reintroduce sexual discrimination in dressage.

What should the reform of sports look like in more detail? I will leave this as an open question. The examples I have given (additional weight and height classes, the abolition of the winning service in tennis, and so forth), are mere speculations on my part. To develop this line of thought takes a kind of expertise that I do not possess. And the method of reform must of course be piecemeal rather than utopian. The various different sports events should be put under scrutiny, one at a time. However, the direction of change should be the same all over the field of sports events. Three desiderata of moderation should be met, when interventions in the development of sports take place:

- Non-moral virtues (such as strength) should be given a less important role, and moral virtues (such as playfulness, inventiveness, sensitivity, cooperation and wit) a more important role, within sports.
- Sports should be developed in a direction that renders our admiration for the winners of sports competitions more decent.
- Sports should develop in a direction that makes it possible to abolish without any cost all kinds of sexual discrimination within sport.

If, and only if, these desiderata of moderation are met, sports will be able to thrive and flourish in the future and continue to add to the quality of our lives.

If these desiderata are (arrogantly) rejected, then, in a world where genetic engineering is quickly becoming a reality, the future prospects for athletics are bleak.

Arrogance and continued sexual discrimination will mean the marginalisation of athletics, or so I suggest here. In particular, unless women are given an equal chance to compete with, and defeat, males within elitist sports, they have a good reason to turn their backs on elitist sports. And unless sports are made immune to the threat posed by genetic engineering, they will be looked upon with little interest by the general public, and will lose their role as important cultural phenomena.

Notes

1   I use the word 'discrimination' in a neutral, purely descriptive sense. Sexual discrimination takes place whenever men and women are treated differently, no matter whether or not this difference in treatment is warranted.
2   Hans Mathlein, Stockholm University.
3   I defend the right in this strong form – which forbids insurance companies and employers to ask for information about the genotype of people or to use such information for any purposes whatever – in my book *Coercive Care* (Tännsjö 1999).

Chapter 8

Gender verification in competitive sport

Turning from research to action

Berit Skirstad

Evolution of gender testing

In order to stop the rumours that males dressed as females were competing in the women's competitions, the International Olympic Committee (IOC) introduced gender verification testing, the so-called 'femininity test', in 1968. This test was intended to prevent cheating and unfair competition.

The best-known cheater was an Austrian skier who won the women's downhill in 1966. After a medical examination and surgery in 1967, she changed sex. This athlete later married and became a father (Ferguson-Smith and Ferris 1991: 17). In 1957 a German former female athlete with a world record in high jump (from 1938) admitted publicly that he had been forced by the leaders of the Nazi youth movement to compete as a woman. This athlete had both female and male genitals, and the German Track and Field Association later banned him from female competitions. In 1980 another case of cheating was discovered by coincidence. Stella Walsh, a Polish emigrant who lived in the US and had won a 100m gold medal in 1932 under the name of Stanislawa Walasiewicz, was killed in a gun shooting at a shopping centre. An autopsy indicated that she, too, had both female and male genitals (Hay 1981).

With very few exceptions, women have no chance to compete on equal terms with men, because of their biological makeup. Men's performances are better than those of women, generally by 8 to 17 per cent (Carlson 1991: 28). In equestrian events, however, there exists complete equality, and women and men take part in the same competitions.

Gender verification and dope testing started at roughly the same time. Rumours reached the IOC that pseudo-hermaphrodites, with varying degrees of developed testes, did not get proper treatment in Eastern European countries, and were chosen in some sports because of their competitive edge.

The question of gender tests goes a long way back. Already in 1948 the British Women's Amateur Athletic Association required a letter from a medical doctor to confirm that the athletes entered in women's competitions were female. This was later characterised as too simplistic. In 1966, at the European Track and Field Championship in Budapest, the female athletes had to make a 'nude parade' in front of three female doctors. All passed the test, but the test was felt to be very humiliating. Five world record holders did not show up for the test, including the sisters Tamara and Irina Press from the Soviet Union. Their absence strengthened the suspicion that they were not qualified for women's competitions.

At the European Cup in 1967, the responsible body for the first time tried to look upon chromosome patterns as a possible method. A Polish sprinter (Ewa Klobukowska) was the first female athlete not to pass the gender test. This athlete had won gold and bronze medals at the 1964 Tokyo Olympic Games, and she held the world record for the women's 100m. She had passed the naked parade the year before. The organiser informed her about her irregular chromosome pattern (XXY), and a committee consisting of six persons did further testing. An ironic fact about her case is that, had she been tested at the next Olympic Games in 1968 in Mexico, she would have passed the test and would have been allowed to start. Ewa went through several medical treatments in order to be able to restart in women's competitions. The International Amateur Athletic Federation (IAAF) deleted her from their record books, however, and in 1970 it took back her Tokyo medals (Ferguson-Smith and Ferris 1991).

The IOC introduced the so-called 'buccal smear' test (or Barr test) at the Olympic Games in Grenoble and Mexico in 1968. From that time female athletes have needed a gender certificate with photo, height and weight and the athlete's accreditation number. The results from the tests have since then been treated confidentially, and are handed over to the doctor of the national team by the president of the IOC Medical Commission. The results are then immediately destroyed. The uncertainty of this test is considerable (approximately 20 per cent), which is the reason geneticists gave up this method long ago.

The test that is used today – a PCR (Polymerase Chain Reaction) test – was introduced in Albertville in 1992. Two samples are taken from cells on the inside of each cheek with a small brush. In order to make sure that no mistake is being made, two tests are taken. The security level is 99 per cent (Dingeon et al. 1992). A positive sample is mixed into each series, according to Bernard Dingeon, a French biologist, who was in charge of the tests in Albertville as well as at Lillehammer in 1994 (Dingeon 1994). French, Spanish and Norwegian geneticists did not want to have anything to do with the tests.

The IAAF abolished gender testing in 1992 after a long process. Its premise was that any athlete who legally, socially and psychologically was raised as a female should be allowed to compete in female activities. The national federations are responsible for the health of the athletes and to confirm their gender, and the IAAF medical delegate at international comptitions has the right to have suspicious athletes tested.

Interviews during the Lillehammer Winter Olympic Games

Methods

Based on the existing literature, eleven simple questions on gender testing were used by the present author at the Lillehammer Olympics in February 1994. The questions were short, in order to secure responses from the athletes. The interviews were conducted in English, Norwegian, German or other languages, with the help of a translator, who usually was either the team leader or the team doctor. The weakness with using another person, who was superior to the athlete, was always going to introduce the risk of influencing the answers. The interview was performed when the athletes appeared for the gender test, in the neighbouring room. No one refused to be interviewed. On the contrary, the athletes reacted positively, since the IOC wanted to have their opinion.

Sample

A sample of 115 female athletes (21 per cent of the total) from 42 countries representing 9 different sports at the 1994 Winter Olympic Games in Lillehammer were interviewed. The initiative stemmed from the IOC Medical Commission; the athletes were informed about this fact, and were told the identity of the interviewer.

Results

From time to time the IOC has used the argument that women themselves want the test. This is a considerably modified truth: when asked if the tests were necessary, 66 per cent of the women said that gender verification was necessary, and approximately the same number found the test useful in that it prevented rumours. Of those interviewed at Lillehammer, 20 per cent expressed the view that the test was humiliating.

The interviews at Lillehammer showed that a majority of the athletes had received very little information about the tests in advance. Those who had little or no knowledge about the gender tests were most supportive of the test, and the more knowledge athletes had about the test, the more sceptical they were. Half of those who had some knowledge about the test claimed that it was necessary. One reason why the athletes supported the test may have been that they knew that, unless they passed it, they would not be allowed to take part in the Olympic Games.

Information

Geneticists are the ones who have protested most strongly against these tests. The athletes in general have not known enough about the complications attached to the tests to question them; they tend to think that the test protects them against male intruders in female competitions, and they do not want to exchange it for a gynaecological test (80 per cent were against such a change). If gynaecological tests have to be performed, the requirement is a female doctor and, again, resistance against the test was strongest among those who knew more about it. The argument that women want the gender test is not automatically valid: as much as 80 per cent of the women wanted more information about the test.

Lacking harmonisation

Many of the leaders and doctors accompanying the athletes during the 1994 Lillehammer Winter Olympics believed that the FIS certificate (International Ski Federation) would suffice, but the IOC only recognises their own certificate, except when the IAAF had filed one. Thirty-three per cent of the interviewees had a certificate from a former Olympic Games, but in order to get a different emblem on the certificate they claimed to have forgotten these. If they had known how unstable the tests were, they probably would not have taken the chance.

Unnecessary test

I believe that no gender tests are needed in order to reveal men dressed as women. The outfits worn by today's athletes, together with close media exposure, would easily reveal the obvious cases of cheating. In addition, athletes have to urinate under surveillance when they undergo dope controls.

The athletes interviewed at Lillehammer focused more on frequent dope testing than on gender testing. A few were concerned about the test, since they had never tested their gender. Unlike the dope test, where they *knew* they would pass since they had not taken any forbidden substances, those who had never previously tested for gender identification were more concerned about the test than those who had been tested before.

'Positive cases'

No one knows how many athletes have withdrawn after they have received the first information from the test both nationally and internationally. Since public 'positive cases' are not available, as they are in doping, our knowledge about them and their frequency is restricted. The IOC has refused to publish the 'positive' cases since the test was introduced. However, the results from the 1992 Barcelona Olympics *were* published: 2406 athletes registered as women were tested; eleven cases of Y chromosome were discovered; and the SRY gene was only found in five women. Of the five, four did not pass a gynaecological test, and one did not show up (Serrat and Herreros 1996). Most of these women will be athletes who have grown up as women and lived as such, but have special gender characteristics. In many cases they have no competitive edge at all. Many times their advantages are no bigger than the variation found in the genetic 'normality'. Some of them would not even stand to gain from the use of anabolic steroids, even if they had tried.

For all we know of the gender issues, probably 1 out of 400 women (0.25 per cent) has been excluded from the Olympic Games since the test was introduced. In most cases they have been discriminated against unfairly, and they have had no competitive edge because of their abnormalities. Ironically, a man with Klinefelter's syndrome (i.e. with XXY chromosomes) could pass the gender verification and take part as a female. According to Fox (1993), there are other conditions, such as 'congenital adrenal hyperplasia' or 'polycystic ovarian syndrome' with endogenous production, which can facilitate performance, so perhaps we should be testing for these instead.

Of the interviewed athletes at Lillehammer, 13 per cent thought they had competed with men. Most of these cases were mentioned in skating for juniors, where the athletes had been from Asia. In all these cases the athletes had never met the male athletes again.

A 'victim'

One of the few publicised cases where the athlete has been reinstated is that of the Spanish hurdler Maria Patino. Until she was 24 years old, she thought she was a woman; she got her gender verification card during the 1983 Athletics World Championships in Helsinki. Two years later, when she was about to start in the World University Games in Kobe, she left her gender certificate at home, and because of this she was tested again. This time some irregularities were found in her test. Her federation forced her to lie and invent an injury in the warm-up period, so she could not start.

The Spanish Track and Field Federation pushed her out in the cold, and many months elapsed before they contacted her. However, she continued to train for the indoor season, and just before the opening competition of the indoor season the president of the federation told her that she would have to withdraw from competitions for ever. She was asked to 'fake' a career-ending injury, because otherwise there would be lots of gossip in the papers. Maria did not obey. She competed, and the newspapers claimed that she was a man. A scholarship was taken away from her. She lost her coach, her boyfriend, and her records in track and field were abolished, and people in the street pointed at her, asking if she was a man.

Three years later she became rehabilitated, after pressure from the media and the Finnish geneticist Albert de la Chapelle. Patino was the first woman to protest publicly against her disqualification and to be reinstated (Carlson 1991). She has warned against apathy in the fight against gender testing, and has expressed the following opinion: 'What happened to me was like being raped. I'm sure it's the same sense of incredible shame and violation. The only difference is that, in my case, the whole world was watching' (Carlson 1991: 29).

Actions planned in order to abolish the test

The Norwegian Biotechnology Advisory Board decided to evaluate the existing test. The background of this initiative was the new Norwegian law in the Biology Act no. 56 of 5 August 1994 – it was not clear why permission had been given for gender testing in connection with the 1995 Junior World Championships in alpine skiing at Voss, Norway. The evaluation from the sports angle (Loland *et al.* 1995) made me look once again through my material from Lillehammer. At this time I became an activist. From then on, the Norwegian Confederation of Sports (the umbrella organisation for sport in Norway) became involved in the fight against gender tests, and tried to convince IOC to stop the test. Since then, a strategic planned action has evolved.

The starting point was a seminar in March 1996 organised by the Norwegian Biotechnology Advisory Board. A geneticist (van der Hagen 1995), a lawyer (Vold 1995) and a sports researcher (Skirstad 1996), who had all analysed the issue, gave their evaluation in the seminar. It was made clear that gender testing was already forbidden in Norway, according to the new law of 1994. Before the 1997 World Championships in nordic skiing held in Trondheim, an international seminar for the media was organised. During the championships, no gender tests were carried out. This was in full agreement with the FIS, for pragmatic reasons and because of the new law.

The Norwegian Olympic Committee and the Confederation of Sports (NOC) then contacted the five Norwegian federations (basketball, judo, skiing, volleyball and weightlifting) having international federations using the test with the message to contact them. The NOC raised the topic of gender testing at the ANOC meeting in Mexico, and a ban was adopted by the general assembly, which consisted of representatives from 197 countries.

Three consecutive women conferences have resolved to abolish gender tests (the IOC's Women's Conference in Lausanne, November 1996; the Second International Women's Conference in Windhoek, May 1998; and the Third European Women's Conference in Athens, August 1998).

As a direct result of this action, the European Judo Federation abolished the gender test in 1997. At the first EOC meeting (of all European Olympic Committees) in 1997, the gender test was 'sacrificed' in order to get consensus about blood-doping tests in the Nagano Winter Olympics (1998).

From 1 January 1998, gender testing was forbidden in Norway for all purposes other than for medical reasons. An amendment to the law of 1994 states this explicitly. The gender tests reveal sensitive information about the athletes, which the athletes have not asked for, and therefore should only be used for medical purposes. Such information can also have serious consequences for other members of an athlete's family.

The last strategy used against the gender test was to send a plea from Norway's top athletes to the IOC Athletes' Commission, asking them to send a letter including the arguments for stopping the test to the IOC president. They agreed to do this in February 1999. If this attempt to abolish the test fails, then it seems to me in order to force the IOC to surrender, international media and leading geneticists of the world should be called upon to stress the point that the test is not scientifically valid.

Conclusions

No simple laboratory test exists that can decide a person's gender. According to psychologist John Money, 'The difference between male and female is not black and white. It's a biological continuum. Any dividing line is a matter of context' (Carlson 1991: 29).

In the fight against gender testing, one of the NOC's tasks is to inform as many athletes and sport leaders as possible about the facts of the gender test and all the problems it can create for the individual athlete. It is my hope that this chapter can spread some knowledge about the gender test to a greater audience. Gender verification is an outmoded notion, and I suspect that very soon we will hear no more about it.

Chapter 9

On the definition of 'woman' in the sport context

Angela J. Schneider

Any discussion of the status of women in the sport context would benefit greatly from examining the underlying premises regarding the definition of 'woman' within (and outside) that context. Even on the surface level it becomes readily apparent to even the less-informed reader that the story to be told of women's participation in sport in general is the story of two ideals in apparent conflict. For example, from inception, the ancient and modern Olympic Games, and the ideal of the Olympic athlete, applied specifically and exclusively to men. From Pausanias' references to dropping women from the side of a cliff if they even observed the ancient Olympic Games, to de Coubertin's ideal that the goals that were to be achieved by the athletes through participation in the Olympic Games were not appropriate for women (de Coubertin 1912), one can easily see that the place of women in sport has been, for the most part, foreign at best. It is this basic idea, the idea that sport (or sometimes even physical activity), particularly high-level competitive sport, is somehow incompatible with what women are, or what they should be, that must dominate any discussion of the unique issues for women in sport. Philosophies of ideal sport, and ideal women, lie behind discussions of permitting women to compete, of choosing the types of sport in which women can compete, in developing judging standards for adjudicated (as opposed to refereed) sports – contrast gymnastics and basketball – in attitudes to aggression, and competition, and indeed to the very existence of women's sport as a separate entity at all.

Before examining some of these issues in detail, it is worth making a point and a distinction at the outset. The point is that many of the issues, even moral issues, that arise in sport, arise equally for men and women. At the personal level, the decision whether or not to cheat, or what attitude you will take to your opponents or the unearned win, are moral problems any athlete must face. At the institutional level, decisions about rules prohibiting drug use, or equipment limitations designed to improve participant safety, should apply equally to women as to men. As such, those concerns common to the realm of sport, important as they are, are more appropriately discussed elsewhere.[1] This chapter is devoted to the issues that arise because it is women, by virtue of the definition of who they are, who are the athletes. Thus the discussion that follows below will be focused on gender and sport, and the inter-relationships between them.

The philosophy of 'woman' versus the ideal athlete

Ideal woman

The battles that represent the basis for contentious issues for women in sport will be fought over conceptions of women – their bodies and their minds. The traditional ideals of woman during the ancient Olympic Games and the revival of the modern Olympic Games (up to and including some current ideals) are intimately tied to a particular view of woman's body. Some of these characteristics are soft, graceful, weak and beautiful. The desirable qualities for a woman in the time of the ancient Olympics can generally be summarised as beauty, chastity, modesty, obedience, inconspicuous behaviour, and being a good wife and a good mother (Lefkowitz and Fant 1985). Of course, these characteristics are tied to the roles of wife, mother and daughter. They are not similar to those of the traditional ideal of man, as hard, powerful, strong and rational, which are tied to the roles of leader, warrior and father. But, more importantly, if we examine the underlying characteristics of the traditional ideal athlete, we can plainly see that the ideal man and the ideal athlete are very similar, particularly in the role of warrior.[2] Conversely, we can plainly see that during the times of the ancient Olympic Games (and during the rebirth in the modern Olympic Games) the ideal woman and the traditional ideal athlete are almost opposites, so much so that women were hardly ever mentioned in conjunction with sport.

In contrast to these infrequent and casual references to women's sport, accounts of men's sport and athletics abound in ancient Greek literature. Homer vividly describes events from chariot racing to boxing. Pausanias furnishes a detailed account of the Olympic Games, and Herodotus, Thucydides and other Greek authors refer to the Olympic Games and athletic festivals such as the Pythian, Isthmian and Nemean Games (Spears 1988: 367).

There were also some exceptional counterexamples from ancient Greece – in the writings of Plato, for example – even though it is not well-known that girls competed in athletic festivals in ancient Greece. Plato, at the peak of his writing, argued that women should be accorded the right to soar to the highest ranks he could conceive of in human excellence – the philosopher ruler; and be equally educated in the gymnasium by exercising naked with the men (Bluestone 1987). Other exceptional counterexamples from ancient Greece that stress physicality and a warrior nature for woman are the archetypes of Artemis, Atalanta and the Amazons, who all rejected the traditional role for women (Creedon 1994).[3]

Of course, book V of Plato's *Republic* is not nearly so well cited by feminist critics as Aristotle's 'On the Generation of Animals' and 'Politics', and quite rightly so, because of the extremely negative philosophy of woman put forward by Aristotle. However, the fundamental issue in this entire discussion is who gets to choose which images of woman are permitted, desired or pursued in life and in sport. The primary question behind the role for women in sport is inextricably linked to the question of power and autonomy. At the institutional level, if it is the case that men decide, for example, the sports that women are permitted to attempt; the standards of physical perfection that are to be met in adjudicated sports; or the levels of funding accorded to women's as opposed to men's sport, then women have a legitimate grievance that they are not being treated with due respect. Just as it is the responsibility of each male to decide for himself, his conception of the type of body and, indeed, the type of life he wishes to pursue, moral or otherwise, it is the responsibility and right of each woman to deal with the challenges female athletes must deal with.

Paternalism and autonomy

The *Oxford Dictionary of Philosophy* defines paternalism as 'government as by a benign parent'. Paternalism is not necessarily sexist, although it often has been in sport and sport medicine (it could be called maternalism in a case where it was another woman making the decision on behalf of the individual, or perhaps parentalism), and it is often well-meaning. It occurs when one person makes a decision on behalf of (or speaks for) another, in what he or she takes to be the latter person's best interest. In the case of children, this is of course a necessary part of the parenting process until the child becomes an adult. Paternalism is also morally acceptable in cases where the person concerned is unable, for good reason, to speak or make decisions for himself or herself. It becomes morally troubling when it occurs on behalf of competent adults.

The concept of autonomy in ethical decision-making is very important. Autonomy is defined as the 'capacity for self-government'; furthermore, 'agents are autonomous if their actions are truly their own'. The crucial point here is that an essential part of being human is having the right and the capacity to make the choices and decisions that most affect oneself. Each competent human adult has the right to choose to pursue the projects and endeavours that he or she most cares about. That right is naturally limited by the rights of others to pursue their own desires and interests, but what the concept of autonomy takes for granted is that no one is entitled to speak on another's behalf, without that person's permission.

Sport paternalism and women's participation

Is there any reason why women should not participate in sports that men have traditionally played? It is instructive to look at what could possibly count as a morally acceptable answer. If there were a sport practised by men that was physiologically impossible for women, it would count as a reason for women not participating. But there is no such sport. To qualify, the sport would probably have to centrally involve male genitalia – funnily enough, we have no institutionally sanctioned sports of this type.

A second possibility would be if there were a sport, played by men, that no women in the world actually wanted to play. It is logically possible that such a sport might be invented, that not one woman anywhere would want to play, but then the reason the women would not be playing would be that they had *chosen* not to play, not that someone else had decided that they should not. Morally unacceptable answers for prohibiting women from playing sport would include: 'It would be bad for women to participate', or 'There is not enough money to allow women to participate'. Each of these two responses requires independent examination.

'It would be bad for women to participate' is the standard line that has been used throughout the history of sport. The exact nature of the harm that would befall women changes. It could be that it 'defeminises' (which might mean that it would make some women less attractive in the eyes of some men – either physically or mentally), or that it would be harmful for women, that they (or sometimes their not-yet-conceived children) would suffer some physiological damage. (For a good discussion of these points, see Cahn 1994.) There are two points to be made here. The first is practical. Assertions that strenuous physical exertion harms women, but not men, are simply not true. But it is the second point that is more important – women have the right, just as men do, to decide what risks of harm they will run. Subject to the normal limitations on every person's freedom, it is immorally paternalistic to decide, on behalf of another competent adult, what personal risks he or she can choose to accept.

The argument that 'There is not enough money to allow women to participate' can be more difficult to answer. It cannot be morally required to do the impossible, however 'There is not enough money' often masks an inequitable distribution of the resources that are available. If there is money available for anyone to participate in sport, then that money must be available on an equitable basis for both women and men. Men's sport is not intrinsically more important or more worthwhile than women's sport, and therefore has no automatic right to majority funding.

Specific challenges to women athletes

In the discussion that follows, some of the challenges faced by women athletes will be examined from a philosophical point of view. Some challenges are a result of the institutional climate for women in sport (e.g. biased, resistant and 'chilly'), and will thus require policy and practice changes in sport. Others – physical, mental and indeed, spiritual – occur at a personal level.

From a physical perspective these challenges may include, but are not limited to, body composition and development issues related to the health and wellbeing of the athlete. Three issues in particular – disordered eating, amenorrhoea and osteoporosis – are called the 'female athlete triad'. Some of these problems are a direct result of the demands of a particular woman's participation in her sport. *Citius, altius, fortius* – pushing the human limits, male or female, has its effects. For example, many elite-level sports present high risks of injuries and, generally speaking, elite-level training produces fit, but not necessarily healthy, athletes. The results of those pressures can be, and are in many cases, different for men and women, but the choice whether or not to train and compete is parallel. However, there is a special class of cases where the sport (such as gymnastics) is essentially judged (Suits 1988) – here the physical requirements and resulting risks are directly caused by decisions about what counts as excellent sport. The judging criteria for these sports should be tailored so as to minimise the health risks they impose on the athletes.

This is particularly a problem for women's events, as women athletes have a much higher prevalence of disordered eating than men. Women athletes have, at various times, faced different ideals (Creedon 1994; Hargreaves 1995), but the greatest tension is the initial tension – between the traditional ideal athlete and the traditional ideal woman. This modern tension is readily identified in the brief history of women's competitive body building and the conflicting judging practices. Further, if it is true that most women in the general population have eating problems as well (Szekely 1988; Bordo 1990; Sherwin 1992: 189), based on the problem of unattainable ideals (in North America, for example, the two ideals have been the Barbie doll and the super-waif model), then this problem is cultural, and medical control may not be the best, and certainly not the only, way of addressing the issue.

Amenorrhoea and pregnancy are unique to women athletes and raise issues that are tied to the implications that all women have faced when reproductive aspects of their lives have been designated as illness; and the tension between the two conflicting traditional ideals of woman and athlete. An essential part of the traditional ideal woman is fertility, because it is necessary for child-bearing. Fertility and child-bearing are not only not essential to the ideal athlete, they are antithetical to the role of athlete as warrior; for example, the Amazons. In many ways the Amazons were viewed as monstrosities because they rejected the essential biological role of woman as primary.

It is also the case, historically, that some medical authorities have created for women a series of double binds, situations where options are reduced for oppressed groups to a very few, all of them exposing these groups to penalty, censure or deprivation (Frye 1983: 2; Sherwin 1992: 179), through the decision to view menstruation, pregnancy, menopause, body size and some feminine behaviour as diseases (Lander 1988; Broverman *et al.* 1981). For the female athlete the situation becomes even more complicated because she can be classified as even more abnormal when reproductive changes become evaluated in the context of the traditional male sports arena. For example, if the normal healthy woman is standardly, from a medical perspective, an unhealthy adult, because the ideal healthy adult is based on being male (Broverman *et al.* 1981), then it follows that the female athlete starts out an unhealthy adult because she is a woman. But, further, if the female athlete shows signs of becoming masculine, such masculinisation is thought of as further abnormality because it is not normal for a woman to have masculine characteristics. Following this kind of medical classification, when a woman bleeds, she is ill ('Woman ... is generally ailing at least one week out of four ... woman is not only an invalid, but a wounded one'; Lander 1988: 48), and if she does not bleed (due to amenorrhoea, menopause, pregnancy) she is ill, because it is not normal for her to be unable to conceive, thus making successful use of her biological organs (Sherwin 1992; Lander 1988; Zita 1988). Pregnancy, then, theoretically constituting a state of health for the traditional ideal woman, should not be treated as a disease requiring a significant amount of specialised treatment. However, women, and women athletes in particular, are not encouraged to think of themselves, or their lifestyles throughout pregnancy, as healthy. Serious charges of irresponsibility can occur when the relationship between women athletes and their foetuses is characterised as adversarial. (Some countries – Canada, USA and Australia – have begun to imprison women for endangering their foetuses; see Sherwin 1992: 107.) Most pregnant women athletes who are falsely charged with harming their foetuses face, at the very least, moral pressure that is based on the view that being pregnant and participating in sport is a socially unacceptable behaviour. However, in some cases, genuine harm to the foetus may occur with participation in sport (oxygen deprivation, for example). But, rather than licensing interference with a female athlete's reproductive freedom, that denies her interest in the health of her foetus and her role as an active independent moral agent, our focus should be on education.

The classification of these reproductive aspects of women's lives as illnesses can, and have, led to wide-scale paternalistic medical management of women under the claims of beneficence (Sherwin 1992: 180). In sport, these so-called illnesses have been part of the basis for excluding women. This does not mean that serious complications requiring medical interventions cannot occur with any aspect of a female athlete's reproductive life or life-cycle changes and ageing. (For example, that older women athletes have experienced pain during their menopause has always been a fact. Sport physicians and coaches, predominantly male, simply had to learn to take their female Master's-level athletes seriously before they could recognise that this pain was all over women's bodies, not just in their heads.) There will be particular cases where the label of 'illness' or 'disease' is appropriate, provided that ascription does not then lead to harming women athletes from a sport policy perspective (for example, banning them from participation in sport rather than educating them about coping with their illness and participating in sport).

The female athlete must also face challenges regarding the mental requirements of sport competition, aggression and violence. Male athletes also face these challenges, but it is considered 'normal' for men and 'abnormal' for women to engage in violence. Traditionally it has also been predominantly men who have committed sexual abuses against women (and minors) in sport. (Some researchers suggest that this predominance may be linked to the socially and legally accepted high levels of violence in some sport; Kirby and Brackenridge 1997.) The control over, and moral responsibility for, violence, abuse, harassment and discrimination, in sport and surrounding sport, lies mainly in the hands of those in the sport community, and it is a concern for both men and women. Some women, weary of not having their voices heard on these issues (and for a host of other reasons), advocate completely separate sport for women as opposed to any integration at all.

One argument against integration is that women have to accept the current selection of sports, primarily designed for and practised by men, with an established culture with rewarding and recognising values (such as viewing sport as a battleground on which one conquers one's foes) that most women do not hold; whereas separation might allow women the freedom to create sport based on the values they choose (Lenskyj 1984). Capacities that are viewed as unique to women – sharing, giving, nurturing, sympathising, empathising and, above all, connecting as opposed to dividing – are stressed in this argument. Nevertheless, some would urge women to pay the high price of integration, so that they can have the same opportunities, occupations, rights and privileges that men have had in sport. This drive for women's sameness with men has sometimes denied women's qualities and how these qualities might contribute in a very positive manner to sport. The argument is that, if women emphasise their differences from men, viewing these as biologically produced and/or culturally shaped differences, they will trap themselves into ghettos, while men will carry on as before.

If we think that women athletes either act as men, if they accept the male ideal, or must be separate and generate their own ideal, the sport experience is highly gender-specific. But, the two views of sport – sport as competition (agon), test against others to overcome; or as connected co-questers searching and striving for excellence – may well be logically independent of the gender of the athlete.

However, the greatest tension arises for women if we have an 'agonistic' view of sport and women are found to be inherently ('essentially') caring and connected to others (Noddings 1984). In such a model of sport, women may be required to disconnect from their embodied experience. This could be the case for some form of alienation. Most athletes (male and female) probably find themselves torn between conflicting views of sport because pushing oneself to one's limits challenges even the strongest sense of self, and because in their moments of agony and joy they tend to experience themselves as both radically alone (because no one else can really understand what they feel) and fundamentally united to their team-mates, their competitors, particularly when this experience happens during a major competition.

The logic of gender verification

Entirely separate sport, and even just separate women's events, inevitably leads to the question of the logic of gender verification. If we are to have separate sport, or sporting events for women only, logically it must be possible to exclude any men who may wish, for whatever reason, to compete. This means that there must be a rule of eligibility that excludes men. (Conversely, if we have such a rule for excluding men, should we, for consistency, have such a rule excluding women from men's events even if the women believed they would inevitably lose, but wanted to take part anyway?) This in turn requires that we have a test of gender and/or sex, that can be applied fairly to any potential participant. There are at least three methods of applying any such test: the first would be to test all contestants; the second, random contestants; the third, targeted individuals.

Before looking any more at testing, we must first deal with the response that we do not need to test because a man would never wish to compete in a women's event. 'Never' is a very strong word. It is not beyond the realm of imagination that a money-hungry promoter might decide that it was a great publicity stunt to enter men in a women's event. A male may even, with good intentions, choose to enter a women's event (such as synchronised swimming) as a form of protest against gender discrimination. Without a test to decide just who is eligible, we could be forced to accept, in women's events, participants who were quite obviously and unashamedly male, but who merely professed to be female.

There is a great deal of debate about how sex roles and gender are established (Tavris, Hubbard and Lowe, Schreiber, Blau and Ferber, and Lindsey). Mercier, in her gender verification report (1993), takes the position that sex is one's biological characteristics, and gender is one's socially learned characteristics. The standard practice in the Olympic Games is to have medical experts verify gender. But, as we have seen in Chapter 8, by delegating gender verification to medical experts, the sport community (and society in general) has given great power to medical experts on an issue that is in great dispute by researchers. Gender may not be merely a medical question, though it involves medical questions. Dialogues on gender, and gender in sport, have serious social, political and legal dimensions, making the medical story only part of the story.

In Chapter 8, Berit Skirstad gave several examples to illustrate the conceptual and moral issues that litter gender verification. Here is another. In 1976 a new player, Renée Clarke, appeared on the US women's tennis circuit, who 'soundly thrashed' the defending champion in the women's division. She was subsequently shown to be Renée Richards, who had recently undergone a sex-change operation and who had previously been a male elite-level tennis player (Birrell and Cole 1994: 207–237). The US Women's Tennis Federation wanted to exclude, as unfair competition, a player who was genetically male, but was reconstructed physiologically and now (presumably) psychologically female. The United States Tennis Association, the Women's Tennis Association and the United States Open Committee therefore introduced the requirement that players take a chromosomal test called the Barr test (Birrell and Cole 1994: 207). Richards refused, and went to court to demand the right to participate in women's events. In court she was deemed to be female on the basis of the medical evidence produced by the surgeons and medical professionals who had overseen his transformation from male to female. In the media this story played as an example of a courageous individual fighting for personal rights against an intransigent and uncaring 'system' (Birrell and Cole 1994). There are other ways of viewing the story, however.

What makes a woman a woman? Is it chromosomes, genitalia, a way of life or set of roles, or a medical record? It is not clear why medical evidence of surgery and psychology should outweigh chromosomal evidence. In fact it is not clear why any one criterion should be taken as categorically overriding any other.

How to approach issues for women in sport

In the field of bioethics, Rosemarie Tong (1995) has suggested that there are three standard elements of a methodology that can be used to deal with concerns for women. I believe this methodology may also be very useful for issues regarding women in sport. The first element suggested involves asking what was originally referred to as 'the woman question' and is now called by some researchers 'the gender-biased question' (Tuttle 1986: 349). This question challenges the supposed objectivity of scientific research findings regarding the nature of woman and the objectivity of the professions (such as sport medicine) based on that research (Dreifus 1977; Corea 1985;

Okruhlik 1995; Schiebinger 1989, 1993). Underpinning this question is the suggestion that many of the 'facts' about female 'nature' actually result from values founded on biased social constructions.[4] The precepts and practices of sport can be, and are, misshaped by gender bias.[5] This gender bias works almost unconsciously and occurs when decision-makers, physicians and coaches in sport treat all athletes, all human bodies, as if they were all male athletes and male bodies. They would then view athletes, or their bodies, as dysfunctional if they failed to function like male bodies, or expressed little or no curiosity or interest in the problems unique to women. There are issues in sport that are, for the most part, unique to women (for example, the female athlete triad — eating disorders, amenorrhoea and osteoporosis; and gender verification, reproductive control and pregnancy, sexual harassment, etc.). There are issues unique to men. There are issues unique to certain sports. There are common issues for participants across regions, sports and particular quadrennial cycles. Physicians, coaches and sport organisers need to be aware enough of sex/gender similarities and differences to deal with these issues.

The second suggested part of this methodology is that of consciousness-raising, which requires that women be seriously invited to contribute their personal experiences into sport, so that it has wider meaning for all women. It is postulated that women who share sexual stereotyping or harassment stories in sport, for example, often come to realise that their feeling of having been treated as a girl, rather than a woman, or treated as a man, are not unique to them but common to most women. Such women, if given the opportunity, routinely gain the courage and confidence to challenge those who presume to know what is best for them, as they become increasingly convinced that it is not they, but (in this case) the sport 'system', that is crazy. The purpose of this consciousness-raising is to achieve fundamental changes by connecting the personal experiences of women to developments in sport. Consciousness-raising suggests that women, sharing among themselves, will become empowered and able to take on some of the responsibility of changing the sport world.

The last part of Tong's methodology is based on at least three philosophical moral theorists: Aristotle's *Nicomachean Ethics* (1976: book 8), Rawls' *A Theory of Justice* (1971) and Mill's *Utilitarianism* and *On Liberty* (1972). She suggests it is an attempt to gain a Rawlsian reflective equilibrium between principles, rules, ideals, values and virtues on the one hand, and actual cases in which moral decisions must be made on the other.[6] It is also proposed that Aristotelian practical reasoning assumes that moral choices are made, for the most part, between several moral agents, rather than isolated within one individual. Finally, Mill's views on the importance of listening, as well as speaking, in the course of a moral dialogue is stressed. Tong's claim that the practice of ethics requires communication, corroboration and collaboration, and that we are not alone when we grapple with applying ethics, is true and can be utilised in the realm of sport.

Such a methodology may assist us in discovering mutually agreeable ways to weaken patterns of male domination and female subordination in the realm of sport. As suggested, this type of discussion requires adopting a particular stance and raising a particular set of questions. The answers to these questions must be dealt with and understood within the context of women's experiences in sport. If we truly seek understanding of these issues, we must understand the perspective, and thus the social, psychological and political predispositions, that we ourselves bring to the discussion. For example, differences in race, gender, education, social/political position, nationality, religion and sexuality are going to bring different perspectives and contexts to the questions of gender, ethics and sport. This fact does not mean that we cannot reach some agreement on important issues, but it does mean that we must be willing to listen, and give due respect, to differing perspectives in our search for justice. This search for justice also requires an understanding of where the power to make changes lies, and the willingness of those who hold it, to share that power. So far the predominant male power-brokers in sport have not demonstrated this willingness.

If we apply this methodology to the questions surrounding gender verification in sport – by taking the three steps of asking 'the woman or gender-biased question'; raising consciousness by connecting the personal experiences of women to developments on gender verification in sport and sport medicine; and using practical reasoning that attempts to gain a reflective equilibrium and accepts our limited ability to explain and justify our decisions, while simultaneously insisting that we try harder to find the appropriate ways – women themselves will (and should) be the guardians and decision-makers concerning women's sport.

Some women argue that any gender or sex test is demeaning (especially visual confirmation of the 'correct' genitalia) and discriminates against women athletes if it is not also applied to men. Clearly the use of any test, given the complexity of human sex and gender, may lead to anomalies and surprises. Yet many women wish to have sporting competition that excludes men. The best result we can achieve will be one that arises through discussion, debate and consensus and it will be the fairest we can reach. A coherent understanding of the causes of women's subordination to men in sport, coupled with a refined programme of action designed to eliminate the systems and attitudes that oppress or neglect women in sport, must guide this complex approach. A detailed analysis of the distribution of power in each case can identify a particular factor as the primary cause of women's subordinate status in sport, which, for the most part, has traditionally been based on biology. Researchers can, and should, attempt to ascertain the actual status of women in sport and determine how far that condition deviates from what justice prescribes.

The current sport conditions may be made more objective by providing more facts, as opposed to myths or stereotypes, about women athletes, thus alleviating or even eliminating the past and ongoing injustices. The knowledge required to create good, just and rational sport practice can be acquired; it is a matter of discovering and acknowledging all of the true facts. Everyone's knowledge about sport, sport science, and the health and wellbeing of all athletes, including women athletes, is limited. If we wish to understand a broader experience in sport than just the dominant male one, we must talk to, and take seriously, as many athletes as possible. Women athletes are now beginning to be credited with being able to see things about the reality of sport that men do not typically see (Messner and Sabo 1990). The dominant position in any set of social relations – the general position of men *vis-à-vis* women in sport – tends to produce distorted visions of the real regularities and underlying causal tendencies in social relations. Men experience their power over women in sport as normal – even beneficial – and this is not women's experience. Women see systems of male domination and female subordination in sport as abnormal and harmful.

Political, social and psychological position are not irrelevant. These criteria contribute significantly to the way in which we see the fundamental facts about the athlete's body and mind. Women in sport may possibly find truth and justice, but right now they are nebulous and, unfortunately for women athletes, it may still be some time before they emerge. Right now, however, not all reasonable people necessarily see the same thing when the facts about women and sport stare them in the face.

A POSTSCRIPT TO TÄNNSJÖ'S RADICAL PROPOSAL

Imagine a world where men and women are treated equally. Imagine a world where boys and girls are brought up together, where they learn the same things, participate in the same activities, and where they are taught to share the same hopes and aspirations. Imagine that in this world all forms of human excellence are encouraged, valued and rewarded. Imagine that in this world there is not a huge disparity in wealth and power between those who excel at a given activity and those who merely strive to do their best. Imagine also that in this world many activities are valued, that activities that exhibit grace or dexterity are as cherished as those that display speed and power. In such a world as this I would be the first person to stand side by side with Torbjörn Tännsjö to celebrate sport that did not distinguish on sex or gender lines, but merely on the basis of ability.

In a system like this people would be able to develop at their own pace and to their own level. In this system young boys would not get discouraged as they watched their pre-adolescent female peers systematically beat them in academic achievement or the full range of sport. Nor would they get discouraged knowing that in certain activities – in particular those that value cooperation over competition, or grace over power, or extreme endurance – they would never do as well as their female counterparts. They would know that, in certain highly circumscribed areas, those that rely on strength and power, they will have their turn.

Nor, of course, would girls and women get discouraged. In this society, because all forms of excellence are equally valued, and because there are as many ways that women are likely to excel as men, and because the rewards for excellence are not targeted towards a small set of predominantly male activities, women as well as men would be motivated to strive for the common good.

Tännsjö's vision in Chapter 7 – of sport transformed – fits into a long line of utopian visions of societies transformed. If we lived in Plato's Republic, where philosophers were kings, there would be no reason to segregate men's and women's sport. (Plato himself included the revolutionary proposals that not only should women be guardians – for there are no relevant differences between women and men in the business of being guardians – but also that women should go through precisely the same sort of training as men, with the men, including naked gymnastic exercises. If we lived in a utopia like Plato's Republic we might be able to have Tännsjö's vision of sport. But unfortunately we do not.

We could imagine another society, one rather closer to our own. In this society there are great disparities of income and power. Some activities are cherished, valued and rewarded. Let us imagine that those cherished and rewarded activities include the bearing and rearing of children. Let us also imagine that some sports are valued. Those who achieve the pinnacles of excellence in these sports are treated and rewarded as heroes or, rather, treated and rewarded as heroines. Let us imagine that the popular sports, the sports that attracted the big audiences, the sports in which athletes could command huge fees in endorsements, were extreme long-distance swimming, ultra-marathons (or triathlons) and synchronised swimming. (It happens to be the case that in extreme endurance sports – events over about twenty-four hours in length, women currently hold the world records.) Imagine how boys and men would feel knowing that in this society the activities that are rewarded all happen to be dominated by women. How would they feel, knowing that they could never hope to compete at the highest levels in the sports that dominate their culture and that bring huge personal rewards? What would they do?

In this society, men might say: 'Look at us – we can do some things really well; we can fight, for instance. Look at us,' they would say, 'when we hit each other as hard as we can, we can get up and do it some more. Please give us some money so that we can go and practise our sports, the activities we are good at.' Would the women who administer and control sports in this imaginary community mind if sport were desegregated? Probably not, but why would they? The sports that everyone cares about would still be dominated by women. Women would still make all the money and enjoy all the glory and prestige.

The proposal contained in Tännsjö's chapter is dangerous, because it masquerades as a genuine proposal for changing sport as it is currently practised, whereas it is really a utopian fantasy, first of a society – and then of sport – transformed. If the world were a radically different place, then yes, the vision of sport where discrimination is based on ability not on gender (or weight or size, for that matter) would be good.

But let us look at the world in which we live. In our world sport plays a whole variety of functions and is played for a great variety of reasons, at a wide range of levels. Let us look first at sport for young children. Their sport exists primarily to give them an opportunity to experience the joy of physical play. Sport for children is about creating opportunities for pleasure. There is no reason to segregate sport for young children. Boys and girls can play perfectly well alongside each other. There are some worries about the ways in which boys are socialised to play competitive games and girls tend to be socialised to play cooperative ones. But, if we leave those aside, the fact that young girls tend to be bigger and stronger than boys the same age tends to be countered by boys' greater desire to play, and their unfounded (and unbounded) self-confidence. Boys and girls ought to be able to play together to the best of their ability, and the experience ought to be enjoyable and challenging for both.

In adolescence things start to change. By this time our acceptance of gender roles is rather more fixed (probably more fixed than it will become in later life as we become more comfortable with who we are as individuals). Girls may start to be self-conscious around boys. Boys may feel that they have to be aggressive and 'masculine' in order to attract the attention of girls. At this age girls, who until now have been self-confident and have generally been beating boys at the full range of academic pursuits (including mathematics), begin to defer to boys in the classroom. What is sport for at this age? I would argue that its primary function is still to allow young people to experience the joy of physical activity and competition. Should we segregate sport at this age? If this is the means of encouraging young people to continue to play and enjoy sport – then yes.

Let us skip a few years and look simply at elite sport. Should it be segregated? In some sports, no. There are some sports where women and men can compete equally against each other, and here there is no good reason to continue to segregate. (In fact, one sport that attempted to desegregate – shooting – rapidly reversed their policy when they found out that women were winning medals.) But in many of the other sports that go to make up the professional leagues, or the Olympic Games, women at present would systematically lose at the highest levels of competition. That probably would not matter if there were as many sports we really cared about where women tend to excel as there were sports where men tend to excel. But there are not. If we desegregate sport we eliminate women from sporting competition at most Olympic events. Would this be a good thing?

Even at the very highest levels, sport is about something more than merely being the fastest, or the strongest, or jumping the highest. Sports are complex social institutions that partially shape and define our images of who we are and what is possible for human beings. Given the sports that currently dominate our attention (and why we value these sports rather than others is an interesting inquiry), it would not help our view of either women or men only to see images of men in elite athletic competition. Seeing, and valuing, strong athletic women provides not only an example to younger women of the range of the possible for women, but it also changes our social views of what is appropriate and good for women to do. This *is* a good thing.

In a society where men's interests and strengths dominate cultural attention through the media, in a society where our social institutions are structured and controlled by men, and in a sport culture where male-dominated sports are the best-funded, most powerful and most-watched, excluding women from elite sport (on whatever grounds) would have the morally disastrous consequences of further restricting the realm of what is possible for women. Tännsjö looks at one little argument based on the pursuit of excellence, in one small context – that of sport functioning at the highest possible level – and he concludes that there is no place for discrimination on the basis of sex. In a world that was fair, and where there was no systematic discrimination on the basis of sex, he would be right. But we do not live in that world. We live in a world where women are systematically denied positions of power and public attention. We live in a world where men's efforts are systematically praised and rewarded. We live in a world where the aptitudes and achievements of women tend to go largely unrecognised and unheralded. In our world, excluding women from the publicity that comes from the highest levels of sporting achievement would merely serve to reinforce women's systemic subservience to men.

I assume that that is not Tännsjö's intention. I assume that, perhaps like in Plato's *Republic*, he wishes that women could play their full roles in all aspects of human life and endeavour. I assume that Tännsjö's vision of philosophical purity momentarily clouded his perception and knowledge of the world in which we actually live. Other things being equal, I'm sure the picture he paints would be good. But other things are *not* equal.

Notes

1   See Schneider (1992, 1993), and Schneider and Butcher (1994, 1997).

2   For a current personal account of the relationship between masculinity and sport in North America, see Messner and Sabo (1994).
3   However, Coubertin apparently never saw women as having central roles in Olympism. He preferred them as spectators and medal-bearers for presentation to the victors.
4   See Ehrenreich and English (1989) and Fausto-Sterling (1985) for this critique of medicine.
5   See Tong (1995) and Sherwin (1992) for this discussion in the profession of medicine.
6   Tong has suggested this for the area of bioethics (1995: 27).

Part IV

The rules of the game

Chapter 10

Against chance

A causal theory of winning in sport

Gunnar Breivik

Introduction

The correspondence theory of truth states that a proposition is true if, and only if, what the proposition states is the case. My statement 'It is snowing on the North Pole right now' is true if, and only if, it is actually snowing on the North Pole right now. But my statement may be a guess and nevertheless true. I may be right; I may make true statements just by chance. Only if my statement is caused by the snowing on the North Pole may we say that I have knowledge. In the famous Gettier examples, this goes much further. The statement 'It is snowing on the North Pole right now' must not only be caused, but it must be caused, in the right or the relevant way, by the snowing on the North Pole.[1]

In a similar way, we want also in other areas of life, that things must come in a certain way, happen in the right manner. If I want to take risks, the risks must come in a relevant way. If I meet risks that are quite unforeseen and irrelevant, I feel dissatisfied or frightened. For instance, most risks should come in a way that is relevant for my mastery and coping.[2]

How is it in sport?[3] Should winning be the result of a process that determines victory not only in a formally fair, but also a causally relevant way? Does that exclude chance factors, and how? If sport is taken in a wide sense, one may point to climbing, where we see different forms with different types of logic. Himalayan climbing includes both skill factors of various types – like stamina, climbing skills, route-finding – and also chance factors – like wind, weather and avalanches. In competitive climbing one has moved indoors and eliminated most of the chance factors. Should other sports follow the same strategy? Should sport competitions eliminate chance factors because they are unfair and irrelevant? Or is there a place for chance, luck and uncertainty? In soccer there is a saying that a winning team also has luck on its side. Is that fair? Of course it is superstition, but if it was true would it be fair? Should not luck rather be a compensation and help the underdog, like in the fairy tales?

Another aspect of the problem has to do with process and result. Fraleigh (1984) and many others discuss how value may be placed on the process (playing well) versus the product (winning), and the possible orderings of values. These two aspects may be independent of each other. The process, the hard and even fight, the well-played game, may be followed by a victory that was won in a 'wrong' way, just by chance. Or a big and important victory may be the fair result of an uneven and badly played game.

My purpose in this chapter is to discuss whether there is a place for chance and luck in sport, or whether a causal theory of winning means that such factors as far as possible should be excluded from sport, at least in serious competitive sport.

Two types of sport

I think we have at least two different structures, or types of logic, that are manifested in sports. One is the idea of sport as a sort of contest or fight, where the result is impossible to foresee, where betting may take place, where uncertainty is a value, where the suspense and excitement is important. Cockfighting, boxing, horse racing and motor sports are all examples from this tradition, which goes back to the horse races in Olympia. This type of practice is also important in many non-Western societies. The other tradition has to do with the testing of individuals' or teams' skills. The point is to decide through a fair process who is best. The first type of sport may include chance and luck, but it need not. By giving horses a handicap in horse racing the uncertainty of the result is increased, but there is no extra element of luck. There is just harder competition and more unpredictable results. However, in soccer the wind may suddenly blow the ball into the goal and the score is accepted, even if an element of complete luck may then decide the winner. No one has control over gusts of wind and therefore chance reigns, or at least strongly influences the result under such circumstances. According to a causal theory of winning, this is problematic. As mentioned earlier, I parallel winning with finding the truth. Truth has to cause my belief in the right and relevant way in order to become knowledge. Risks have to come in the right and relevant way to make me satisfied in my risk taking. Winning should come in the right way in sport, in order to count as victory. According to such a view, chance factors should be eliminated in sport as far as possible.

Seen from the athletes' point of view, chance factors may enter in various ways. Goffman has analysed chance-taking in various contexts of life, building on the life in gambling casinos as the prototypical model. He develops a special terminology to describe what goes on 'where the action is'. It is interesting that he regards commercialised competitive sport as the first place where action can routinely be found. Obviously he is thinking of team sports like American football when he comments, 'First, contenders find action in commercialised competitive sport. Perhaps because this activity is staged for an audience and watched for fun, it is felt that no fully serious reason could exist for engaging in the activity itself' (Goffman, 1967: 195). This is typical for the circus and entertainment sport, but is not characteristic of the experiment type of serious sport. It is not chance-taking we seek in serious sport, but self-efficacious performance.

In principle, all factors one is unable to control, predict or master may be experienced as chance. They may, however, include factors with quite different types of logic:

- the wind in a soccer game, which is related to chance or rather unpredictability in nature and outside one's environmental control.
- a bad starting position in a skiing race, which is determined by a sort of lottery and therefore outside one's organisational control.
- equipment, which is less than satisfactory and therefore outside one's economic or technological control.
- differences in body build, which are outside one's genetic control.

In one sense only the first and last factor are chance factors, related to what we could call 'ontological chance'. The second is related to epistemological uncertainty. The third is related to lack of resources and not to chance in the strict sense. The consequence of unsatisfactory equipment is that I am placed in a less favourable position and the winner is therefore decided by an unfair process.

It may seem a paradox that some of the problems with chance are eliminated by chance. For instance, the disadvantage of playing with the late afternoon sun in one's eyes is given to one team by a simple toss of the coin. Would it be better to eliminate the sun? One could, in some instances, do this almost instantly by moving a roof over the arena, like in the Sky Dome in Toronto.

Chance and skill

Some things in life we are not able to control, while other things are outside our control. In order to control things we try to develop certain skills that enhance mastery and self-efficacy. What lies outside our control happens by chance or luck. Once chance or luck enters, we are not able to causally influence what happens.

In sports, skills encompass a variety of factors, such as strength, endurance, motor control and psychological skills. Skills are enhanced and prepared through training, in order to be used effectively during competitions.

In the same way, chance factors encompass a variety of things. Basic is a distinction between ontological chance and epistemological chance or uncertainty. In the first case, 'nature itself' is affected by chance. It may, for instance, be impossible to determine whether a process runs in this or that direction, or whether it happens or doesn't happen (like Prigogine's bifurcation processes in chemistry). Or one may point to Heisenberg's principle of indeterminacy, to recent theories of chaos or complexity.[4] Under some interpretations, 'nature itself' is here seen to be indeterministic, affected by chance.

In the second case, in epistemological chance, the ontology may be deterministic but we have no possibility of knowing how things will happen, and therefore it may seem to happen by chance, for instance like in gusts of wind or avalanches. This again can mean several things. It may be that we are not able (even in principle), with our present faculties, to understand or foresee what happens. Or it may mean that we are not normally able (in most circumstances) to foresee what happens. But this may be due to our human limitations, and has nothing to do with chance in an ontological sense. For instance, we say that it is impossible to foresee what happens in a situation in soccer where a lot of players are involved just before one of the goals. But there are not necessarily any ontological chance factors here, just fast and complex interactions that we are unable to follow, control and cope with. There is epistemological uncertainty, due to a lack of information-processing capacity and other skills.

However, our discussion in sport is related to what we may call 'anthropological chance'. It is not the inner nature of the universe but the action space of human beings we are exploring. We talk of 'luck' when chance is linked to human action. One may have good luck or bad luck when things turn to one's favour or disfavour without oneself being actively involved in the outcome. One is not causally active or central in what happens. Rescher (1995), for instance, maintains that luck characterises a certain development for someone when the outcome comes about 'by accident', and that the outcome has an evaluative status, either positive (benign) or negative (malign). One has good or bad luck.

In relation to human action (the anthropological dimension of chance) we may distinguish between

1   Chance elements – ontology
2   Uncertainty – epistemology
3   Luck – outcome by 1 or 2
4   Skill – outcome by certainty or probability
5   Mastery – ability to handle certain elements of 1, 2 and 3.

Chance elements are things which we are unable to influence, control or foresee. Uncertainty is related to a situation where we do not know the possible outcomes, whether this is based on ontological determinism or indeterminism. We are affected by luck when things happen by chance or through uncertainty to our favour or disfavour. Skill is characterised by the ability to control actions with certainty or high probability. I use the concept of mastery to describe the ability to cope with situations where there is a mixture of elements – both skill and chance. Mastery is the ability to handle complex or new situations.[5]

What is measured in sport competitions?

Some people argue that we should allow chance factors to play a central role in sports. That makes them unpredictable, and produces fun and good entertainment. Against this view one could say that suspense and excitement, without foresight of the result, can as well be produced by hard competitions among evenly matched opponents, where the result is completely dependent upon skills and with almost no chance, like a good 100m heat in athletics.

Others think that sport competitions should try to eliminate chance factors and luck, and make the result as much as possible dependent upon skills. That means that some sports, as they are arranged today, should be changed in a direction where non-relevant chance factors are eliminated.

I mentioned earlier that there seem to be two different logical structures underlying sports. Let us discuss the ideal types behind the two views.

The most extreme eliminator of chance factors is the scientific experiment. All chance factors should be removed. Complete control is the ideal. The more complex the experiment, the more difficult the task.

The other extreme is the circus or entertainment in various forms, where the point is to hold people in suspense, to impress, to be unpredictable, sometimes to let chance factors decide. There are various forms – from complete chance in lottery or gambling, to mastery and skill in the circus (for instance, by trapeze artists). But the point in the circus is not the performance *per se*, but the ability to impress, to entertain, to hold the audience's attention. The unbelievable performance is just a means.

How should one evaluate the situation? There are two clear ideal types here, in a Weberian sense. One 'ideal type' is the 'pure test of skills', modelled like a sort of scientific experiment. The other is the 'exciting game'. Accordingly, sport can be modelled as a scientific experiment deciding who is the best, or as an exciting game with suspense and entertainment. The driving force behind the circus model is the public: 'We want to be entertained, to have an exciting game, a thrilling fight.' The driving force behind the scientific experiment is the athlete: 'I think I am the best. Who can beat me? I have trained for years for this, I want to test myself.'

Should sports be experiments or shows?

A first view would be that some sports are circus or entertainment and others are experiments. It seems that athletics and gymnastics belong to the experiment division. The point is to exclude chance factors. Let the best win. A lot of the ball games, like soccer and American football, belong to the circus tradition. Some sports mix circus and experiment, like downhill skiing and ski jumping. The best athletes are placed in seeded groups and normally have better equipment, better support, better genetic makeup – a lot of advantages. The entertainment factor demands that (say) skiers should be placed together in seeded groups, and that the best skier after the first round competes last in the second. That way, the public is kept in suspense until the end. Nevertheless, there is a certain compensatory lottery inside the groups. Chance decides the starting order inside the groups in the first round. It is a mix of science and circus, taking care of the interests of the public but also that of the skiers. According to this view, both experiment and entertainment have a place.

A second view holds that all sports should become experiments and should try to get rid of the chance factors. Sports should be a testing place for athletes and their skills, and not a place for entertainment and show.

A third view would be that chance has a very important role to play. It could even mean that we should go in the other direction and make all sports more entertaining by actively introducing chance elements.

A test case for the realism of views in relation to the athletes' interest is the investment problem; athletes' investment in their sport career has increased enormously in elite sport. When you have devoted your life from age 12 to 38 to being the best in the world, and you are a true professional in every sense of the word, would you let chance factors decide how much you win? Even if chance factors were spread out in a fair manner and you had the same number of victories, would it be satisfying for you if you won by a mixture of skill and luck? Would it not be better if you won by skill and mastery alone?

A critique of the praise of chance

Some people think that chances are inherently important for sport. De Wachter (1985) has argued strongly, but not convincingly, for the inclusion of the element of chance in sport. He thinks that sport without chance would degenerate into scientific measurement of physical and strategic capacities. This would reduce sports to the world of labour or transform it into pure entertainment. Sport is, according to De Wachter, a form of play that goes alongside life and portrays the mixture of skill and chance elements in life. However, De Wachter has a very wide definition of chance, which includes unforeseen effects of actions, the *petit causes, grands effets*. He also includes failed actions, like the player who misses an easy shot. He says that 'Chance always denotes an incongruence between the result produced and the intended action produced from the skill and effort of the player' (De Wachter 1985: 55).

This would actually mean that we should not welcome high-performance sport in general, because it increases prediction of performance and lessens chance. I think what we want is exactly the opposite. The athletes strive to control performance and make the result dependent upon their own intended actions. As spectators we want that the best team wins, or that the team that wins is the best. De Wachter's view leads to a sort of nostalgia. This becomes evident in his Tour de France example. In the 'good old days', the participants had to repair their own bicycles when they broke down. The strong element of chance has today been eliminated by the following cars, the extra bicycles, the mechanics, and so on. I think this view is totally untenable. Neither we nor the cyclists themselves want to praise the one who was lucky enough not to have a mechanical problem. Nor do we want to test in a bicycle race who was the best cyclist and mechanic, and who had most luck (or least bad luck). We want to praise the one who was best in the relevant sport skill; in this case, the ability to cycle the Tour de France in the shortest time (according to prescribed rules and so on).

Skill and chance – one-tailed or two-tailed

Suppose skill and chance were the two relevant factors deciding a game or a contest. If skill increases, then chance decreases; if chance increases, then skill decreases. Skill and chance would then be opposites on a continuum. But this is not always the case. Chance and skill may both be two-tailed. Skill may decrease, but what increases is not chance, but lack of skill. It is even more obvious with chance. If chance decreases, it is not necessary that skill increases. There can be both little skill and little chance. We can also have a situation with both skill and chance increasing at the same time, as when better players enter the soccer field and play at their highest level, but the wind increases and blows unevenly and in gusts. It would make the skill demands more complex, but it would lead to a less well-played game with a causally less relevant winner.

Do we want chance factors to play an important role in sport? This is a different problem to not being able to predict or foresee the result. As we saw earlier, by matching two or more even opponents one may get a very exciting and unpredictable game. One may also get a well-played game. There is no chance element, no winning by luck, but there is still uncertainty about who is going to win. That is optimal. When people speak in praise of chance I think most of them confuse chance with uncertainty. We want a win to be caused by skill and not by chance, but we want it to be uncertain. We do not want it to be predictable. And that is achieved when athletes and teams are set up in evenly matched ways. Therefore, in sport we should not praise chance, but skill. And we should praise uncertainty and unpredictability.

Skill and unpredictability

What is the relation between skill and chance? Suppose you have a Player A who is going to make a pass to Player B in a soccer game. If the player is very good, he is able to give the pass with higher precision than a less skilled player, who may send the ball in a completely unforeseen direction. From Player B's perspective, the chance factor increases when the less skilled player makes the pass. However, it is not chance in the strict ontological sense, since everything follows the laws of nature, but the execution is less skilful and therefore less precise. However, is a lack of precision and skill (which means more unpredictability) something that we want? Do we want less skilful players and more chance elements? Does that give better entertainment? I think not.

Loland thinks that in some sports, such as football, the element of chance is important (Loland 1989). He welcomes this and thinks that it adds excitement and thrill to the game in a positive way. He mentions the wind, the failed pass, the below-normal achievement, as examples. I think that several different types of factors are mixed together here. One thing is the failed pass, which is not a chance factor but poor skill. The problem is to predict when poor skill is happening, but not chance. The wind is another matter: it is an external factor affecting the game in the form of a chance factor. But this is something I think should be excluded as far as possible. I see no positive element here. We do not want unpredictability based on chance. Suppose you have a very talented player who is trying to dribble around another player. Because he is very good he is very unpredictable: he is able to hide his intentions, camouflage his moves. A less skilled player is less able to hide his intentions, easier to read and more predictable. What do we want? We want the unpredictability based on skills. And this is not chance. The player executes very skilfully what he intends to do, but since he is skilled in various ways he seems unpredictable. We want unpredictability or uncertainty, but not chance. Chance would interfere if the ground was very uneven and the ball moved in unpredictable ways. Do we want the soccer grounds to be more uneven to introduce chance? I think not.

Another problem is how we organise chance. Chances can be accumulated or spread out. If we arrange soccer games in cup competitions, there may be chances during games that tip the game in a certain direction and the lucky team can win. This means that a good team can be unlucky and be out after the first round. Most people find that a series is more just because the chances are more evenly distributed over time in a series. And in a series you can have a bad day, a bad game, and yet still win. In cups, you cannot have a bad day or a team with a lot of luck playing against you and still win. This means that cups are especially problematic in sports where chance plays a great role, like in soccer. It is less problematic in sports with little chance, because if you lose it is because you played badly. The loss was caused by lack of skill, and not another's luck.

In cups we measure acts. In a series we measure an accumulation of acts, and therefore consistency over time. Therefore we normally admire the winner of a series most. That does not mean that the cups are less exciting. Often, quite the contrary. It gives the underdog a chance. But that belongs to entertainment. In scientific experiments we can accept entertainment based on good performance, but not too many chance factors.

Pre-game and in-game factors

There is skill and chance both during the game and before the game. Genes are important, both to determine the capacity for a certain sport and the capacity to improve from training. People therefore speak of the genetic lottery. A lot of other factors are important: growing up in the right place, having the right friends, having the right facilities, a good coach, being able and motivated to train hard, using the right equipment, getting backup from the sport system.

What do we test in a sport competition? Indirectly we are, of course, testing all the above. And it is impossible to say how much each of the factors has contributed. We also like to think that we are testing the athlete himself – his person, his character, his skills or whatever we might call it. We think that an athlete somehow integrates the various factors into his unique person. It is this integrated athlete who really performs and therefore deserves to win, as a person. That is the tacit assumption lying behind the worship of sports heroes.

However, it is increasingly obvious that what we are really testing is not the person, but a system, the performing team with coach, medical support team, psychological team, equipment producers, sponsors, etc. And, of course, we are indirectly testing the genetic makeup, the socialisation. We are testing a lot of factors that influence the performance in unpredictable ways. Do we in any way want to interfere with these factors? I think not. It is exactly the various unique combinations of factors that we are unable to control that make for the variation of athletes trying to excel and win in sports. So why do we test for doping in sport, in the preparation period? Do we want to test for genetic engineering in the future? What if other unknown factors were introduced? I do not think we should test other things than those which can be tested, and I do not support testing in the preparation period.

This means that one can win a game in the right and relevant way by a lot of different factors being used in the preparation period. I maintain that what happens in the preparation period is irrelevant for the competition itself, how we evaluate winning and the causality. If I say that there is snow on the North Pole right now, the truth is not dependent upon *how* the snow fell.

This means that I am in favour of chance, luck, uncertainty and the various combinations thereof in the pre-game period. Let the training subcultures grow, the diversity flourish. However, in the game, in the fight, in the competition, the chance factors related to what is relevant for winning should be eliminated as far as possible. The game should be a test – but an exciting test. And what is tested, for instance, in a 100m sprint? What is tested is the ability to run 100m as fast as possible – with other competitors, set up in heats in certain ways, with certain regulations, on a certain track, on a certain day. We are not testing the genetic makeup, not the training, not the technological support, even if they all influence the result. In that sense we test these factors indirectly but indiscriminately. We do not know how much each contributes, especially not on that day and in that event. That, however, is what training science has to find out and control. The winner in a certain 100m race is the winner of *that* particular 100m, that is all. In this sense I go for minimalism and nominalism. Sport as a test is a test of who is the best in exactly that event that is set up in that sport, on that day, in that special way. Only indirectly is it a test of a general ability to run 100m across different situations, with different opponents. Upon this event structure we build a lot of structures, introduce contexts, write a lot of scripts, tell a lot of tales. Since sport is embedded in societies, there will be differences in the ethos of games, the moral character of heroes, the social importance of winning. There will be stories of winning streaks and unlucky losers, of efficiency of doping and drugs, of training maniacs and efficiency of equipment. But this belongs to what we could call the 'mythology of sports' and is based upon the primary event, competing in the right way, in a certain event, on a specific day.

This is an extreme view. An argument against this would be that if we want to test not only who is best in one 100m race, but over a season or a year, we have to set up tests, say every month, to see who is consistently the best. Why should not sport be seen as testing over a series of events? No, why not? A World Cup winner in a certain sport is a winner across a series of events. But winning the World Cup is parasitic upon the single events. The ontological priority of single events is what I call 'nominalism' of sport competitions. The minimalism relates to what is tested. I claim that what is tested is exactly stated by the purpose of the event. In a 100m race it is the ability to run 100m as fast as one can and faster than the others. But it is not 100m in general, but 100m on a specific day, in a specific competition, with specific competitors, a specific application of rules and regulations, and so on. There is no testing of general abilities, character, background, etc. This is only done indirectly, and is hypothetical.

It is a bit like the state/trait discussion in psychology. Traits are just accumulations of states across situations and time. The problematic jump is from series of states to traits as inherent qualities. Loland maintains that what we measure in sports is 'sport ability' or 'potential for achievement in sport' (Loland 1989). This seems to be a hidden general factor that becomes instantiated in specific sport events. 'Sport ability' is defined as 'technical and tactical skills based on basic physical and psychological qualities and which are limited by the rules of the specific sport contests' (Loland 1989: 131, my translation). I think this leads to essentialism of general sport abilities. I am in favour of nominalism here. What we measure in the 100m sprint is the ability to run 100m as fast as possible, and only that. By looking at parallel skills in other distances (60m, 200m, and so on), we may make inferences about a general sprint talent. But this is only an inference based on performance in specific events.

In sports we are not able to jump from the series of situations to qualities of an inherent character. When we say that Manchester United is the best soccer team, do we thereby refer to a sort of inherent quality, a special soccer trait? I do not think so. 'Manchester United is the best soccer team' just means that across a series of matches they have won more matches than the other teams and have got the most points. It means nothing more and nothing less. No Platonism here.

Examples of chance

Let us return to the concept of chance again and take a new round after our discussion so far.

If winning means being the best in a certain event, on a certain day, and so on, how should we handle chance factors that interfere with the causal process.[6] Our list of chance elements included:

- the wind in a soccer game – related to chance elements in nature
- differences in starting order – outside one's organisational control
- differences in equipment – outside one's economic or technological control
- differences in body build – outside one's genetic control.

The common characteristic of these elements is that they are outside the athletes' control and are experienced as chance factors affecting the possibility of athletes to influence causally the sport event. They are related to what we called 'anthropological chance'. Some of the problems here have to do with lack of control over outcomes, and all of the problems are related to fairness and even chances to win.[7] Let us look at some examples.

Natural elements

One team was the stronger in a soccer game, but did not manage to score. The wind grew stronger during the second half and in the last minute a high ball that was played towards the goal of the best team blew into the net, just by chance. Wind, rain and snow may affect soccer games in various ways and represent typical chance factors. There are two ways to avoid this.

One is to build indoor halls with predictable conditions. The other is to change the rules so that more goals are scored. Chance goals would then not affect the result as often and as dramatically. It would also be possible to have the referee annul the score if it was obviously caused by chance. But it would often be difficult to decide whether the wind really was the decisive causal factor.

Weather and variability in outdoor conditions affect the results of competitions. If winning or being able to show your best was really important – for instance, if one was playing for a lot of money or for a decision about life and death – one would want equal and just conditions. It is especially important to have fair conditions if one is the better athlete or plays on the better team, for instance in a soccer match. A team that is less good would be able to get some help from chance. But do they deserve it? If they were losers in the genetic lottery they may, but if they have been lazy and skipped training, why *should* they get help?

Starting order

In a speed-skating competition the ice is watered and the next pair gets better ice than the others. If the ordering of the pairs is made by lottery, the inequality is more acceptable. In slalom, however, the best skiers have the best conditions in the first run, and also better than most others in the second run. And this is consistently so. In addition to the best starting position, they also have the best equipment and the best support. This is an example of unfair competition, where the deteriorating condition of the track, which is difficult to avoid, influences the result. And because of the other advantages for the best skiers, there is an accelerating effect. The difference in snow conditions is accelerated by differences in equipment, and vice versa. In addition, we may have differences in wind, it may start to snow, fog may enter, and so on. It would be more fair if all the skiers took part in an open lottery to decide starting numbers. However, that would not be good for the public and the media, for they want a concentration of the best in one group. And the organisers know that the best must come last, if the public is going to stay to the end. We see here a good example of the mixture of circus and experiment. The skiers and the public have deep differences in interest. It seems that, increasingly, the public, the media and economic interests decide how competitions are to be set up.

Differences in equipment

In cross-country skiing you have no chance to become the best if you have the wrong wax or the wrong surface structure under your skis. This means that the best skiers from the most technologically advanced countries will have the best equipment most of the time, and therefore the competition is influenced by the quality of the equipment. This is a problem mainly related to unfairness and not chance. But the chance element comes in because, under some conditions, usually around zero-degree conditions with snowfall, the wax and surface problem becomes much more important. The problem could be avoided if there were ready prepared skis of different lengths, and related to different weights, and where the skiers picked skis from inside their body-size group by lottery. Over a season that would have been fair. But there would not be the same competitive interest to produce new and better skis, and the ski producers would not have the same incentive to produce them. But should athletes tolerate chance and unfair competitions in order that the ski market should thrive?

The genetic lottery

In ski jumping we have an uneven wind, which will make some skiers have good luck and some bad, and some middling. Ideally all the skiers should pick starting numbers through an open lottery. But again the market, the media and the public want an exciting setup with the best in one group. And in the second round, the best should start last inside their group.

A more serious problem for fairness in ski jumping is body size, especially weight. If you are heavy, you have no chance of becoming a top-level ski jumper. The rules favour the smallest and lightest. The rules have now been changed in the right direction, but not far enough. It is the same problem in other sports. Through the genetic lottery some people have advantages, and some disadvantages, in relation to specific events and disciplines. In some sports weight classes compensate for the genetic lottery and make it possible for all to compete at top level in their class. This is the case in weightlifting, boxing, wrestling, karate and judo, but not in sumo, shot put, discus or hammer throwing. No height classes have been introduced (even if height is a decisive factor at elite level) in basketball, volleyball or gymnastics.

Loland (1989) maintains that both non-relevant variations in the environment (wind, rain) and the arena (ice, track, ground) should be compensated for. In the same manner, body build and body composition (that in a non-relevant way influence performance) should be eliminated as far as possible by classes based on weight or height. I agree with this, but when he also thinks that non-relevant factors of a pre-game type, like social and cultural environment, the resources of the total (national) sport system, should be compensated for or eliminated, I think he mixes in-game and pre-game factors. We want maximum variation in pre-game factors, including climate, economic resources, cultural values, social environments, sport organisations. But we want minimum variation of non-relevant in-game factors.

Do the sports organisations have an obligation to make it possible for all, not only to take part in a certain sport but also to compete at a high international level? I think so. This means that classes based on body build should be introduced. One argument against this would be that sport organisations have the right to set up what they want. They just open up possibilities. They do not need to meet certain moral or rational obligations. Against this, one could argue that sports should be considered as goods also at high level and should be open and available to all, not only in principle but also in practice. There is, then, an obligation for the nation to arrange this, be it through the state sector, the civil sector or the market.

Relevant winning in the future

Kantian ethics say that we should be able to want to make our norms and rules universal (universalising). I think this should be true also in sports and for sports. One should try to realise the same goods, rights and obligations in sports as in other parts of civil society. Elite sport should not be an island ruled by the IOC, with its own traditions and rules. Sport should be open to public criticism. Also in elite sport there should be a discussion of social and individual goods that belong to an open society.

Everybody should have the same chance of winning. By this we mean that chance should be eliminated, or at least be evenly distributed among the participants. We have seen some examples where chance factors favour certain athletes, usually the best ones. There are other examples where some athletes are deliberately favoured, and that can and should be avoided. It is the public, the media and the sponsors who strongly focus on the best, and therefore make the best have the advantages.

In addition to the fairness argument, which demands an even distribution of chance among the participants, I think the causality argument implies that chance should be eliminated as far as possible. We want an athlete to cause his or her victory. Winning should be caused by the relevant sport-specific performance and not by accidental factors. Therefore chance should be eliminated as far as possible in serious international sport competitions. But this is confined to what happens inside or during the competitions. What leads up to the event should be as many-sided and complex as possible, with variations in all relevant factors, including chance factors. Athletes of all builds and types should have the chance to excel in as many sports as possible. I am therefore in favour of classes related to body build or other relevant factors. We will have better performances when the medium-sized basketball players and the big ski jumpers enter the arenas.

Today's sport is too laden with tradition and suffers from a lack of creativity. I welcome more creativity and new competitive sports forms and events, as we see it in the new forms that are emerging in youth and adventure sports.

I have argued that what we measure in competitive events is just who is best, which athlete, which team, in that special event, on that specific occasion. The addition and accumulation of events to series and world cups are secondary structures. Both the primary single events and the secondary structures should be rebuilt and revised. In the future, at top level we should get rid of the entertainment notion, the show factor. Let us eject the 'sport as show' traditions and get more exciting athletic tests, more experiments. The folklore, the rituals, the sport as entertainment belong at lower levels, in national and local environments, with fans and supporter clubs. The serious business at top international level – where athletes use twenty to thirty years of their life, full-time, to become the best, to test their skills – is quite another matter. And this will be most interesting in various ways in the future.

Let me sum up my position. Beliefs are true if they are caused in the right and relevant way by the conditions they represent. Risks are taken deliberately if they enter in the right and relevant way, and can be coped with or mastered. Winning should be based on the relevant skills, and be the result of the sport-relevant skills and behaviour of competing athletes. Therefore chance has no place in elite sport.

Notes

1   These showed that a theory of knowledge as 'justified true belief' (Gettier 1963) is problematic. A causal theory of knowledge, as proposed by Goldman (1967), takes care of most problems. According to Nozick (1981), the causal theory is the best as far as it goes, but is not able to handle knowledge in mathematics and ethics. The causal theory of knowledge is relevant, I think, as a model for a theory of sport competitions and winning in sport.
2   Sometimes, however, I may, as in Russian roulette, take risks that are impossible to control. I take chances that are blind. And that is the whole point.
3   I use 'sport' in the sense of 'competitive sport' that includes sports with formal competitions. I include the Olympic sports and events. I also discuss climbing, as an example of a sport with various forms or types of logic. Leisure, outdoor recreation, exercises and training, etc. are not competitions and are therefore excluded.
4   When we speak about ontological chance, this is already a problematic notion. It may relate to determinism versus indeterminism. Is there a strict causality in nature with uniform laws? For Einstein, the indeterminacy was related to our knowledge and not to physical reality. God does not play with dice. The Copenhagen interpretation of the Danish physicist Niels Bohr suggested an ontological indeterminacy. Recent theories of complexity and chaos may be ontological or epistemological in their dealing with indeterminism and chance.
5   I have not introduced the concept of 'risk', which in game theory describes a situation with knowledge of the possible outcomes, but not of the probabilities of each of the outcomes. Risk is in some other contexts used as meaning the same as objective danger. It may also mean the possible loss of something valuable, like life, health, money, etc. The last meaning is used in daily language and is different from the game-theoretical usage. The game-theoretical meaning is very relevant in sport contexts. I have avoided introducing the concept

because I think the concepts of uncertainty and chance cover most of the substantial issues and problems.

6   I speak of winning in this chapter and do not discuss reward alternatives. For instance, should only the winner be rewarded, or should we rank the three best with gold, silver and bronze, or a bigger number of participants? The points I make are relevant for various situations. Any ordering would be affected by my arguments against chance.

7   That competitions should be fair is a tacit assumption at various points in this chapter. One of the problems with chance elements is that they may be distributed unevenly among contestants. Another problem is that chance interferes with the causality of winning. If I test myself against other contestants, I want ability or skill, not chance, to cause victory.

Chapter 11

Justice and game advantage in sporting games[1]

Sigmund Loland

> Justice is the first virtue of social institutions, as truth is of systems of thought.
>
> (Rawls 1971: 3)

Introduction

Questions of justice arise regularly in game playing as in other areas of life. Was this a fair game? Did the soccer team deserve that goal? Did the better competitor win? Sometimes, the claim is even heard that the best team actually lost, that the game was unfair and that the loser was the 'moral' winner.

At first sight, these questions and claims might seem insignificant from a moral point of view. Games and play are voluntary, non-serious arenas for excitement and fun. Discussions of justice deal with how to allocate fundamental goods in a society; basic liberties and obligations, income and wealth, positions and offices, and so on. On second thought, however, games and play may appear to be of more significance. To the child and the dedicated amateur, games can be sources of joy, friendship, self-development and self-respect. The paid performer has turned a passion into a profession and competes for, among other things, fame and fortune. Indeed, in this sense, games and play can be of moral relevance. As Albert Camus wrote in *Resistance, Rebellion and Death*, 'I learned all I know about ethics from sports'.

In this chapter I suggest an interpretation of the role of justice in sporting games in which participants strive for a mutually exclusive outcome and in which 'goods' and 'burdens' are distributed according to performance of athletic skills as defined in the relevant rules of the game. Hence, the chapter can be seen as a case study of what Elster (1992) calls 'local justice'; of particular schemes of justice which, on a relatively autonomous basis, are designed and implemented by institutions and practices to meet their own preferences and goals.[2]

First, a framework is suggested for examinations of schemes of justice in particular institutions and practices. Second, an attempt is made to articulate a set of requirements that have to be met in order to characterise a sporting game as just. In conclusion, it is argued that the basic justification of these norms is to be found in the concern for fair and good games that can provide experiences of meaning and value to everyone involved.

Fairness and justice

'Fairness' is commonly understood as a moral obligation regarding rule adherence, or at least as a norm on adherence to a commonly agreed upon interpretation of the rules; an ethos.[3] According to Rawls, the main idea of fairness is this:

> ... when a number of persons engage in a mutually advantageous co-operative venture according to certain rules and thus voluntarily restrict their liberty, those who have submitted to these restrictions have a right to a similar acquiescence on the part of those who have benefited from their submission.[4]
>
> (Rawls 1971: 343)

In short, the idea is that it is wrong to benefit from the cooperation of others without doing our fair share.

However, the obligation of fairness does not arise unconditionally. One basic premise is that the parties are voluntarily engaged. They have chosen participation in favour of non-participation and have thus more or less tacitly agreed to follow the commonly accepted rules and norms of the practice.[5] Another basic premise is that the practice in question is just. If goods and burdens are distributed in arbitrary or autocratic ways, there is no definition of what is our fair share and there is no clear idea of what each of us should contribute to, or receive from, our cooperation. An unjust practice does not take seriously the idea of persons as free and equal moral agents. The very idea of fairness is undermined.[6]

What, then, are the requirements of justice that have to be met for the obligation of fairness to arise? A formal understanding of the idea of justice, already given by Aristotle, can be articulated as follows: 'Equals ought to be treated equally, unequals can be treated unequally, and unequal treatment ought to be in reasonable accordance with the inequality in question.'[7]

This formal norm provides merely a framework for elaboration of distributive justice. The norm is external to the procedure through which it is implemented. As Elster (1992) has shown in his many case studies, local norms for distribution of goods and burdens are of a great variety. Substantive criteria of what is to be considered equal, and what are to be considered relevant inequalities that qualify for unequal treatment, have to be formulated with reference to the preferences and goals of each particular practice or institution. Still, however, it is possible to establish an overview of norms and procedures that enables a systematic and critical discussion (see Table 11.1).

Norms and procedures of justice

Let us take as a simple example a situation in which a certain amount of money is to be distributed among a certain number of persons. This can be done on the basis of: an egalitarian norm – all parties get the same amount of money; a meritocratic norm – the parties are awarded according to performance or merit of some kind; or a norm based on dedication – each party is awarded according to devotion and relative effort. Moreover, the money can be distributed according to needs, according to social position or rank, according to what is considered a legal entitlement, or according to combinations of the norms mentioned above.[8]

As with the formal norm for justice, distributive norms are idealised concepts. They belong to the system of ideas (rules, norms) of a given practice, defining it as a possible form of conduct. To see their practical relevance, we need to consider the practice as a system of action – as the realisation in the thought and conduct of certain persons at a certain time and place of actions specified by these norms. Within the process of realisation, we may distinguish between three different procedures.[9]

Perfect procedural justice realises completely the distributive norms that are supposed to guide practice. If, based on an egalitarian norm, we want to distribute a hundred dollars among four persons, they each get twenty-five dollars.

Imperfect procedural justice indicates that a given distributive norm cannot be realised completely. An example would be the Scandinavian system of progressive taxation. A perfect realisation of a norm prescribing all to be taxed according to ability to pay seems practically impossible.

Pure procedural justice is characterised by the fact that there is no distributive norm or independent criterion to guide practice. The procedure itself guarantees a just outcome. The standard example is a lottery: if the participants are voluntarily engaged, and if the lottery and the final draw are conducted in a fair way, each lottery ticket has an equal chance of being the winning one. The distribution of goods will be fair whatever the outcome may be.

On this basis, what can be said of justice in sporting games?

Game advantage

First of all, we need a better understanding of the particular nature and distribution of 'goods' and 'burdens' here. In sporting games, inequalities in performance lead to inequalities in the distribution of game advantage. Or, to be more precise, successful performances lead to an increase in game advantage, whereas unsuccessful performances and violations of rules (if detected) usually lead to game disadvantage and penalties.

Table 11.1   A systematic overview of norms and procedures of justice

	System of ideas	System of actions
Formal justice	Norms for distribution: • egalitarian • meritocratic • according to effort • according to need • according to position or legal entitlement • combination of the norms above	Procedures: • perfect procedures • imperfect procedures
		• pure procedural justice

Game advantage is distributed in two different ways. Informal game advantage arises throughout a competition as a result of good performance, but is not recorded and implies only a potential for accumulating further advantage. After a good start, the 800m runner can choose the inside track for good tactical running. After a well-executed dribble, a soccer player reaches a better position for a successful strike at the goal.

Informal game advantage often leads to formal advantages that are distributed according to the rules, and recorded and accumulated to count in the final ranking of competitors. In tennis and in soccer, formal advantages are given in the process of play in terms of points and goals. In other competitions, such as in track and field, there is no distribution of formal advantage, except for a final ranking of all participants.

Game advantage and equality

The first part of the formal norm of justice stated that equals ought to be treated equally. Substantive criteria of what is to be considered equal in sporting games have to be formulated on the basis of their own particular goals. There are many sorts of goals like this. Participants are engaged based on subjective, intentional goals, competitions have their own objective logic that to a certain extent guides conduct for all competitors, and there are intersubjective, moral goals linked to ideas of the fair and well-played game.[10]

In terms of intentional goals, there is a great variety among participants, ranging from process-oriented amateurs who focus primarily on experiential values like joy, excitement, challenge, and a feeling of community, to hard-core instrumentalists striving for prestige and profit only. For a social practice to be intelligible, however, its constitutive norms and rules have to be known and acknowledged by all. Such a socially shared understanding defines what kinds of conduct are permissible, what kinds are prohibited, and what kinds are awarded.

A socially shared understanding of sporting games is linked to their logic as competitions. What we may call the institutional goal of these practices is to measure, compare and finally rank the participants according to performance of athletic skills as defined in the rules of the relevant game. In other words, in sporting games, the predominant distributive norm is meritocratic. The norm on equal treatment, then, becomes a necessary condition for a game to be realised at all. To be able to evaluate the relevant inequalities satisfactorily, participants have to compete on the same terms. The specified equality norm is this: 'All competitors ought to be given equal opportunity to perform.'

At first sight, there seem to be no significant problems here. In most games, players compete according to the same rules that, among other things, require all parties to start out with no game advantage at all.[11] The concern for equality is followed up during the competition. Points in tennis and goals in soccer are distributed according to the same standards for all competitors.

But, on closer inspection of actual practice within sports, problems arise. A first problem is linked to the fact that sporting games are hardly ever realised in full accordance with the rules. Rule violations, both intentional and unintentional, may cause unfair distribution of advantage. The point, then, is to eliminate or compensate for unjust advantage. In the case of unintentional rule violations, such as an accidental handball in soccer, the initial situation has to be restored to the greatest possible extent through, for example, a free kick. In the case of intentional violations, for example a deliberate handball, restoration of the initial situation is not enough. The 'contract to compete', in which participants voluntarily restrict their liberty in order to compete in a setting of mutual trust, is broken. Intentional rule violations call for additional penalties which, in soccer, are given in terms of a warning (a yellow card) or a red card (which means that a player is expelled from the game). However, no penalty can completely restore the initial situation or the fair contract. It can only compensate up to a certain extent for the injustice that has been done.

Here we see that the norm on equal opportunity is realised through imperfect procedures. The gap between ideals and reality, or between a sporting game as a system of ideas and as a system of action, is hard to bridge. But if the rule system and its realisation as a whole seem to satisfy requirements on equality of opportunity to perform, and if injustices caused by rule violations are sufficiently compensated for, a game can be considered to be as just as it is reasonable to demand under the circumstances.[12]

A second challenge to the norm on equal opportunity comes from the fact that a particular kind of non-meritocratic element is allowed to influence the outcome. In outdoor events, competitors have to perform under varying external conditions. A strong wind from the side may change the course of a soccer ball and blow a good shot just outside of the goalposts. Due to temperature changes and slower tracks, a cross-country skier can lose a tight competition because of a late starting number. How are we to deal with inequalities of this kind?

Many sports take place in outdoor arenas exposed to uncontrollable external influences. The ideal of identical conditions is hard to realise. But inequalities in external conditions can be accepted within certain limitations.

First, such inequalities ought never to exert significant influence on performance and outcomes in sporting games. Under extreme weather conditions, soccer games and skiing competitions will end up as pure games of chance. Therefore, most outdoor sports operate with clear limitations outside of which no competitions should take place.

However, even within these limitations inequalities due to variations in external conditions occur. Second, then, if we accept outdoor competitions at all, the possibility of being influenced by such inequalities should be distributed in a just way. The only fair procedure, therefore, is to distribute the possibility of such influence through pure procedural justice; that is, through chance. And, indeed, this is exactly what is done in a series of sports. The most common procedure is (as in skiing) to draw starting positions or (as in ball games) to draw pitch or court halves through a lottery.

To sum up, we can say that the norm on equal opportunity to perform is met if unfair advantages due to rule violations are eliminated or compensated for in the best possible way, if inequalities due to uncontrollable external conditions do not exert significant and systematic influence on the outcome, and if the possibility of being affected by unavoidable inequalities of this kind is distributed through pure procedural justice or chance.

Game advantage and inequality

The norm on equal opportunity is designed to secure a just distribution of game advantage based on a particular kind of inequality – inequality in performance of athletic skills. The second part of the formal norm of justice prescribes a reasonable accordance between relevant inequality and unequal treatment. In the setting of sporting games the specified norm goes like this: 'There ought to be a reasonable accordance between inequalities in performance of athletic skills and unequal treatment in terms of the distribution of game advantage.'

What are the procedures upon which this meritocratic norm can be realised in practice? In sporting games, there are principally two different ways of rewarding performance. A ranking can be based on physical-mathematical measurements of performance, or good performances can be rewarded with what we may call game-specific advantage.

Advantage based on physical-mathematical measurements of performance

In some sports, such as in the 100m sprint, in javelin throwing or in weightlifting, advantages are distributed in terms of a ranking of competitors based on exact quantification of performance in physical-mathematical entities such as seconds, metres and kilogrammes. Provided with exact and reliable methods for evaluation, it seems at first sight that we come very close to perfect procedural justice. A ranking list of runners on a 100m sprint illustrates the point. We have here an ordinal scale with the accuracy of a hundredth of a second. If the norm on equal opportunity is realised in practice, there seems to be almost complete correspondence between inequalities in performance and advantage gained.[13]

Upon further consideration, however, the picture is not so clear. Exact quantification of performance must be based on valid scales of evaluation. One problem with modern hi-tech measurement methods is that they perhaps include too much. For instance, to use tenths of a second to distinguish between competitors after 50km of cross-country skiing seems unreasonable. We are dealing here with a two-hour outdoor event that necessarily involves slight changes in weather and snow conditions. The outcome of a tight race is not based on inequalities in performance of skills but, in the final instance, on climatic changes that strike randomly among participants.

Another example illustrates how non-meritocratic elements are parts of the very logic of exact measurement of athletic performance. Two 100m sprinters perform almost identically. One athlete is the necessary hundredth of a second in front and wins. Athletic skills, of course, are predominant. Still the victory is not based on merit alone. The chest that breaks the finishing line a few millimetres in front of a competitor is not only an outcome of a well-planned race and deliberate tactics. One hundredth of a second is beyond the margins within which a sprinter, perceptually and cognitively, can be in full control. The paradox, then, is that, whereas the intention is to increase the accuracy of performance evaluation and the degree of meritocratic justice, finely tuned measurement technology seems to increase the degree of randomness. How are we to deal with this?

To win games with small margins, we usually need luck. Rescher (1995) distinguishes a pure-chance process that per definition cannot be predicted (like that of a lottery) from various kinds of luck. Luck seems unpredictable from the affected person's points of view due to ignorance of some kind (for example, when confronting a fork in the road and not knowing where the different routes are leading, we choose the right one).[14] Luck can be influenced by reducing the degree of ignorance and by increasing skill. For instance, the appearance of a strong sun that implies a softer and slower course in the alpine skiing race can be compensated for with psychological stamina and more risky, aggressive skiing. But luck always implies unpredictable elements that, from the affected person's point of view, come about 'by chance' or 'by accident'. Risky, aggressive skiing results in smaller margins between, and less control over, success and failure. The alpine skier who, in spite of a slower course, wins by five-hundredths of a second performs excellently. At the same time, such a small margin of victory can never be fully controlled by the skier, who therefore experiences good luck as well.

The institutional goal of sporting games is to measure, compare and rank competitors according to performance of athletic skills. In tight games, finely tuned calibration of measurement technology helps in distinguishing a winner. The price to pay is to accept luck as part of our evaluations. Still, however, this does not mean that sporting games necessarily become unjust. Again we can say: As long as the outcome of most games is based primarily on merit – that is, as long as chance and luck do not exert significant and systematic influence on the outcome – this represents no serious threat to the norm on a reasonable accordance between skills performed and advantage given.

Game-specific advantage

In other sporting games, distribution of game advantage is of a more complex kind. In ball games, advantage is distributed in terms of points and goals. It is not possible to quantify these performances in exact terms. They qualify for what we may call game-specific advantage that is defined in the constitutive rules of the game and has no meaning outside of the context of game playing. And here the correspondence between skills performed and advantage gained is not always as easy to discuss as in the examples above. In fact, non-meritocratic elements do not just decide the outcome of tight games. Once in a while they can decide uneven games in favour of the lesser performance. A tennis player might win the majority of games (7–6, 7–6, 0–6, 0–6, 7–6), but still lose the match if the opponent, due to good luck and a couple of net touches, wins the decisive rallies. A soccer team might control a game and have several shots on goal but still lose by one randomly scored goal by the opposing team. It is usually in the context of games with game-specific advantage that we hear statements about 'unfair results' and about the loser as 'the moral winner'. What can be said here of the correspondence between skills performed and advantage gained?

Again, luck is involved in various ways. Luck and skill are often tied together so closely that they are difficult to distinguish. In good performances, luck is often marginal. Is the tennis champion Steffi Graf really lucky when she hits the line with a perfect volley, or are her skills in fact so close to perfection that this is pure merit? Where good luck follows skill, there is no serious threat to the norm on meritocratic distribution of advantage.

In a similar manner, the influence of bad luck can be compensated for by skill. After an easy goal in favour of the opponent, a good soccer team can adjust their tactical dispositions to get a quick equaliser. An expert tennis player who realises that her shot will be (too) low can compensate with a strong topspin to increase the chance of a net touch point.

However, even if good luck and skill often come together, and even if the influence of bad luck can be reduced by skill, this is not always so. In games with game-specific advantage, the influence of luck sometimes contradicts merit. A soccer player may attempt to pass to a team-mate in a better position, but miss and instead hit the goal and score. To everyone's surprise, a technically lousy shot on the tennis court can drop down on the right side of the net. To use De Wachter's definition of chance in sports, there is '... an incongruence between result produced and the intended action produced from the skill and the effort of the player' (De Wachter 1985: 55). What can be said to this?

The answer of the game cynic is as follows: 'The point in soccer is to score goals. The point in tennis is to win the important rallies. Whoever does this, is always the better performer.' Likewise, 'The point in soccer is to score goals. The team that scores the most goals is the better team.' The cynic's view is built on the premise that in all games there is complete correspondence between performance of skills and advantage gained. Our evaluations are completely reliable and valid. Performance of skills *is* advantage-gained. Sporting games are per-definition cases in which an ideal norm on meritocratic distribution is realised through perfect procedures.

This standpoint is unreasonable. First, as said above, rule violations and a certain element of chance and luck are unavoidable. Non-meritocratic factors cause inequalities that are impossible to eliminate. We can merely compensate for them up to a certain point. In sporting games, perfect procedures are utopian ideals. Second, the cynical position leaves us with no critical possibilities. It accepts no idea of the well-played game. The best playing team is simply the team that is winning. The score tells it all. As the game cynic rejects game ideals, there is little basis for critical reflection on good play in spite of a loss, on how winning performances can be improved, on changes and developments of games, etc. Paradoxically, the cynical view is naive, as it shows no sense of the way games are understood and practised in real life.

But even if we disagree with the cynic, we can still tighten the correspondence between skills performed and advantage gained in some sporting games. The scientifically inspired game enthusiast could argue that, to increase the validity of our game 'experiments', we should differentiate to a larger extent between ways of distributing such advantage. The ideal would be games with physical-mathematical measurements of performance. Soccer could follow the example of basketball. Penalty shots could give one point; shots from within the penalty area, two points; and shots from outside the penalty area, three points. In tennis, points could be awarded by a much more precise operationalisation of the quality of play, for instance by a board of referees. On a longer-term basis, advanced operationalisations could increase accuracy of performance measurements in all ball games. Even if our procedures are still imperfect, we come closer to the ideal: pure meritocratic distribution of advantage.

But this position represents an unfortunate reductionism as well. There is more to a sporting game than the evaluation of performance. We must not confuse the institutional goal of these practices; to evaluate and rank players according to performance, with intentional goals among participants and with their status as experienced and 'lived'. What we may call the ludic argument tries to incorporate this point.[15]

The ludic argument

The ludic argument provides a rationale for accepting non-meritocratic influence on the outcomes of sporting games in general – both those that measure performance in exact physical-mathematical entities and those that are based on game-specific advantage. The argument goes as follows.

Games have, in principle, no external purpose. The rules and norms that constitute them give little meaning outside of the practices. Searle (1979: 33) says of such rules that they '... constitute (and also regulate) an activity the existence of which is logically dependent on the rules'. He explains:

> The rules of football or chess ... do not merely regulate playing football or chess, but as it were they create the very possibility of playing such games. The activities of playing football or chess are constituted by acting in accordance with (at least a large subset of) the appropriate rules.
>
> (Searle 1979: 33–34)

This point corresponds with an empirical fact. Most players compete for the sake of values realised in the games themselves – experiential values such as fun, joy, challenge, excitement, a feeling of togetherness, experiences of opposition and rivalry. Games have primarily autotelic value. To most of us, games have not just the logic of play but are realised accordingly.[16]

According to a long tradition of play theorists, among them most notably Johan Huizinga (1950), a non-utilitarian, playful attitude is the origin and core of cultural practices like art, dance, literature and games. Play is considered fundamental to human existence as its basic themes are fundamental, existential questions on who we are, to whom we belong, and what we can achieve. The thrill of cultural practices is linked to their openness to interpretation of answers to these questions, to their ambiguity, to their 'genuine humanism' (to use a somewhat old-fashioned expression).[17]

Good games seem to be permeated by an exciting openness and uncertainty linked to outcome. The uncertainty arises through a delicate mix of predictability and unpredictability. Games have a predictable framework in terms of rules. We know that soccer players will kick the ball without using their hands and try to score in the prescribed manner. We know that a tennis player will try to hit the ball over the net and on the opponent's court half, but still out of her reach. At the same time, every move in a game has an element of unpredictability. Does the attack in the soccer match end with a goal? Who is in the lead after the first half? Where will the tennis player place the ball? Who will win the tennis rally, the game, the set? Who will finally win the match?

So far, the influence of chance and luck has been treated as a problem that ought to be eliminated or compensated for in the best way possible. From the ludic perspective, however, the argument is that chance and luck are not problematic, but represent valuable parts of sporting games. If kept within the frameworks sketched above, chance and luck enhance the complexity of the skill challenge and intensify the thrilling unpredictability of the answer to the question 'Who wins?' – what is sometimes called 'the sweet tension of uncertainty of outcome'.[18] Does the soccer team handle the disadvantage (distributed by pure chance) of playing against an increasing wind in the second half? Which one of the sprinters has the good luck of breaking the finishing line in a tight race a few hundredths of a second in front of a competitor? Is the tennis player able to give the low ball the necessary topspin to achieve a point after a net touch?

From this perspective, even in situations where luck contradicts merit, such as in the case of the lucky soccer goal or a tennis point, it can be accepted. Luck is experienced as outside the control of the persons affected, its outcome is unpredictable and it seems to strike blindly among participants. Hence, luck exerts no systematic influence on the outcome and will usually even out during a game, or at least during a series of games.

The ludic argument illustrates a particular local scheme of justice in sporting games in which chance and luck have a limited but important role to play.[19] Moreover, insights into the particular local scheme of justice in sporting games help to distinguish them from other social practices with which they are sometimes compared. For example, sports are neither scientific experiments aiming at valid, or scientifically 'true' knowledge, nor are they like a court of law striving towards perfect procedural justice. Their particular value is to be found in their delicate mix of meritocratic justice, chance and luck. The primary distributive norm is meritocratic, whereas chance and luck enhance the skill challenge and the 'sweet tension of uncertainty of outcome'.

Game advantage based on aesthetic criteria

There is a special case in the area of game-specific advantage that ought to be mentioned in this respect. In some sporting games, the distribution of advantage is based on aesthetic evaluations. In sports like dance, figure skating, rhythmic gymnastics and ski jumping, performance is in part evaluated on the basis of criteria like 'artistry' and 'style'. What can be said about a reasonable accordance between skills performed and advantage gained here?

First of all, what does an aesthetic standard include? What do we actually evaluate? In most 'aesthetic sports', we find expressions like 'the overall impression' or 'the artistic expression' of the performance. Indeed, successful performances include strong aesthetic qualities such as harmony, rhythm, float, precision and the dynamic use of force. Experts play with ease and grace, and at the same time forcefully and decisively. No doubt, aesthetic qualities play an important role in the good game experience.

However, from the perspective of justice, the problem with aesthetic criteria is that these qualities are hard to operationalise. As is indicated in the terms used ('an overall impression', 'an artistic expression'), we deal with holistic qualities that are by definition non-analytic and impossible to quantify. Evaluations rest, to a larger extent than analytic ones, on subjective interpretations of performance.

Of course, subjectivity is not wrong *per se*. A judge in gymnastics or ski jumping may be subjective but still follow his or her honest conviction about the criteria of perfection of the sport. Moreover, in most aesthetic sports, there are several judges involved and the final score is based on an average of their evaluations. If all judges follow their own views, and if the group of judges is representative for views in the sport community, evaluations of performances are based on sound premises.

A greater problem is that evaluations based on holistic criteria are open to the possibility of partial outcomes. In gymnastics, refereeing scandals with secret agreements among judges have ruined many competitions.[20] In other sports, the criteria for aesthetic evaluation are constantly a step behind the development of taste; the 'unwritten' and commonly accepted standards of aesthetic excellence. A good example is ski jumping, in which in later years new movement patterns such as the so-called V-style were accepted among athletes, coaches and spectators long before they were given credit in the rules.

Aesthetic qualities are important both to players and spectators in most sporting games.[21] From a critical point of view, the aesthetic qualities of Michael 'Air' Jordan's jump shots in basketball, or of a wonderful 'double play' on the baseball field, seem to be just as strong as those of champion Katarina Witt's movements on the ice in the so-called aesthetic sport of figure skating. Aesthetic evaluation of performance could be a criterion for distributing advantage in many sports. However, any evaluation criteria should be based on intersubjectivity and should be open for critical examination in terms of their application. If aesthetic evaluations are done in terms of holistic qualities, proper evaluations become impossible. In addition, such evaluations increase the possibilities for partiality and unfairness. Perhaps the best solution would be to abandon aesthetic judgments as a basis for distribution of advantage in sporting games as a whole?

Concluding comments

This chapter started out with questions on justice in sporting games. Through a discussion of the distribution of game advantage, I have outlined a local normative scheme of justice in these practices.

Sporting games are competitions in which we try to measure, compare and finally rank participants according to the performance of athletic skills. Strict norms on equal opportunity to perform provide a framework for a clear meritocratic distribution of game advantage. The primary distributive norm is meritocratic.

However, in all sporting games non-meritocratic elements arise. Rule violations are almost unavoidable. During outdoor events, advantages and disadvantages arise due to changing external conditions. And, in all sporting games, outcomes are open to a certain influence of chance and luck.

I have argued that such non-meritocratic elements do not necessarily make sporting games less just and fair. As long as inequalities caused by rule violations are eliminated or compensated for in the best way possible, as long as non-controllable inequalities in external conditions are distributed on the basis of chance (as in a lottery), and as long as chance and luck do not exert significant and systematic influence on the outcome, sporting games must be considered to be as just as it is reasonable to demand. Moreover, as long as all participants know of and commonly acknowledge the role played by non-meritocratic elements as a basis for their voluntary engagement, sporting games also satisfy requirements on fairness.

The influence of chance and luck in sporting games is sometimes considered to be a problem that has to be eliminated or compensated for in the best way possible. I have argued for a different view. According to the ludic argument, a certain influence of chance and luck adds value to sporting games. The skill challenges become more complex and exciting. The 'sweet tension of uncertainty of outcome' is intensified. The optimal blend of merit, chance and luck in the good game expresses a particular 'ludic rationality' aiming at maximising values in sporting games in themselves.

In this way, fair and good games can become paradigmatic examples of what Rawls (1971: 520–529) calls social unions. They become collective achievements in which all participants share the final goal – that there should be a good play of the game. All players find satisfaction in the very process of pursuing this common goal, in ways allowed by the rules and norms agreed upon by all under fair conditions.

The experiential qualities of sporting games establish links to more fundamental values. A fair sporting game should perhaps be understood on the basis of the etymological root of 'fair', *fæger* (Old English), which refers not only to what is just, but to what is admirable, beautiful, and performed with dignity as well. In games, as in cultural practices in general, we pose existential questions about who we are, to whom we belong and what we can achieve. The fair and good game opens a variety of interpretations of these questions in a meaningful and valuable way.

Notes

1 Thanks are due to Gunnar Breivik, David Heyd, Mike McNamee and Tony Skillen, for valuable comments on earlier versions of this chapter. In addition, I have received helpful comments from two anonymous reviewers of *Ethical Theory and Moral Practice*.

2 Elster (1992: 4) contrasts local justice to global justice. The latter deals with globally redistributive policies designed centrally (nationally) and intended '... to compensate people for various sorts of bad luck (resulting from the possession of "morally arbitrary properties")'. Global justice takes typically the form of cash transfers. Local schemes of justice are not, or at least only in part, compensatory, and they concern the distribution of goods and burdens other than money. This essay is inspired by Elster's discussion of local justice but departs from it as well, as it aims not only at descriptions and explanations, but at a critical, normative discussion of the fair and good game.

3 For an elaboration of the idea of ethos of games, see D'Agostino (1981). For a critical reinterpretation of this idea, see Loland (1998a).

4 For an elaboration, see also Rawls (1971: 108–114).

5 Rawls (1971: 113) explicitly mentions games in this respect: 'We acquire obligations by promising and by tacit understandings, and even when we join in a game, namely, the obligation to play by the rules and to be a good sport'. There is, however, a long philosophical debate on the premise of voluntariness for the obligation of fairness to arise. We could argue that even those who benefit from a cooperative practice without prior consent should bear some of the burdens. For an overview of the discussion, see Arneson (1982). I am indebted to an anonymous reviewer for this point.

6 See Rawls (1971: 112.)

7 See in particular the discussion of distributive justice in book 5 of *The Ethics of Aristotle/Nichomachean Ethics* (1976: 177–184).

8 Elster (1992: 62ff.) offers a detailed overview over a series of principles and norms applied in local schemes of justice. The overview presented is based on Perelman (1980: 1–23) and is much simpler but sufficient for a systematic discussion of the practice under consideration; sporting games.

9 For the distinction between systems of ideas and systems of actions, see Eckhoff and Sundby (1988: 22–23), and Rawls (1971: 55). For the distinctions of different kinds of procedural justice, see Rawls (1971: 85–86).

10 See Rawls (1971: 525–526) for a discussion of the different kinds of goals in games. A detailed discussion of the various goals of sporting games can be found in Loland (1989).

11 Of course, there are sporting games in which inequalities in initial conditions are defined in the rules, e.g. handicaps in golf. However, in most games, this is not the case. Moreover, if the norm on handicap is followed in detail, we end up with pure games of chance.

12 In a similar vein, Rawls (1971: 343) says that, in addition to voluntariness, the obligation on fairness depends upon the institution in question being just, or '... if not perfectly just, at least as just as it is reasonable to expect under the circumstances'.

13 This is not to say, of course, that the external rewards as results of victory such as profit and prestige in any reasonable way are related to the actual difference in performance between the winner and the other competitors on the list. An Olympic gold on the 100m dash can be won by a hundredth of a second, but in terms of external rewards we are close to the norm 'winner takes all'. The discussion here focuses on the inner logic of competitive games, or local justice within the game itself.

14 See in particular, Rescher (1995: 19–40).

15 The term 'ludic' is based on Latin *ludus*, meaning 'play'.

16 For an overview of research on motivation in sporting games, see Roberts *et al.* (1997).

17 There is, of course, a sociocultural component here. Different games thematize existential questions in different ways. In a series of studies Sutton-Smith (1974) has shown the relationships between the basic norms and values of a culture within which the games are played. As many sport historians and sport sociologists have argued, among them most notably Allen Guttmann (1978), sporting games are based on equality of opportunity to perform and are thus typical expressions of an industrialized, capitalist culture with focus on quantifiable progress measured under standardised conditions.

18 The idea of 'the sweet tension of uncertainty of outcome' as a characteristic of good sporting games is originally Warren Fraleigh's. Elsewhere I have used the expression to characterise what I have called the phenomenological structure of the good game experience. See Loland (1998: 100ff).

19 Here, then, we see how sporting games are related to other kinds of competitive games, like bridge, in which the chance element in the dealing of cards plays a role that can be influenced by intellectual skills. In contrast to bridge, however, sports deal with bodily movement skills. To an athlete, the relationship between intended actions and outcomes is more complex and admits to a larger extent of luck, as the very carrying out of the intention is a complex motor-skill demand. The intention is hardly ever realised in its perfect form. Moreover, competitive games like sports and bridge are different from the competitive game of chess, in which luck in the sense discussed here plays no role at all. On local schemes of justice, see Roger Caillois (1961).

20 One of the more recent examples can be found during the 1999 World Championships in figure skating in Helsinki in which a Russian and a Ukrainian judge were captured by TV cameras communicating extensively with gestures and signs during the evaluation of competitors. Such communication is strictly forbidden in the rules. They cooperated, of course, to improve the rankings of skaters from their own countries. The Russian and Ukrainian judges will probably be expelled and the routines for judging will be critically re-evaluated.

21 There is a significant body of philosophical literature on the aesthetic elements in sports. For a selection of essays, see Morgan and Meier (1995: part 8).

ling

An indirect reflection of sport's moral imperative?

Graham McFee

The moral imperative sometimes located within sport (and rightly so, in my opinion) is often not a direct consequence of the rules or laws of particular sports, and this fact is recognised when appeal is made, not to those rules themselves, but to the *spirit* of the rules, or to considerations of *fair play*, or some such. But how do these matters manage to impinge on sport performance? In this chapter, I argue that they stand to the rules of sport roughly as Ronald Dworkin's (legal) *principles* stand to his (legal) *rules*: recall that it is the *principle* that one should not benefit from one's crime that prevents the grandfather-killer, Elmer, from inheriting his grandfather's wealth – there is no *rule* here (Dworkin 1978: 22–28, 71–80).[1] In just this way, the principles underlying a sport provide a *learned* background essential for appropriate participation in that sport. But this seems rendered problematic once the *constitutive* role of the rules of particular sports is granted.

In Dworkin's own example, that of the rule in baseball, '... that if a batter has had three strikes, he is out' (Dworkin 1978: 24), a sporting case illustrates human situations (especially legal ones) where there are *rules* but no *principles*, and (therefore?) one where such moral considerations do not apply.[2] Or so Dworkin thinks. For the decision to select *three* strikes (rather than, say, four) is arbitrary: if so, there would be no need for further justifications. But this is misleading if we view sport more realistically: these moral(ish) principles do apply in at least some sports, as illuminated by the possibility of contravening the 'spirit of the rules' (for example, by what I shall call 'spoiling'). Even in Dworkin's example, there are many factors. For instance, one motivation for the rule must relate to the proposed/intended duration of a game – the rule '300 strikes and you are out' would make a typical game too long – but even here there might be *some* consideration of fairness; that one strike did not give the batter a *fair* chance to display prowess, for example. So there is an implicit appeal to (principled) fairness.

To say this is to stress the importance of the *possibility* of winning (etc.) where this means more than just the logical possibility. I use the term 'spoiling' to characterise approximately behaviour that, while not contrary to the rules of a game/sport, is nonetheless not how one *ought* to play it, for 'participating in the game/match' should mean participating in ways that respect one's opponents, showing due regard for them.[3] Plays which involve spoiling do not permit opponents the possibility of playing the game according to its spirit, a possibility one *must* grant to opponents taken seriously. Although permitted by the rules, such plays are recognised – at least by knowledgeable audiences – as inappropriate ways to play the game/sport: an arena where players who 'spoil' may legitimately be criticised by the audience, team-mates and the media, but not by referees.

Nor should we think of this as an impossible burden on referees – their problems are not the key ones here. One of Dworkin's own examples to illustrate this point runs as follows:

> Suppose some rule of a chess tournament provides that the referee shall declare a game forfeit if one player 'unreasonably' annoys the other in the course of play. The language of the rule does not define what counts as 'unreasonable' annoyance …
>
> (Dworkin 1978: 102)

His example could readily be replaced by one about sport; about cricket or soccer, for instance. And his point would be ours – that the rules do not circumscribe the exact behaviours they permit or prohibit.

In referring to the need for what, following Dworkin, I am calling 'principles', my point is not one about the completeness/incompleteness of rules as represented by rule-formulations (the kind of thing better drafting might be thought to cure) – there is always an element of judgment in the application of a rule, and in 'knowing how to go on'[4] on the basis of a rule. Rather this distinction is employed to highlight a species of more general constraint on *appropriate* sporting behaviour (for some sports, at least), but one not required (nor prohibited) by that sport's rules.

As Dworkin (1978: 103) continues, such rules '… are not incomplete, like a book whose last page is missing, but abstract … ' This means that they must be filled in, *particularised*,[5] to a given context. And that immediately licenses disputes about the appropriateness of the various cases offered. For how exactly do the rules apply – and how should they be applied – in this (testing) case? There will always be room for dispute here, since no application of a rule is uniquely determined by the rule-formulation. Nor should we think of such disputes as rare, for they are driven by questions of *principles*. And, as Dworkin remarks, 'Once we identify legal principles as separate sorts of standards, different from legal rules, we are suddenly aware of them all around us' (1978: 28). For we see the normativity of such principles in many of the social behaviours of human beings.

A crucial thought here is that one learns at least *some* of the principles through learning how to '… *construct* the game's character' (Dworkin 1978: 103) when we learn the *rules*. Dworkin's exposition takes the acquiring of principles as somehow prior to, and the basis for, such learning of rules; as he puts it, the principles provide a '… gravitational force' (1978: 115) operative within the rule. But, in sporting cases, this cannot be quite right. The interlock between the moral metaphors of justice – 'level playing field', 'fair play', etc. – and the specifics of sport mean that, in learning how to make sense of these ideas *as they apply in particular sports*, one is learning the general moral principles, by learning how to apply these key metaphors more exactly. (If this is true, it places a particular obligation on teachers of sport: they can be teaching the 'rules' of a moral laboratory – see below.)

Through a consideration of cases of 'spoiling' plays, this chapter defends both the thesis that, properly understood, such principles offer essential moral constraints on (some) sports and the idea that, *for this reason*, some sports have the capacity to provide examples of those concrete particulars that alone permit the learning, and learning to apply, of moral concepts; in short, that some sport can function – as I put it earlier – as a *moral laboratory*, in which moral concepts are acquired, but with less risk than in genuine moral confrontations.

Key differences between principles of this kind and typical rules constitutive of sport highlight the 'framework' character of those principles. And, since the principles regulate human interactions (in the sense of headlining what one ought or ought not to do), it cannot be far off the mark to call them 'moral'.

Since my argument is for the *intrinsic* moral possibilities of sport, as we will see, it is interesting to note a typical explanation of spoiling: for example, the case of someone bowling underarm and along the ground the last delivery of a limited-over cricket match – to preclude the *possibility* of the opponents winning. For – as later – these explanations point to the externality or extrinsic-ness of the counter-forces here, thereby suggesting the internality of the principles against which spoiling (etc.) offends. And my concern is with the *nature* of sport (what is intrinsic to it) rather than what is extrinsic – for example, its ability to make money.

In this way, one sees how sport's claims to be genuinely beneficial to human beings (in an *intrinsic* fashion) might be sustained, and thus how a commitment to sport's (broadly) educative potential, which *parallels*, say, that of Pierre de Coubertin, might be defended – although in a more realistic version.

Yet arguments for particularism in morality (here accepted) might make us doubt the possibility of acquiring *moral* principles through learning in *sporting* situations. For, surely, particularism emphasises the *sporting* character of these situations. But a more realistic account of the relation of the particular to the abstract can resolve this tension.

Before returning to these abstract considerations, it is useful (perhaps essential) to have a concrete example in front of us. As my central example is from cricket, I will spell it out at some length, drawing rough parallels to baseball. The situation is the end of a limited-over cricket match: there is one delivery (one 'ball') to go and the batting side needs *six runs* to win. Now while, in principle, six runs might be scored in a large number of ways from one delivery, in practice these runs can only be scored by the batsman hitting the ball over the boundary rope without its bouncing; 'on the fly', as people say. Typically the bowler in cricket delivers the ball overarm, where it bounces *roughly* in front of the batsman. Such a delivery might be hit for six, hit over the boundary rope, 'on the fly'; and this is especially likely, given that the relevant batsman is a *good* hitter of sixes.

To give names to the players (fictional names), let us call the bowler 'Trevor Chappell'. What he does – following the instructions of his captain (who we will call 'Greg Chappell', and designate to be his brother) – is to bowl underarm, along the ground. This facilitates the batsman's *hitting* the ball, but effectively precludes his hitting it 'for six'. As a result, Chappell's side wins the match.

Now, one *is* permitted to bowl underarm in cricket – there is no rule precluding it. Further, one is permitted to bowl along the ground; again, there is no rule prohibiting it.[6] But the net effect of the action is to win the match with a technique which – as people say – 'is not cricket': it is a *spoiling* gesture.

Notice that this is not a technique one could always use: first, it would not always be necessary. But it is effective in this case partly because here one is trying to preclude (exactly) *six* runs, and would be quite happy to concede, say, *four* runs: that would still leave the Chappell team winners! Second, it would be counterproductive if all teams used it, either *throughout* the game (which would destroy much of the excitement) or *at the end*, where its predictability would make it useless as a *match-winner* – everyone would be doing it!

This example is powerful *partly* because cricket is regularly offered as a model of fair play – although today's high-class game, with its 'sledging' (that is, behaviour designed to unsettle the opposing player by, say, commenting on his skill or his mother's virtue) is often far from that.

It is granted on all sides that spoiling behaviour in cricket is permitted by the rules of the sport. But if this spoiling behaviour really were acceptable, why not do it *all* the time? The idea of only doing it on this (strange) occasion is tacit acknowledgment that it is not OK. (Also, as noted above, there are practical issues about the effectiveness of it as a long-term strategy, one consequently to be adopted by one's opponents, say.)

This is an example of *spoiling* because bowling in that fashion at that point in the game does not give the opposing side a *fair chance*. So spoiling has a direct connection to the 'spirit of the game' idea – to the *essence* of a sporting contest, as we might put it. But here there is a pun on the term 'sporting', both to mean conforming to the rules of the game (and hence part of that sport) and to mean played appropriately!

Spoiling comes about when there is a *conflict* between the letter of the rules (the written rule/statute) and the *spirit* of the rules – that is, the principles (for instance, of fairness) on which the rules rest.

In determining the relevant principles here, notice the (*conceptual*) importance, within cricket, of the idea of a 'wide', a delivery beyond where the batsman can plausibly hit the ball. Here we see the commitment, within cricket, to the bowling of deliveries from which the batsman *can* score, if he is sufficiently skilled. That its rules allow the concept of a *wide* therefore indicates something about the principles underlying cricket. Further, the penalty for bowling a *wide* is twofold: first, the bowling side automatically gains one run for the wide and, second, the ball is delivered again. In this way, the bowling side *simply* loses one run and *still* has to bowl that delivery. Its importance here, though, lies in the connection of sport's rules to its principles being visible here – as the case of spoiling identifies. In recognising the place of (effectively) moral principles here – and thereby of the preservation of the integrity of the sport – we begin to see how the hoped-for connection of sport to the moral might be defended. (Notice, though, that this concerns what sport can do, not what it must, or inevitably will, do.)

But need there be *one* account here for sport in general? Suppose that we resolve this case: how far *need* that commit us? To what degree are there *precedents* being set here? Well, we began from the interpenetration of moral notions with our lives – what we are adding is the thought that they (also?) have a role in sport – a role recognised in the moral metaphors from which we began.

Of course, this parallel also makes plain a limitation of the moral laboratory – not a problem for the theory but for the practice. For, just as someone might be a master of pure mathematics but unable to 'manage' elementary applied maths (say, unable to check one's change quickly after buying a round of drinks), so one might be a master of the moral concepts in the sporting context but unable to apply them outside the 'laboratory'. There is no theoretical safeguard here, no guarantee that generalisability won't be thwarted (*pace* de Coubertin) – although eternal vigilance might work against this being a regular occurrence; and valuing sport partly as a moral laboratory might make such vigilance easier to organise!

But those 'moral metaphors' are either *not* metaphorical or are *less* metaphorical in the sporting context, where there really can be fair playing and the levelness of actual playing fields. Seeing how these ideas interact with the rules (and spirit) of sport can show us how such notions might *apply* – and hence, perhaps, how they might be applied more generally. And saying this is acknowledging a kind of generality of *application*, which is *very different* from simply generalising – as we might put it, it is the generalisability of the particularist (see Travis 1996).

If particularism in morality is granted (i.e. true), principles could only be acquired ('learned') in concrete situations: that is, learned 'concretised'. This is one reason why one cannot (usefully) write down such principles. Or, we can write them down, but not helpfully. The principle against spoiling might be, 'Play the game' or, more exactly, 'Do not act so as to impede your opponent's playing to the spirit of the rules'.

Of course, one is here formulating *in the abstract* the objection to spoiling, but this simply reflects the contours of the relevant principle – it certainly would not be exceptionless. So that if I render the principle against spoiling as 'Play the game', I do not give useful guidance as to what to *do* in a particular situation, nor how to judge what someone else does. And this is especially true when the principle applies to more than one sport, as well as to different situations *within* a sport. But, if I am an experienced cricketer, being told 'play the game' may be informative – it might highlight ways in which my behaviour to date was less than exemplary. Even more revealing is when I am told, say by my captain and older brother, to *not* 'play the game': I might know what to do *then* just because I *do* know 'how to go on' without contravening this principle – although on this occasion I do not do so. The point, though, is that formulating the abstract principle is doubly unhelpful. Of course, like any 'rule'-formulation, the application of my principle-formulation is a matter of judgment (as noted above). But, more crucially, the application here is circumscribed by the specific nature of the sport itself. Unsurprisingly, this conclusion reinforces the particularism (explicitly) assumed earlier.

A good question here will be how we learn such (sporting) principles, and this will be especially important *for me*, given my account of the connection between understanding and explaining.[7] For what is involved in *learning* X surely has a bearing on *explaining* X. So how does this happen? How do we (typically) learn sporting principles? My most general answer is that this happens in *appropriate* teaching of the sporting activity. It follows that what one learns is not – and could not be – just a formulation of the principle (a principle-formulation), but how to *behave* in accordance with the principle; for instance, how to manifest 'fair play' (which is, of course, no guarantee that one will then actually play fairly). In effect, then, my thought is that principles are taught when rules are properly taught – where the term 'properly' makes just that point!

We have a sense how, in teaching the rules of a game (for example, cricket), a teacher sensitive to the principles might inculcate those principles too; indeed, those of us who were well taught can remember this process. So, if we cannot *say* how to teach these principles, we do at least know. But now a further issue intrudes. How, given the teaching and learning of sporting principles, does this apply to morality? The model here is of an abstract principle learned from (and in) concrete instances in sport, then applied to concrete moral situations where – perhaps for theoretical reasons – we might also formulate abstract moral principles.

Notice the way principles of (roughly) rule-application are moral: for instance, there is a moral obligation to mean what one says, in two senses: first, that one *does* mean what one says, because (other things being equal) one means what one's words mean – to put it roughly; and second, because the alternatives are lying or frivolity (or self-deception) – that is, they are moral failings.[8]

Of course, one must acknowledge the limitation of my argument here: spoiling is at best *one* such index of moral connection; moreover, it is for some sports only.[9] But it is not for that reason a useless or trivial index. For these cases illustrate why someone might misconceive the relation of sport to moral development as well as offering some 'fixed points' for many discussions (although not all). As we might say, they point to answers to *particular* perplexities. The particularism thus exposed – that there are no wholly general problems here – reinforces a conception of philosophy on which the concerns that philosophy should address are the philosophical puzzlements of particular individuals: that is, a therapeutic conception of philosophy.

To return to the main thread, it was noted earlier that there is something 'fishy' about spoiling procedures: for, otherwise, only tactical considerations would preclude their being used throughout the game – and this is not so. Might we make some more of this, by asking whether such a procedure is as obviously within the rules of the game as it appears? Here we would be looking at the nature of rules or statutes.

At first sight, this behaviour is certainly permitted by the rules of the sport – in the sense of not being explicitly excluded. But a more radical solution might be considered. In line with some of Dworkin's remarks, we might ask whether the behaviour is actually excluded by the 'real' rules – that is, the rules on their 'best' interpretation, the interpretation that maintains the 'integrity', as Dworkin puts it (1986: 94) of those rules; what he elsewhere calls the *principles* underlying it (typically moral/political principles and, for games at least, concerned with fairness/justice). For Dworkin illustrates how, in legal disputes over the correct decision in a difficult case, the opposing judges are disagreeing about the correct interpretation of the law – over *what the law is* (Nagel 1995: 196). For instance, they might dispute '… how to construct the real statute in the circumstances of that case' (Dworkin 1986: 17). The point, of course, is that if this were also true of the statutes of our game, we might with justice argue that the rules of the game, its *real* rules, do have a bearing here – and find against the legality of spoiling!

As Dworkin says, one is here recognising '… implicit standards between and beneath the explicit ones' (1986: 217). And these standards – enshrined in the *principles* – will typically be moral ones. Preserving *integrity*, in this sense, amounts to 'reading' the rules of the practice so as to show that practice in its best light – thereby preserving its principles – in the light of what has gone before in that practice. Here, as Dworkin (1986: 227) records, 'History matters because ... [the] scheme of principles [appealed to] must justify the standing as well as the content of ... past decisions'. We need such integrity 'all the way up'!

Three points are of interest for us. First, as Nagel (1995: 197) notes, *integrity* in this sense is ' ... an ambiguous virtue', so construing the law and its purposes '... makes decisions flow from a coherent set of principles, even when those principles are not your own'. So, in this idealised version, we have an explanation of consistency requirements as well as a basis for disputes about what counts as consistently interpreting a rule of sport. Second, such a model of integrity fits practices like sport, where the rules (and even some of the principles) have explicit formulation, at least as well (and perhaps better) than it accords with Dworkin's preferred case, municipal legal systems. And this is revealing, since it cannot be far off the truth to say that the *integrity* being preserved is the integrity of the sport itself – and this accords with earlier talk of its *spirit*. Third, we know where to look for the 'interpretative' acts here; namely, to the decisions of umpires and referees, as well as to appeals concerning those decisions. Here, a crucial *difference* is that, in contrast to typical judicial decisions, the decisions of umpires (etc.) will always be required in a fairly brief time span: the players (etc.) cannot wait for ever ... (This just places yet more importance on the umpires as *informed* judges, and hence places yet greater weight on their appropriate training.)

In the context of Aristotle's discussion of rule/case thinking, McDowell (1998: 26–27) considers the possibility that, if one has the rule, that only leaves open questions of 'interpretation'. But, first (as above), one must acquire the rule via cases; second, as Dworkin (1986: 20) illustrates, the general separation between cases and rules is spurious – finding out how to treat *this case* can be finding *what the rule is*.

Dworkin urges that legal rules, as regularly conceived, '... are not themselves programmes *of* interpretation' (1986: 226). As Nagel (1995: 197) notes, this constitutes a *substantive* theory of law; and we could, of course, reject it.[11] But suppose – at least for the sake of today's argument – that we do not. What follows about the rules (the *laws*, as they are often rightly called) of sports?

First, we should have to rephrase our account of spoiling – it would be contrary to the rules on their real interpretation (that is, roughly, with the principles imported), although not on a more conservative or literalist interpretation.

Second, and more important, Dworkin is here offering a different perspective on the fact that any *written* statute requires 'interpretation' (that is, understanding) for its implementation in *this* case. But it invites us to see this as an *essential*, and as a *productive*, feature of such law. We have already noted that – on pain of regress – the applications of rules cannot themselves be a matter of rules. Here we see its weirder sister: that what is and what is not a *real* rule is an *essentially* 'interpretative' process, such that pointing to *the wording* of some statute cannot (typically) decide the matter. And if this were true of the statutes of a legal system (*any* legal system, as a matter of logic), how much more likely that these points apply ('in spades') to the rules of sports?

This, then, addresses two points: first, as others have recognised,[12] one cannot resolve *all* of the moral problems (potentially) occurring in a particular sporting situation by tinkering with the sport's rules; and second, the *pressure* here genuinely is pressure from the *principles* (in Dworkin's sense) that drive those rules – and that is a way of asserting that these genuinely are moral concerns.[13]

A crucial point here is hard to get *exactly* right: on the one hand, there is a sense in which the fact that no rule (or law) can deal with *all* cases must be acknowledged. So one cannot, for instance, resolve *all* difficulties in a particular sport by making new rules for that sport (or new codes of professional ethics, for that matter),[14] rules which deal with every situation unequivocally. Now, one way to make *that* point would be to emphasise the role of judges (say, referees) in *interpreting* rules in real cases. Equally, and on the other hand, we must recognise (as Dworkin does)[15] that what can *look like* the making of law by judges is in fact the kind of judicial discussion that determines *what the law is*; at the least, judges are not *free* to 'make the law' – say, in these 'hard cases'. And one way to articulate this point would be to see judges as *looking for* the law. The difficulty, of course, is that these two images of legal practice (and legal decision) *seem* to run in opposite directions. And what is true of law generally conceived is – by extension – true of the laws of particular sports. Some might say 'So what?' Our reply is that we want (or perhaps need) to say both of these things, on different occasions; that the same form of words can be different questions in different mouths, with each being resolvable, taken case by case – yet without there being some *general* resolution! So there will be some occasions when the revealing answer will point in one direction, and other occasions when it will point in the other. As Gordon Baker and Peter Hacker comment, of a similar difficulty, '… The question is misleading but the facts are clear' (Baker and Hacker 1985: 47n.).

A key question (one *you* may have been asking for some time) is 'Can one spoil in sports other than cricket?' The crucial characteristics of spoiling – as I have characterised spoiling here – might make one doubt this. The spoiling behaviour must be *within* the rules of the sport (so attracting no penalty, nor gaining censure from the governing body) yet contrary to that sport's *spirit*; and this will mean, roughly, contrary to how it *is* played, rather than to how it *might* be. And the activity must give the perpetrators an advantage – at least in that context. I do not know enough about *all* sport to answer with confidence the question of whether it applies elsewhere.[16] Nor can we produce some 'transcendental argument' to determine the matter once and for all. But we progress by, first, considering the *upshot* of spoiling for our view of sport (roughly, the insight it provides) and, second, considering cases which are *not* spoiling.

My suggestion is that spoiling – in illustrating the place of (roughly) *principles* in sport – illuminates some of the ways sport might be thought generally valuable. But that suggestion turns on sport's use as moral laboratory, an idea made concrete through consideration of spoiling but not (of course) limited to it.

Now consider some cases which are *not* spoiling. If I waste time in soccer (say, by kicking the ball away prior to a free kick), I may be penalised; at the least, a competent referee will simply add on the time wasted. So I will have gained nothing. Thus what I do *is* contrary to the rules, and is recognised as such. Therefore this is not spoiling as I have explained it, since this is contrary to the letter of the law. (Still, given that there was no penalty … well, there is *really* no advantage either, if the referee is 'on the ball'.) Correspondingly, a quarterback who 'throws the ball away' to avoid being sacked is not *spoiling*, because his behaviour is *not* censured (by players or officials). But a basketball player who fouls an opponent in the act of shooting is doing something both *expected* of him and (as the rules are 'read' by referees) not contrary to the rules – as the imposition of fixed penalties for this behaviour is taken to illustrate; indeed, to call this *foul* is to use the term 'foul' in a way quite different from its everyday use. For, far from being a behaviour censured, it is behaviour *applauded* (or at least required) within the contemporary playing of the game.

What we learn, then, – if we attend to the contemporary version – is that sport retains the possibility of an engagement with morality (in line with the *moral laboratory* concept); the spoiling cases both show this to us and give us insight into its basis in what, following Dworkin, have been called 'principles' – a moral underpinning not divorced from the contexts of realisation in sports practice.

Notes

1 See Dworkin (1978: 72) for his own comments on the distinction, and its importance. See also Dworkin (1986: 15–20) for a discussion of Elmer.
2 Dworkin is, of course, alive to the number of exceptions which must be recorded for a 'full' statement of this rule.
3 This may be cashed out in terms of *lusory goals* (if it were clear what that expression amounted to). See Suits (1978: 36–37). Notice that the pre-lusory goal is there characterised as '… a specifically achievably state of affairs' (1978: 36); we might see this as a discussion of its achievability!
4 See Wittgenstein (1953: 151, 179).
5 See Dancy for particularism as including the view '… that no set of principles will succeed in generating answers to questons about what to do in particular cases' (1993: 56), but also '… that the moral relevance of a property in a new

case cannot be predicted from its relevance elsewhere' (1993: 57) with 'predicted' the key term. See especially the discussion (and rejection) of switching arguments (1993: 64–66), attempts '… to determine what to say here by appeal to what we say about something else' (1993: 64). Particularism is opposed to *substantial* moral principles, not to moral principles *as such*.

6   A subsequent rule change, arguably as a result of the events described, simply made a different (and more complex) way of spoiling possible.

7   See Baker and Hacker (1980: 76–85).

8   See Cavell (1969: 32).

9   If one thought that the summer Olympics were too large, one might use this as a basis for selecting Olympic sports: those with a role in the moral laboratory are in; the others are out. In this way, some of de Coubertin's commitments might be maintained.

10   See Wittgenstein (1953: §309). I explored this topic in my inaugural lecture, 'A Nasty Accident with One's Flies', University of Brighton, May 1996.

11   See, for instance, 'Postscript' to Hart (1994: 238–276).

12   See, for instance, McNamee (1995: 166–167).

13   For what sports can there be spoiling? Certainly not all … for it requires conflict between letter and spirit of the sport's law. (Does basketball lack such a spirit? Or consider chess, a sport in Cuba – we do not need face-to-face contact *at all*, so is there no necessary *moral* contact?)

14   See McNamee (1995).

15   In both Dworkin (1978) and Dworkin (1986); see McDowell (1998: 62, especially n.).

16   One might think of 'walking' a batter in baseball as akin to (or as quasi-) spoiling. As Haugeland (1998: 162n.) explains: 'Generally, the opposing pitcher would try to avoid giving a batter a free "balls on base" (also called a "walk"); but in certain threatening situations, especially when the current batter is on a "hot streak", then that batter is "walked" intentionally'.

Part V

The scientific manufacture of winners

Chapter 13

A philosophical overview of the arguments on banning doping in sport

Angela J. Schneider and Robert B. Butcher

A great deal of time, energy and money is spent on enforcing bans on doping in sport. There is, however, growing evidence that enforcement of bans is not only doomed to failure, but also somehow misses the point. The argument is that we need education programmes that would show how doping is antithetical to sport; why it is that doping does not fit sport and thus prevent its occurrence rather than punish offenders.

For this educational task to be successful there have to be demonstrable and sound reasons for banning doping and then enforcing those bans. This chapter includes a critical review of the justifications currently available for banning doping, and proposes why athletes and the broader community should support doping-free sport.

All banned substances and practices are first identified by the International Olympic Committee (IOC), the rest of the world then follows suit. What the IOC has in its Doping Charter is a list, of substances and practices that are banned from the Olympic Games. The use of the substances and practices on the banned list is referred to as 'doping'. What the IOC lacks is a clearly stated ethical framework that could justify the banning of the items on the list by showing them to be relevantly different from other, permitted, substances and practices.

Though the IOC does not present a cogently argued philosophical justification for its banned list, it does refer to some general reasons:

> A   Considering that the use of doping agents in sport is both unhealthy and contrary to the ethics of sport, and that it is necessary to protect the physical and spiritual health of athletes, the values of fair play and of competition, the integrity and unity of sport, and the rights of those who take part in it at whatever level ...

Thus, protection from harm (both physical and through the violation of rights), together with defence of fair play and the integrity of sport, are the three underlying justifications in this passage. In addition the IOC refers to its role in the larger, social 'war' against drugs (it sees doping in sport as a symptom of a larger problem of social drug use), and to supporting athletes' calls for more stringent doping controls and sanctions. However, as they stand these do not constitute reasons or justifications for banning doping.

Each of the reasons listed in the IOC preamble can be found in more fully developed forms in the literature of the 'philosophy of sport'. The reasons can also be expanded into arguments to attempt to justify bans in more than one way. Those arguments can then be categorised on the basis of the type of appeal they make. We thus have arguments from cheating and unfair advantage, from harm, from the idea that doping perverts the nature of sport and from the contention that doping is dehumanising. We will look at each of these categories in turn. We will finish by looking at what we call an 'athlete-driven' model of testing, and by sketching the outline of a view of the intrinsic goods of sport, which we believe can (when taken together) form the basis for a potential coherent and enforceable ban on doping in sport.

The inadequacy of current arguments to support bans

There are four clusters of arguments generally proposed to justify banning drugs in sport. All of them have some merit. As they stand, however, none of them provides a sufficient justification for banning doping.

Cheating and unfairness

This apparent argument merely forms a neat circle – doping is banned because it is cheating, and it is cheating because banned.

This argument was used by Justice Charles Dubin in the Canadian Royal Commission established by the Canadian Federal Government after the Ben Johnson scandal in Seoul 1988. The written summary of this Dubin Inquiry, called the *Dubin Report*, and the Federal Government of Canada, through the policies of Fitness and Amateur Sport, all used this argument. The first sentence of Section 23 in the *Dubin Report*, the section on 'Rights and Ethical Considerations', tells us that the most vigorous opponents of cheating in sport are those who insist that it must be conducted in accordance with the rules. The rest of the section goes on to denounce cheating. Our moral disapprobation of doping is thus seen as coming from the fact that doping is cheating. Defenders of this argument claim that doping should be banned because it is cheating, relying on the unstated premises that all cheating is wrong and wrong things should be banned. Upon closer examination it is clear that some forms of this argument, such as the one Dubin uses above, are only a purported justification, for they beg the question. The major problem with this position is that an activity only becomes cheating once there is a rule prohibiting it. So, while the fact that doping is cheating may well provide a reason for enforcing the rules against doping, and while the fact that doping is cheating may well give other athletes a reason for having an extremely negative attitude towards those who dope, there is not yet a clearly argued reason for creating the rule banning doping in the first place.

But there may be alternative interpretations of this argument. One suggestion is that there is something in the concept of 'cheating', which captures a notion of 'unfair advantage,' that, if properly understood, would enable us to see that the use of certain substances and practices fall into this category, whereas others do not. Clearly, for this type of move to work, the notion of 'unfair advantage' must be independent of the rules of sport in the way that our first formulation was not. That is, if 'unfair advantage' turns out to be just rule-breaking, then it cannot do the work that the concept of 'cheating as rule-breaking' could not do. This raises a variety of philosophically interesting questions: What is cheating? Why is cheating wrong?, and independent of the answer to these questions, Why should doping be banned? For the purpose of this chapter – namely, the search for a philosophically acceptable justification for a ban on doping – it will not do to say simply that one should not dope because it is banned. What is significant is the justification for banning it in the first place. But this is not as clear as it might be because of the difficulty in understanding the notion of cheating.

Similarly for the argument of unfairness. The simplest idea of fairness is one connected to adherence to the rules – an action is unfair if it is against the rules. This position suffers the same fate as that above. An alternative notion of fairness that is independent of the rules of sport has been postulated. But this notion would have to show how doping was somehow inherently unfair, even if the contestants agreed to do it and even if the rules of the game permitted it. It is not clear how an argument like this could succeed. We have not seen, nor do we think there is available, concepts of cheating or unfair advantage, grounded outside of sport, that could be used to show that doping ought to be banned.[1]

Harm

The second most commonly cited category of arguments used to justify the bans on doping are those from harm. In this section we will look at four types of arguments from harm: harm to users, harm to other clean athletes, harm to society, and harm to the sports community. We will also look at harm *caused* by the bans. It should be pointed out that the arguments from harm cannot be expected to provide a general justification for prohibiting doping. If the argument from harm works, it works sport by sport and practice, or drug, by practice.

Harm to athletes who dope (the users)

The argument from harm to the user, in its simplest form, looks like this:

Premise 1	Substance or practice X harms its user
Premise 2	Its user needs to be protected
Premise 3	The user can be protected by banning the substance
Conclusion	Therefore the substance should be banned.

If we consider, for example, this general argument in respect of adult rational athletes and the particular substance, anabolic steroids, we can examine it in three quite different ways.

The assertion that steroid use harms the user is, as yet, scientifically unproven. At best the medical evidence is mixed. Much of the evidence concerning harm is derived from anecdotal testimony of athletes using very high doses in uncontrolled conditions. On the other hand, the hard medical evidence from controlled low-dose studies tends to show minimal harm (Dubin 1990). Our society's abhorrence of the practice has prevented the gathering of hard, scientifically validated, evidence because such research has yet to pass ethics committees. For Premise 1 of the argument to work, we would require far better data than is currently available. There are two elements to the harm charge: bad effects and the causal linkage of these to doping. Currently it has not been scientifically proven just what bad effects there are from doping. This doubt about the truth of the first premise is, however, insufficient for us to dismiss the argument. So let us grant, for the sake of argument, that steroids do indeed harm their users, because it is not implausible. There are, however, other performance-enhancing substances for which this assumption would be implausible, e.g. over-the-counter cold remedies. This argument from harm cannot, therefore, be used as a general argument against doping. Thus, we must deal with each substance separately.

Premise 2 fails for different reasons. The desire to protect some other 'competent' adult from the consequences of his or her own actions is paternalistic. The basic notion is that individuals are deemed to be competent to make their own decisions unless they are minors or are demonstrated to be 'incompetent' from a medical/legal perspective. Banning doping, in the present context, would be a form of paternalism if it was done in order to protect the athlete. Paternalism has acceptable and unacceptable forms. For example, some argue that banning doping for minors is acceptable and banning doping for adults is unacceptable. However, there are cases in society where we ban practices for adults, and view ourselves as justified in doing so (in Canada, for example, we ban driving without seat belts). The question that must be addressed is: Is banning steroids and other substances and practices an example of acceptable paternalism?

Paternalism is acting on behalf, and in the best interests, of another. Although 'paternalism' now has negative connotations, not all examples of paternalism are bad. For instance, acting on behalf of a minor, or on behalf of someone not competent to make a decision, is paternalistic, but not morally wrong. Acting on behalf of an adult who is competent to make a decision is rather different. At least since Mill, those in the liberal tradition have accepted that actions on behalf of a competent adult, in that person's presumed best interests, are unwarranted intrusions into that person's liberty. Feinberg calls these two types of paternalism 'soft' and 'hard' respectively. Justifying hard paternalism is difficult, although clearly not impossible, as we can see from the evidence of seat-belt and motorcycle helmet legislation. In this study we have concentrated on the case of adult, competent athletes. We accept that quite different problems are raised in the case of children. We are also assuming that the notion of 'competent' is uncontroversial. To address that issue would require a separate book entirely.

Generally we foster and value independence and the right to make the important choices that affect one's own life. We value autonomy.[2] Much of the thrust of modern North American medical ethics has been directed precisely against medical paternalism. It may be argued that to ban steroids solely to protect their adult competent users is to treat those athletes as children unable to make the choices that most affect them. As Miller Brown points out in all of his writings on this topic, this position is generally inconsistent with the limit-pushing nature of high-performance sport. The question to be asked is: Why the inviolable boundary of doping? This question will be covered in more detail in later sections on the perversion of sport (see pages 195–196) and the dehumanisation and unnaturalness arguments (see page 196).

Premise 2 is unsuccessful for other reasons too. It is inconsistent at the least, and maybe even hypocritical, for sport governing bodies to attempt to justify a ban by appealing to the athlete's well-being. There are many training practices, and indeed many sports, that carry a far greater likelihood of harm to the athlete than does the controlled use of steroids. If the reason for banning doping in sport really were a concern for the health and well-being of athletes, there would be many sports and many more practices that should be banned. So, at the very least, it seems inconsistent to argue in favour of the bans on doping and not the myriad other practices which are also harmful to the athletes.

One might try to argue that risks that are incurred by the nature of the sport, such as brain damage from having one's head pummelled in boxing, are different from risks that are incurred from practices that have nothing to do with competition in the sport *per se* – liver damage from steroid use, for example. The basis of this argument might be tied to MacIntyre's internal/external goods distinction, where internal goods are gained from participation in the activity itself for intrinsic reasons (skill, strategy, etc.) and external goods are gained from societal recognition of success in the specific sport (fame, prestige, money, etc.). The only way one can gain the internal goods of the sport is to take the risk involved when competing. We will see more on this issue in later sections, but for now this distinction won't work if the justification for the ban is harm and harm operates on sport from the outside, because the athlete is harmed in either case; that is to say, both brain damage and liver damage are harmful.

Finally the third premise fails because there is no evidence to suggest that banning steroids really will protect athletes. All the time that a subculture exists that indicates that steroid use brings benefits and that it is an occupational hazard of high-level competitive sport, athletes will continue to use them in clandestine, unsanitary and uncontrolled ways. This is not just a matter of better enforcement of the ban but, rather, it requires a change in values, and this will only happen after a logically consistent position for the ban has been put forward and the subculture in some Olympic sports changes.[3] Presumably the ban would be intended as part of a larger process aimed at producing just such a change in values.

Taken singly, the counterarguments motivated by our antipathy to paternalism and the inconsistency of a ban predicated upon the desire to protect athletes, are sufficient to show that the first argument from harm does not work. Our rejection of the argument is strengthened by the lack of unequivocal scientific evidence for harm and the contention that athletes are probably not benefited by a ban anyway. The justification for *banning* steroids, based on protecting 'competent' and consenting adult users from harm, stands in need of considerable strengthening.[4]

Thus, the particular argument from harm that suggests that doping should be banned to protect the athletes who dope is, as it stands, paternalistic, inconsistent and incomplete. It is paternalistic because we do not generally permit the intrusion into the lives of competent adults in order to protect those people from harms they may inflict on themselves. It is inconsistent because sport, in particular elite-level sport, is (necessarily) an extremely hazardous enterprise. It is not clear why adult competent athletes should be protected from the harm that might come from doping when we do not see fit to protect them from the harms of the sports they practice and the overtraining they endure. The argument is incomplete because the evidence of harm for the practices currently considered as doping is mixed at best. While steroids in high doses may cause adverse side effects, steroids in relatively low doses seem not to. Autologous blood-doping has not been shown to have adverse side effects at all.

Harm to other (clean) athletes

The second form of the argument from harm is based not on the harm that the steroids cause to their users, but on the harm their use causes to other athletes. The 'others' in this argument are usually deemed to be other 'clean' athletes ('clean' simply means non-doped). Sometimes this argument is called the 'coercion' argument and it is more difficult to dismiss quickly. The same liberal tradition that prohibits paternalistic intervention permits interventions designed to prevent harm to others. The crucial questions will concern how great the harm is to other athletes and how severe the limitation on personal action. The argument runs like this:

Premise 1	An athlete's use of substance X causes harm to 'clean' athletes
Premise 2	Those people need protection
Premise 3	Banning substance X will protect those people
Conclusion	Therefore substance X should be banned.

In order to assess this argument we need to consider whether or not the potential coercion of clean athletes outweighs the infringement on the liberties of all athletes caused when a substance or practice is banned. Clean athletes are harmed, so the argument goes, because the dopers 'up the ante'. If some competitors are using steroids, then all competitors who wish to compete at that level will need to take steroids or other substances to keep up. The argument here is that drug use is coercive. Because doping may improve results, there is coercive pressure placed on those who wish to compete without drugs. If there are drug-users, then non-drug-users are forced to dope to keep up. This argument has some merits, but is still incomplete, because elite-level sport is already highly coercive. If full-time training, or altitude training, or diet control, are shown to produce better results, then everyone is forced to adopt those measures to keep up. It is unclear why doping is any more coercive, and sufficiently so to warrant being banned than, say, full-time training. The feeling that somehow steroid use is worse than longer and ever more specialised training just raises the question of why it is worse. Some may argue that the question really is, Why can't an athlete accept two 'raises of the ante' but not accept a third, or an unlimited number? The answer to this question relies on a demand for consistency. There must be some reason why this, rather than that, practice is the one that is banned, and that reason cannot be merely that it was the third or the nth raise of the ante. This is a qualitative question, not a quantitative one, that necessarily requires an explanation for the rejection of the third raise of the ante, when there has been no rejection of the first two. It may be argued that the answer could be simply that two is acceptable but three is too many. But then we must ask which two, and the answer will inevitably appeal to a qualitative distinction. (We will look at the special attention given to steroids below, because there may be an implicit belief that they affect our humanness in some especially negative way.)

On the other hand, the coercion argument has merit if it can be shown how doping is irrelevant to a particular view of what is important to sport.

If sport, and sporting excellence and sporting contests, is about testing skills, then it can be argued that the improved performance that comes with doping is irrelevant to that test of skill. (Especially when one bears in mind that if some athletes dope, others will be forced to dope in order to keep up, thus obviating the original advantage that came with doping.) If doping is irrelevant to sport, then athletes can shun it as being unnecessarily coercive, as compared to, for example, extended training, which may improve one's skill at the contest at hand.

Harm to society

This position says that doping harms others in society, especially children, who see athletes as role models. This argument works in two ways. The first is that if children see athletes having no respect for the rules of the games they play there will be a tendency to undermine respect for rules, and law, in general. This argument only works if doping is against the rules and so cannot function as a justification for banning doping in the first place. The second part of the argument sees athletic drug use as part of a wider social problem of drug use. The argument here is that if children see athletes using drugs to attain sporting success, then other drugs may also be seen as a viable means to other ends. The limitation of this argument is that there are many things that we consider appropriate for adults but not for children. Alcohol and cigarettes are obvious examples, as indeed is sex, but, in North America at least, we don't ban these substances or activities for adults because they would be bad for children.

A further response to the suggestion that athletes should be role models, and in particular 'moral' role models, is to ask just why that should be so. We currently expect widely varying things of our public figures. No one seriously expects musicians or actors and actresses to be moral role models, so why should athletes be singled out for special treatment? There is appar- ently quite widespread use of beta-blockers by concert musicians, yet there has not been the hue and cry and media circus that followed the revelations of drug use by athletes (Wolfe 1989). Why do we expect more from athletes than from other public figures?

Some philosophers (Weiss 1969) have argued that sport is one of the very first areas young people experience and in which they hope to gain excel- lence, and these excellences are exemplified by their sports heroes and heroines. (We will look at the concept of sporting excellence in more detail below.) From a societal perspective if this hero or heroine is morally despi- cable, this will be a negative influence, because young people will not separate the athletic abilities of their heroes or heroines from the quality of their personal lives, especially when fame and glamour surround that person. Weiss also points out that the achievement of excellence in athletics is prior to, and will influence greatly, the achievement of excellence in adult arenas such as business, academia and politics. Perhaps for these reasons we are more concerned about the moral image of athletes than other public figures.

First, what is not clear is why drug-assisted performance or excellence is negatively perceived (assuming we can put cheating aside for the moment until we establish a justification for the proscription on doping). Fashion models are not less beautiful (if they are beautiful at all) if they have used diuretics or 'uppers' to lose their weight. Weiss's point is well taken, but what is it about drug use in sport that we find morally repugnant? For example, no one else is prevented from using cold remedies, even if they drive public transport, or from using caffeine as a stimulant to work harder. So it is not even the case that we want athletes to meet the standards every one else meets, but rather (with regard to substance use) we want them to meet more rigorous standards.

It is sufficient to say at this point, as Simon (1995) has clearly stated, that until a clear and cogent reason is put forward to justify treating athletes differently from other public figures, and until a causal link between their actions and harm to others has been demonstrated, we do not have a justification for the ban based on this argument.

Harm to the sports community

One other group that is potentially harmed is the sports-watching public. These people have been harmed because they have been cheated. They expected to see dope-free athletes battling it out in fair competition and they were denied this entertainment. This harm can be removed in other ways than through banning steroid use. One could remove the expectation that athletes are dope-free. If you do not expect them to be dope-free you cannot be harmed if they are not. The feeling of being cheated is dependent *on* the idea that what was expected was a particular type of competition. But this response may be too quick. If what spectators want is doping-free competition, then their desire is not met by warning them that what they want is not to be found at the Olympics. At best, it is simply proposed (if not required) that they settle for less than what they really want. If they do not expect athletes to be doping-free then indeed they do not suffer the harm of deception if they are not. But they might suffer other harms; for example, loss of the chance to watch doping-free competition. The question we need to answer is: Why do they value doping-free competition? We will look for an answer to this and other unresolved questions in later sections.

We have now examined the main variants of the harm argument. None has been found convincing. Of course, there are other possible candidates who could putatively be harmed by athletes who dope. It is doubtful that there will be any candidates who could be harmed sufficiently to outweigh the harm *caused* by banning and testing for drugs and/or other potential performance- or training-enhancing substances.

Harm caused by bans

So far we have looked at reasons for bans based on the harm caused by the banned substances. Unfortunately, because we need to enforce the bans we create there are also harms caused by the bans themselves. Enforcement of bans on substances or practices designed to help one train, rather than improve one's performance on the day of competition, requires year-round random, unannounced, out-of-competition testing. This testing requirement is an extreme intrusion into the private lives of athletes. Thus athletes are harmed by being required to consent to such testing procedures in order to be eligible for competition.

One aspect of the harm caused by bans is abstract. Any time one's choices are restricted one has been harmed; as, for example, the athlete is harmed when deprived of the chance to dope in order to improve performance. On the other hand, the *spectator* is harmed when deprived of the chance to watch doping-free sport. There is, however, a more direct harm. If one bans drugs or practices one must necessarily take steps to enforce that ban. It has become apparent to those involved with doping control that, despite the number of positive tests during a competition, the only effective way to test for banned substances is to introduce random, unannounced out-of-competition-testing. This is because some substances, for instance anabolic steroids, can be discontinued before competition and still retain their effects. Also the use of masking agents and the method of urine substitution with catheters all serve to subvert. The demand that athletes be prepared to submit to urine (or blood) testing at any time is a serious breach of their civil and human rights. That sort of intrusive intervention in people's lives can only be warranted by the need to protect others from serious harm. None of the current candidates come anywhere near demonstrating the depth of harm required to warrant such extreme interference with personal liberty. It could be argued that such interference is just part of the price of being in sports. No one is forced to become an athlete, let alone an elite athlete.

Many who discuss this topic (for example, the Canadian government, Justice Dubin, Sport Canada) suggest that 'sport is different'. They try to argue that, because of this difference, the limitations imposed by the requirements of consent do not apply. The suggestion is that participation in 'high-performance' sport is a privilege, not a right. In chapter 24 of the *Dubin Report*, on athletes' rights, in which an Olympian athlete and Dubin claim that participation in sport is a privilege not a right, it is argued that the imposition of otherwise unjustifiable conditions is acceptable as a precondition of participation in sport (Dubin 1990: 490–491). The argument runs like this: athletes are not deprived of their rights if they are deemed ineligible because they will not submit to a drug test, because they do not have a right to participate in the first place. The serious consequence of this argument is that it would allow the imposition of any rules no matter how absurd, for it says that the authorities may impose whatever rules they like, but would not have to *justify* such rules.

Further, this argument is unclear. It may mean that no person has the right to be selected for a national team or for government financial support. This is certainly true, but it is also true that there is some obligation to select the best available people for national teams and, barring income tests, for financial support too. It could then be argued that the 'best available person' means the best person available, who abides by the rules of the game, one of which is the requirement that athletes consent to random, unannounced, out-of-competition testing. However, the rules of sport are not arbitrary and they are open to moral scrutiny. Just as a rule of eligibility that barred people on the basis of race would be objected to on moral grounds, other rules of eligibility for sport are open to similar moral assessment. If, therefore, the format of the drug test is unacceptable on the moral ground that it invades privacy, it would be unacceptable for there to be a rule of eligibility that required it. Sport may well be different, but nothing is so special or different that it can escape all moral scrutiny from the outside.

One question that needs to be addressed is, Why is sport different? It may be suggested that people think it is different because it is not 'real' life, it is only a game, so it is trivial. In order to address this question, a brief review of the nature of sport is in order. In the next section, on the perversions of sport, we will attempt to determine if there are any grounds for banning doping that come from the nature of sport; that is, from an 'inside-out' perspective.

It is worth pointing out that the first two argument categories have been morally significant; the concepts of cheating and unfairness and harm are moral ones. In the case of cheating and unfairness we saw that the two concepts, when used in sport, presupposed a set of rules for any sport, so logically the concepts could not be used to justify a rule. The concepts of cheating and unfairness we are concerned about *are* 'inside' sport. By contrast, the argument from harm utilised a principle found outside of sport and sought to apply it to sport, working from the 'outside-in'. The next set of arguments, those that talk of the perversion of sport, no longer operate from moral principles, but rather are metaphysical. What the arguments seek to show is that there is some feature of sport which, if properly understood, would be demonstrably incompatible with doping.

Perversion of sport

According to this view doping should be banned because it is somehow antithetical to the true nature of sport. This view requires an account of sport that shows why doping is incompatible with it.

Naturally enough, the prelude to an argument that works from the nature of sport to the conclusion that doping is incompatible with it is an attempt to define the nature of sport. Unfortunately this is not as straightforward as one might hope and is well beyond the scope of this chapter. However, we have argued elsewhere that there is not (as yet) a plausible account of sport available to demonstrate its incompatibility with doping (Butcher and Schneider 1993). Part of the problem one faces when dealing with this question is that sport is socially constructed and there is no obvious reason why it could not be constructed to include doping. We have argued that a view of sport that places at its centre the testing of sporting skills, with sporting skills defined by the nature of the game concerned, will allow us to see why doping is not necessarily antithetical to sport, but rather irrelevant to it (Schneider and Butcher 1994). We argued that doping is irrelevant to sport because it does not improve skill but merely provides a competitive advantage over those who do not dope. But a prerequisite for this justification to begin to fly is that it must come from the athletes themselves, not from sport administrators.

Unnaturalness and dehumanisation

Here the argument is that doping should be banned because it is either unnatural or dehumanising. The unnaturalness argument does not get very far for two reasons. The first is that we do not have a good account of what would count as 'unnatural' and the second is that we are inconsistent. For any account of 'natural' and 'unnatural', some things designated unnatural would be permitted (spiked shoes, for example), while other natural ones (such as testosterone) are on the banned list.

The dehumanisation argument is interesting but incomplete. It is incomplete because we do not have an agreed-upon conception of what it is to be human. Without this it is difficult to see why some practices should count as dehumanising. We also have a problem with consistency. Some practices, such as 'psycho-doping', the mental manipulation of athletes using the techniques of operant conditioning, are not banned, whereas the re-injection of one's own blood is. We attempt, below, to provide some sort of framework that will give us an idea of human excellence. This will permit us to see how the pursuit of athletic excellence can, and should, be limited in ways that exclude doping from the pursuit of sport.

The way ahead

Our proposal is a two-tiered approach for showing why doping can be justifiably prohibited in sport:

Why athletes should not want to dope

The joy of sport

Sports are practices, practices that provide the opportunity to acquire and demonstrate skills. Each sport creates what counts as skill in that sport. So, for instance, a well-executed backhand volley that passes your opponent on his or her approach to the net is a demonstration of skill because of the kinds of things that are necessary to win at tennis. The shot is difficult, and effective, and it is just this sort of manifestation of skill that makes participating in sport so worthwhile. The joy of sport comes from acquiring the goods that are internal to sport, the goods that come with the mastery and demonstration of skill. If this joy is the primary reason for participation in sport, we can see how doping is irrelevant to the internal goods of sport.

The irrelevance of doping

Every sport is a sort of game, a game where obstacles have been artificially created to prevent one from readily achieving the object of the game. Skill is demonstrated in the overcoming of those obstacles, within the limits provided by the rules of the game. We can thus see the irrelevance of doping. What makes sport interesting and worthwhile is the mastery of skill and its demonstration in a fair contest with equally skilled opponents. Doping does not help one to acquire sporting skills, but simply provides a competitive advantage over those who do not dope.

Athletic prudence and the avoidance of unnecessary risk

If doping is irrelevant to sport, if it does not enhance one's skill, it is easy to see why athletes would prudently choose to avoid it. Even if the risks are minimal, or even if the probabilities of harm are small, provided one's competitors do not dope there is no reason for any athlete to dope. Because there is no game-productive reason for doping, athletes would be wise to avoid it as an unnecessary risk.

The self-defeating nature of doping

The coercive effect of doping is that if athletes believe that a good number of their opponents dope, they also will feel compelled to dope in order to keep up. But this has the effect of removing the competitive advantage that those who first doped sought, originally, to gain. Doping is only an advantage, in terms of 'winning', if you dope and your opponent does not. That advantage is lost if everyone dopes.

These four arguments show why athletes should want to choose not to dope. They also point the way to a method of avoiding the invasion of privacy caused by the enforcement of bans. If athletes want doping-free sport, as we have argued they should, they will also want to be assured that the competition is fair, that they are not being taken advantage of by cheats. Athletes, then, would be in the position to request the enforcement of the rules of self-limitation that they themselves have rationally and prudently chosen. We thus have a recipe for athlete-driven testing, a proposal quite different from the top-down imposition of bans we have traditionally seen.

Why the community should support doping-free sport

Given that doping is irrelevant to sport we should support doping-free sport on the basis that we can avoid unnecessary risks to athletes who do not wish to dope. Because doping does not enhance the acquisition of the internal goods of sport, we can prevent the coercive effects of doping by banning it.

The community is in a position to defend a view of human excellence that can put limits on the pursuit of performance excellence in sport. Given that in many countries amateur sport is publicly funded, the community can promote a view of sporting excellence that places it within the context of a complete, and excellent, human life. So, despite the fact that excellence in downhill skiing may require running dreadful risks, the community is in a position to limit those risks because it does not want to promote downhill speed over long and healthy lives. The message from those who support sport should be that an athlete's sporting life is only a part of his or her entire life. While excellence in sport is worthily pursued, it should not be pursued at the expense of one's later health and well-being. Because amateur sport is publicly funded, the community is in a position to put limits on its support; limits that come from the desire to promote human excellence across a complete lifetime.

Conclusion

None of the arguments, taken individually as they are currently presented, are sufficient to provide a moral justification for banning drugs in sport. The intrusion into personal privacy that is required for adequate enforcement of bans creates a high ethical hurdle that any proposed justification has to overcome. In addition there are practical problems in enforcing bans that appear to come as the result of rules imposed on athletes from the outside. But this certainly does not mean that the attempt to remove doping from sport should be abandoned.

From an athletes' rights perspective, our proposal is for a contractarian justification for banning doping. We have argued that athletes themselves – if asked – would voluntarily agree to limit their own behaviour, provided

that adequate assurance could be provided that others will do the same. This proposal, however, is subject to three important limitations.

First, it could turn out that athletes would not agree to limit their own behaviour. The preliminary evidence, however, supports the view that athletes do wish to ban doping. For instance, the athletes attending the IOC conference on doping in February 1999 themselves demanded the harshest penalties for those who betray their trust and are caught doping. However, the real work of athlete consultation is yet to be done.

Second, the list of doping infractions would certainly need to be revised. It is prudent for athletes to seek to ban drugs that enhance performance and run the risk of causing harm. However, there is no good reason to ban drugs that do not enhance performance or which do not bring any appreciable risk of harm. The Ross Rebagliati case in the Nagano Olympics in 1998 is instructive here. Rebagliati had his gold medal removed for testing positive for marijuana. It was then reinstated on appeal, for there is no evidence that marijuana enhances snowboarding performance, so testing for its presence is therefore an unjustifiable intrusion into an athlete's personal freedom.

Finally, the agreement could founder on the difficulties of enforcement and assurance. Without random, no-notice, out-of-competition testing, the drugs that enhance training rather than stimulate performance on the day of competition will never be detected. No prudent athlete would consent to limit his or her own access to doping without reliable assurances that others were doing the same.

But without genuine athlete agreement and support, we believe the current efforts to prohibit doping are doomed to go the way of the fight against amateurism. The crucial difference is that banning doping is demonstrably in the interests of the athletes themselves. The task, therefore, is to gather agreement and support from those to whom the rules will apply.

Notes

1   The notion of cheating does have a life outside of sport. We speak, for instance, of cheating on one's partner or one's income tax. The idea here is that one has broken an agreement, and done so deceptively. But, as we saw above, the agreement that is broken in sport is based on the rules (formal or informal) of that sport.
2   Once again, as with the issue of competence, we will not be discussing all of the philosophical problems with definitions of the concept of autonomy, due to the breadth of the discussion on the topic.
3   Some sociologists of sport propose the concept of positive deviance as an account of this type of behaviour. See Hughes and Cloakley (1991).
4   It should be pointed out that the harm argument needs to be applied separately to each substance or practice. So, while it may not work for steroids, it may work for other practices and substances.

Chapter 14

What's wrong with doping?

Claudio M. Tamburrini

What is doping?

Professionalism and widespread sponsorship brought about for athletes the prospect of getting considerable rewards for their efforts. This, no doubt, puts them under great temptations. Illicit short cuts to victory, though obviously not providing excellence in a sport discipline, might nonetheless secure economic benefits as well as fame and respect, at least as long as the unfair strategy for victory is not uncovered.

Doping is one of those short cuts. To many people, this indicates that the current development that elite sport is undergoing is unsound.

But, what is doping? The term is used to cover different things, with varying effects on the individual's health. When discussing forbidden performance-enhancing methods, it is useful to make the distinction between doping substances and doping techniques.

Among the former group (doping substances) we have those that are:

1 *harmful though legal*, when prescribed by a physician. Within this group, we find anabolic steroids, growth hormones, beta-blockers, ephedrine, stimulants of the central nervous system such as amphetamines, etc. At present, there is no doubt that prolonged and uncontrolled (that is, without medical supervision) use of these substances yields serious health damages. However, the state of our knowledge concerning the effects of their short-term and properly dosed administration is still deficient.

2 *harmful and strictly illegal* (for instance, central stimulants such as cocaine).[1]

3 both *harmless and legal*, such as diuretics and caffeine. These substances are generally used and there are practically no restrictions on their use, other than those imposed on athletes by the International Olympic Committee (IOC).

Among banned performance-enhancing techniques, perhaps the most known is blood-doping. It consists in the withdrawal, storing and re-injection of the athlete's own blood to increase oxygen intake. Although the method – when properly administered – involves no known health risks, it is proscribed by some world sport associations. A similar effect is obtained by altitude training. This latter method, however, is not forbidden by doping regulations.

Now, before this discussion on doping takes off, it could be asked why we need to scrutinise the rationale behind doping bans. Isn't the use of performance-enhancing techniques obviously wrong? In spite of this widespread intuition, actually there are some arguments that support lifting current bans.

First, the prohibition on doping puts arbitrary restraints on the further development of sports. Athletes are thus impeded from perfecting the skills specific to their discipline.

Furthermore, the ban is responsible for our present lack of knowledge on the eventual harmful effects of doping. This is highly relevant, as doping, in spite of the ban, occurs and will continue to occur. Lifting the prohibition would then allow us to conduct research aimed at reducing harm provoked by actual unsupervised doping use.

Finally, doping also deprives professional elite sport from the transparency it so badly needs at present. We know for sure that Ben Johnson and Diego Maradona doped. But we can only suspect that the late Florence Griffith-Joyner also did it. Who hasn't sometimes felt that his admiration for a sport hero was darkened by the doubt whether the victor really was 'clean'? In elite sports, we may have arrived at a situation in which we often celebrate not the most excellent, but the most sly athlete, the one who dopes and gets away with it. The significance of this lack of transparency for the educational role of sports cannot be exaggerated.

In spite of all these reasons, the ban on doping apparently has wide support among athletes, sport officials and the public. It thus seems reasonable to ask, What's wrong with doping?

Different reasons are advanced to support the ban. A first reason is that doping is damaging for athletes' health. Objectors to doping argue, then, that the ban should be maintained in order to protect sports practitioners from getting harmed by their own free decisions.

A second argument states that the ban on doping is required to prevent noxious effects on society at large. With free doping, the objection runs, performance-enhancing methods will yield great social harm, as they will be adopted by a vast number of amateur and young sports practitioners.

Doping can also be opposed to on grounds of fairness, and could be said to be unfair because it grants competitive advantages to some athletes but not to others. The latter are thereby unfairly deprived of control over their competitive chances.

Sport essentialism lies at the basis of the fourth reason against doping. This objection is two-edged. First, the present argument rests on a widely accepted ideal of sport competition, according to which competitors should be ranked on no other grounds than their natural and (for the sport discipline in which they compete) relevant inequalities. Doping is then said to run counter to this competitive ideal, as it makes the outcome of the contest depend on artificial and irrelevant factors. This position is often summarised in the slogan, 'Sports should be clean!' Second, being a contest between persons, as different from technical products, it is argued that sport contains an element of uncertainty, which explains the excitement it evokes in the audience. The introduction of different doping techniques, however, might be expected to increase predictability in competitive outcomes, thereby weakening the fascination sport exerts over most of us.

In what follows, I will scrutinise these arguments as part of my strategy to support the claim that the ban on doping is not justified and should therefore be lifted.

Doping is harmful to athletes

Now, even if the present objection were tenable, why should we care? After all, we generally accept risks involved in different sport practices. Too intensive training causes physical injuries, and the lethal figures for certain sports (for instance, climbing and boxing) are clearly higher than the number of doping victims.

Against this, it could be argued that those risks are essential to the sports in question: you cannot climb a mountain without pending in the air, or boxing without being hit by your opponent. But, even if essential, these risks might be reduced. However we define the internal goals of these disciplines, there is no need to climb extremely risky peaks or to box without head protection. Those risks are simply unnecessary for developing the specific skills of the sport, or for experiencing the joy of participation.

Of course, it could be contended that climbers and boxers will then be less motivated to engage in their sports. But that simply means that they would not like what they do as much as they like it at present. Well, it is clear that at least some athletes literally get a kick out of doping. Why shouldn't these athletes be allowed to do what they like, then?

As commonly stated, the present objection to free doping is paternalistic: the ban on doping is justified in order to secure the wellbeing of sport practitioners. Thus, sportsmen are impeded from practising their activity, in the way they judge more appropriate. Professional athletes are not allowed to decide for themselves what risks they are disposed to confront in the pursuit of their careers.

We do not do this in any other profession, and in that sense the ban on doping is unique. All prohibitions imposed on professional activities aim, directly or indirectly, to protect persons other than the practitioners themselves.

To this it might be objected that this is not true of safety working regulations, which are compulsory and intended to prevent workers from getting injured. Are they not paternalistic also, then? In a sense they are, for workers are compelled to wear helmets in their own best interest. But this is not why safety regulations are relevant here. If there were none, employers could coerce workers not to wear helmets; in fact, they might even make it a condition for employment, in order to reduce costs. Safety working regulations aim to prevent this unfair coercion. So their ultimate rationale is not protecting workers from their own decisions, but rather protecting them from being compelled by others (employers) to take risks they don't want to take. This justification is totally in line with the anti-paternalistic principle.

Prohibitionists may argue that doping is different, since the sacrifices usually related to career commitments do not constitute risks of the magnitude that doping does. To spoil one's health, they would claim, is a sacrifice of quite another dignity than working overtime.

This observation is not well taken. There are also damaging consequences attached to career commitments. People get stomach ulcers and heart attacks because they work too hard, or they ruin their family life as a consequence of exaggerated professional ambitions. Which is worse: to lack an enriching social life, or to suffer a kidney malfunction? Is it worse for a child to have a parent suffering of a doping-related condition, or to grow up in a home where professional achievements are the first priority? I doubt that prohibitionists can provide a satisfactory answer to these normative questions. However, for their criticism to have any bite, that is *precisely* what is needed.

Rather, when properly analysed, the present argument supports the idea of engaging in other projects than the pursuit of professional success. Professional athletes are no doubt unwise if they ruin their health (through doping or through other training techniques) in order to win. But, in that case, other professional categories are no wiser. We do not see this as a particularly disturbing situation from a moral point of view; it is generally accepted that people should be granted the right to make unwise decisions. Why should professional athletes be denied that right? Thus, though relevant, the argument relating to unreasonable sacrifices backfires.

Finally, supporters of doping bans also argue that it is not accurate to affirm that society never sees it as justified to restrict the personal liberty of individuals exclusively for their own good. They usually point to the obligation for vehicle drivers to use safety belts and the prohibition against recreational drugs. Both these statutes, they affirm, aim to protect the person coerced: in the first case, to prevent injuries when traffic accidents occur; and in the second, to avoid the damaging effects of narcotics.

These two examples, however, are compatible with the anti-paternalistic principle. Vehicle drivers are numerous, so to abolish the safety-belt prescription might therefore increase the number of victims, and the seriousness of their injuries, beyond tolerable levels.

Something similar could be said about the legal ban on narcotics. Legalising recreational drugs would probably lead to a situation where too many people indulged in such practices. This might reasonably be expected to have devastating effects for social life, not only in relation to the population's health but also their service arrangements.

So both safety-belt regulations and the proscription of recreational drugs can be justified on grounds of the *aggregate* social harm they are expected to prevent. The vastness of these noxious effects then turns these banned patterns of behaviour into actions harmful to the whole social body. The regulations are therefore implemented to protect people other than those being coerced.

This, however, is not the case with the ban on doping. Professional elite athletes are by definition few. The aggregate social harm that might follow from their doping use would therefore not be sufficiently large to justify the ban.

Doping harms others

Prohibitionists also affirm that doping does not simply harm the individual athlete. In their view, the ban is justified because doping is harmful to others. To begin with, they contend that doped athletes coerce reluctant colleagues into doping. Otherwise, they will not be able to reach the same competitive level as those who dope. Second, athletes (especially successful ones) are social models to the young. There is then a risk that young people will try to emulate their sport heroes and go for doping, or even for a drug culture. Finally, there is the criticism that underlines the impossibility of restraining doping to professional, adult sportsmen: if allowed, doping will probably be adopted even by amateurs and junior top athletes. Will these objections suffice to support the ban?

The coercion argument

Due to the situation of hard competition that characterises professional sports, would it be fair to say that doped athletes put their more reluctant colleagues under pressure to dope themselves?

In my opinion, to speak of coercion in this context is an overstatement. Athletes reluctant to dope will, no doubt, be put under a pressure to emulate their less prudent colleagues. But nothing hinders them from still refusing to dope. They will not, then, be among the reduced group of habitual winners. This, however, is not morally problematic. In competitive activities, not everyone can win. In the realm of professional ethics, it is widely accepted that benefits should be distributed in relation to efforts and risks undertaken. An ambitious war correspondent puts her life at risk to obtain interesting news or the most impressive picture. If she succeeds, she will be rewarded. By so doing, she is, albeit indirectly, challenging her colleagues to do the same, if they want to achieve a similar success. Should we prohibit war correspondents from coming too near the battle line, to avoid submitting other war correspondents to such a pressure? The suggestion seems to me preposterous. Every well-informed adult has a right to decide by herself which risks to take in the exercise of her professional activity, so long as this does not harm others. Athletes should not be treated differently.

My conclusion is that, other things being equal, if an athlete risks her health to attain victory, while others are more prudent, it is only fair that the victory goes to the former.

An objection to this line of reasoning might be that pressure is also morally problematic. After all, we should not forget that professional athletes make their living on sports. Reluctant athletes, however, are deprived from this possibility, at least as long as they refuse to dope – or so objectors could reformulate their argument.

One could dismiss this argument by pointing out that the current high level of professionalism and commercialisation in elite sports activities allow even non-top athletes to have a respectable professional career and make their living on sports.

In fact, one could even speculate on the possibility that, if the doping ban were abolished, many second-order athletes might get advantageous sponsor contracts precisely on the grounds of their reluctance to dope. (We should not forget that many people will still believe that sports should be a 'natural' activity, no matter how permissive we become concerning doping. And if there is a public, there will be sponsors interested in addressing it.) So, what we get is that doping, far from depriving reluctant sports practitioners from a professional career, might actually promote their careers even further!

Athletes as social models

A common objection to allowing doping in sport competitions is that sports stars are social models for young people. Thus, without the ban, athletes will probably be emulated in their doping habits by young people, and this might lead to increases in both drug consumption and doping use among the young. Considerable social harm will follow from that.

The first part of the objection assumes that performance-enhancing methods (including doping substances) can be placed on an equal footing with recreational drugs. This, however, is a misunderstanding (though a very common one). It is simply wrong to connect doping and drugs in the way these objectors suggest. Whatever the sacrifices an athlete makes in order to achieve a high level of performance, she will be jeopardising her chances to win if she takes drugs. In that sense, with or without doping, sports still are incompatible with drugs. This is, in my opinion, the correct interpretation of the common saying that 'Sport should be "clean"'. Sport is obviously incompatible with unhealthy life: if you want to engage in physical activity (on a professional *or* amateur basis), you need to adopt a moderate way of living. That is quite other thing from abstaining from doping. Properly administered, doping might even be required to achieve a high level of performance. It is unwarranted to assume that the public, even young people, will be unable to see this fact, or that the misunderstanding cannot be taken care of by means of proper information.

The struggle against illegal drugs is a justified cause. So is the goal of restricting smoking and drinking among the young and the population in general. It is questionable, however, whether athletes should be used as a weapon in that struggle. Athletes should certainly not be curtailed in their professional freedom, no matter how commendable the goals we are trying to achieve in the process – at least, no more than people in other professions are.

The second part of the objection, instead, rests on arbitrary delimitations. Successful athletes are indeed social models for the young. But so are parents; nobody has yet proposed to penalise parents who smoke or drink in front of their children. The aggregate social harm caused by tobacco and alcohol on young people is probably much larger than the noxious effects that might follow if young athletes doped under medically controlled conditions. Many sport stars also smoke and drink in public. Again, why not suspend them from competition? They also are giving a bad example to the young.

Furthermore, rigorous training programmes are often harmful for young athletes. How do we know these damages are less than the injuries doping use eventually might cause them? That would surely not be the case regarding such innocuous doping methods as, for instance, caffeine intake and blood-doping.

Finally, we have no reason either to assume that a ban on doping would be the most effective way of reducing its use among young athletes. Open dialogue and communication between coaches, parents and young sports practitioners might turn out to be a better way to come to terms with doping abuse by the young.

Effects on amateur top athletes

We have seen earlier that doping is no impediment for reluctant athletes in pursuing a professional career. This, however, does not settle the issue for prohibitionists. A further objection to doping runs as follows. Amateur sport practitioners who refuse to dope might be unable to get into the reduced circle of professional athletes if they do not agree to dope. So, while perhaps granting that doping does not necessarily lead to a situation in which reluctant athletes are hindered from pursuing an athletic career, prohibitionists might nonetheless sustain that doping will make the transition from amateur to professional sports more difficult. The consequence of this is that it will be practically impossible to confine doping to professional elite sports – its use will spread to amateur athletes.

Why should this be a problem? As far I can see, the present objection has two different implications. The first is that reluctant amateur athletes will be put under pressure to dope in order to get to the professional top. This, however, does not strike me as a fatal objection. In all professions, as I have argued earlier, it is widely accepted that the most ambitious practitioners (those who are willing to take most risks) should be rewarded most. There is no reason why a similar argument should not apply to practitioners on their way up to the professional top.

However, the present objection has a second problematic implication, one that is harder to meet. Unlike the professional elite, the number of amateur sport practitioners is not reduced. Thus, doping might after all cause a sufficient degree of aggregate social harm as to justify the ban. In other words, the prohibition on doping now ends up in the same category as safety-belt regulations and the proscription of narcotics.

The answer to this criticism is twofold. First, it does not affect harmless doping methods. So, even if it were tenable, the present objection cannot support the ban put on doping of type 3 (see page 200), and such doping techniques as blood-doping.

Second, the objection might prove to be untenable even for doping methods that are harmful to the users' health (types 1 and 2 on page 200). In fact, it is an open question whether medically controlled doping causes health damages of the magnitude assumed by the objection. Ironically, as I have argued already, the main hindrance to having access to that knowledge is the ban itself. With doping allowed, and properly administered under medical assistance, we could begin to establish the real incidence of doping substances on athletes' health. This strategy perhaps would not eliminate the harmful effects of doping totally. But it might reasonably be expected to reduce the effects to a large degree. Thus, without the ban and with medical research and supervision, the aggregate social harm of doping might after all end up at the same level as that caused by alcohol consumption. Some of us like booze. Well, some athletes like to dope. Neither they nor we harm other people.

Effects on junior top athletes

I have already discussed an objection to doping that focuses on the possibility of its use becoming extended among young people. It had to do, let us recall, with the role of athletic stars as social models.

The objection I shall discuss now concentrates on a different implication of my attack on the ban of doping for young people. Up till now, I have been advocating free doping in the realm of professional sports. My stance could be criticised by pointing to the fact that in some highly competitive professional sports (tennis, for instance) many athletic stars today are teenagers. Should they also be allowed to dope? Does my proposal include them as well?

Yes and no. Minors should not be allowed to indulge in practices that might jeopardise their health. Using dangerous doping substances, such as many of those included in types 1 and 2 (see page 200), is no doubt one of these practices. This sort of constraint is reasonable, as teenagers usually lack the maturity to have complete awareness of the risks these decisions might entail. Nor should parents and legal guardians be allowed to decide such matters on behalf of young people. Greedy adults might, after all, be tempted to put the health of their children at risk in order to get material benefits. This constraint is also in accordance with current social and legal practices.

But, with relation to harmless doping methods we also should be liberal in relation to young athletes. My previous arguments, then, apply to them as well. This comprises, it should be noted, all doping methods included in type 3, but it might also include some of the substances listed in types 1 and 2 (see page 200). Though dangerous, we should not exclude the possibility that, in the future, we might learn to neutralise the noxious effects of these substances, at least when they are properly administered. As long as their use cannot be expected to hinder harmonic growth, it should be left to young top athletes to decide whether to use them or not. Otherwise, they would be competing with adult practitioners in unequal conditions.

Doping is unfair

Another objection to a liberal doping policy consists in affirming that doping is unfair; it implies that some athletes will obtain competitive advantages over their rivals.

Now, generally stated, it is not easy to grasp what this objection amounts to. With no prohibition, no athlete will be in a situation of competitive inferiority, as all will have the opportunity to dope. In fact, it is the present situation with harsh sanctions attached to doping that creates inequality in competition. Those who dare to challenge the prohibition get the best results. Eliminating the ban put on doping might allow currently rule-abiding athletes to do something about their disadvantage without fear of being disqualified from further competition.

Perhaps the present objection might be taken to mean that, with doping, not all athletes will have equal opportunity to dope. Some bodies are more apt to assimilate drugs and to make better use of doping techniques than others. Pharmaceutical companies will naturally offer their products to the most promising sport practitioners, which obviously will increase the gap between the elite and the next-best athletes.

Considering the framework in which professional sport is practised at present, this is an amazing criticism. After amateurism was abandoned by the IOC, big enterprises entered the sports field to sponsor athletes. Sponsorship creates, no doubt, a situation of inequality in competitive conditions: those who get a succulent contract with a powerful company end up in a better position than non-sponsored athletes. What creates more inequality than (through sponsorship) enabling one athlete to dedicate himself to hard training every day, while competitors without sponsors have to go to work and must train in their spare time?

Nonetheless, these competitive inequalities are considered by the IOC and most ban supporters as natural, and relevant for sport contests, as they are accepted by current regulations and have not been questioned after the entry of business interests into the world of sports. If sports organisations really cared about equal conditions of competition, rather than banning performance-enhancing methods, what seems to be needed is a selective doping policy. Non-sponsored athletes might be allowed to dope, while those supported by commercial firms would not. Surely this measure would contribute to levelling out all participants' chances of wining much more efficiently than would banning doping.

There are, of course, other methods that would yield the same result. Thus, sponsored athletes might be made to compete with extra weights, or be equipped with worse technical tools (shoes, bathing suits, poles, skis, etc.) than non-sponsored competitors. However, I favour selective doping as a better strategy to level out competitive inequalities. If we chose instead to make athletes use different technical equipment, the transparency effect that would follow from lifting the ban would be lost.

The essentialist argument

A common objection to performance-enhancing methods is that doping runs counter to the nature of sports competitions. According to a widely accepted notion, within the framework of current regulations, a sports contest consists in establishing as objectively as possible the inequalities between athletes that are relevant for the sports discipline. Athletes differ in skills, training motivation, sacrifices made, etc. Fairness requires that all athletes abide by the same rules, and that the outcome of the competition will be settled exclusively by those differences. These restrictions are expected to contribute to the uncertainty of the outcome, which – in its turn – is said to give the activity the excitement that captivates sports audiences. Doping, on this line of reasoning, deprives sports of its excitement, as it makes the outcome of the contest more predictable. The contest, rather than being a challenge between persons, is then transformed into a struggle between bodies, supported by different technological devices.

Doping deprives sport of its excitement

There is an element of tension and uncertainty in play. The player wants something to come off. He wants to succeed by his playing, and all those who take part in the game (participants as well as spectators) wait to see the end of that tension (the outcome of the game) with excitement.

Professional sport shares this moment of uncertainty with play. It is the chanciness inherent in competition that makes sport such an exciting activity. A contest with a predictable outcome – for instance, a competition with a certain winner – will evoke no excitement.

A further objection to lifting the ban, then, might be that, with doping, sports will evolve into a mainly technical activity with almost no room for the unexpected. As competitions will be decided on the basis of pharmacological techniques, the outcome of sports contests will become much more predictable than they are at present. The excitement evoked by sportive contests, which is at the very heart of sport's nature, will therefore disappear in the process.

Now, the first observation to make is that the present criticism simply assumes that a lower level of excitement in sport activities would be regrettable. Personally, I am not so convinced that it *would* be a bad thing if much of the enthusiasm and fanaticism that sport contests arouse in the public suddenly disappeared. So, even if the argument were tenable, and doping actually contributed to lowering the fascination of sports, it still has to be proved that such a change would be for the worse.

Second, the criticism above does not affect all sports. Increased technification (as, for instance, the introduction of pharmacological products in the preparation of athletes) will no doubt reduce chanciness in those sports where the level of performance and success is exclusively assessed within a spatiotemporal framework (in metres, seconds or kilogrammes). Weightlifting, athletics, the javelin, etc. are examples of sport disciplines threatened by doping. However, with more creative sport disciplines, like ball games and aesthetically influenced sports, there is no reason to be equally pessimistic. After all, there is as yet no pill or technique that may ensure increased ball control, rhythm and creativity. So, while lifting the ban put on doping might well be followed by a decay in the public's interest for pure performance sports, such disciplines as ball sports, gymnastics and artistic skating will not only survive, but perhaps even come out strengthened by this process. Again, it is not obvious to me that such a development is undesirable.

Finally, it is also not obvious that measurement-oriented performance sports will be affected very much. Consider, for instance, Formula 1 racing – probably no other sport has undergone such an overwhelming technical development as car racing has over the last decades. Technification has not only transformed engines and produced many mechanical improvements, but it has also radically changed the way in which the work of man is conducted. The working routines in Formula 1 pits are an example.

This notwithstanding, car races still are won and lost on the race track. The human factor, particularly the skill of the driver, lies behind that tiny difference that may decide a victory or defeat. I think this is why car races today are followed with such excitement by the sporting public.

Doping is incompatible with the idea of contest between persons

Another objection to doping is that, if it was allowed, sport contests would not be decided on grounds of athletic ability, but rather on the response elicited by the substances ingested. Thus, the objection continues, what we get is not a competition between persons, but between bodies, as the contest would aim at measuring the capacity of a body to react to different substances, instead of differences in athletic ability between competitors.

This argument has been advanced by Robert Simon in the following terms:

> ... the whole point of athletic competition is to test the athletic ability of persons, not the way bodies react to drugs. In the latter case, it is not the athlete who is responsible for the gain. Enhanced performance does not result from the qualities of the athlete qua person, such as dedication, motivation, or courage. It does not result from innate or developed ability, of which it is the point of competition to test. Rather, it results from an external factor, the ability of one's body to efficiently utilise a drug, a factor which has only a contingent and fortuitous relationship to athletic ability.
>
> (Simon 1995: 212–213)

The conclusion Simon arrives at is that '... the use of performance-enhancing drugs should be prohibited in the name of the value of respect for persons itself' (1995: 214).

Now, what is first needed is a more nuanced account of what doping actually is. Doping is no magic pill that makes dedication, goal-oriented training, motivation and effort completely superfluous. Doping stands for small marginal differences in athletic performance. That means that all the personal attributes in which the winner has to excel in order to get the victory will still be needed in sport contests, with or without performance-enhancing methods.

Simon is well aware of this fact, however, but he does not consider this point as decisive. He says that even 'if all athletes used drugs, they might not react to them equally'. This makes him insist that, in that case, 'outcomes would be determined not by the relevant qualities of the athletes themselves but rather by the natural capacity of their bodies to react to the drug of choice' (1995: 213).

Simon's criterion, however, is problematic; at least, if consequently applied, it would equally condemn standard training techniques. The capacity to profit from a particular diet or training method is also an innate 'capacity of the body'. He has a straightforward answer to this: 'Capacity to benefit from training techniques seem part of what makes one a superior athlete in a way that capacity to benefit from a drug does not' (1995: 213). Thus, Simon manages to condemn doping and save standard training by refusing to apply his criterion in a consistent manner. He simply stipulates his assertion, but gives no reason for it. His move therefore strikes me as question-begging.

Another possibility is to interpret Simon as stating that doping use falls outside the prevailing paradigm in the sport community. Such an argument, of course, cannot be a conclusive reason to reject a new practice. Otherwise, athletes would still be condemned for conducting standard training (as they were at the beginning of the twentieth century). Or professionalism would never have entered into the realm of sports. We have witnessed paradigm shifts in sports before, so why not allow for a new one now, where doping is not banned?

This argument gains strength from the fact that sport, like reality itself, is continuously evolving. However, it would be implausible to derive from this that any innovation whatsoever must be accepted. If doping changed the practice of sports in ways that were, in some respect, unattractive or undesirable, then perhaps we should stick to the current paradigm.

Here is where Simon's previous statement that, if doping were allowed, we would not be treating athletes as persons, can be advanced as a reason to oppose such a paradigm change. But what does it mean to treat someone as a person? According to Simon, this is tantamount 'to reacting to the intelligent choices and valued characteristics of the others', such as motivation, intelligence, courage. However, if sport competitions become more and more of a contest between bodies, then it will seem more appropriate to see competitors as mere things to be overcome, rather than as persons posing valuable challenges. And, in Simon's opinion, 'athletic competition is a paradigm example of an area in which each individual competitor respects the other competitor as a person'. So, 'insofar as this requirement ... is ethically fundamental, the prevailing paradigm does enjoy a privileged perspective from the moral point of view' (1995: 213).

I do not think Simon's argument is successful. Maybe risking the ruin of one's health is not the rational thing to do. If so, doping is no doubt an unwise decision to make. But this does not mean that the decision does not reflect the values and choices of the agent. In that sense, to dope or not to dope belongs undeniably to the kind of choices persons (and only they) can make. So, using performance-enhancing methods does not fall outside the prevailing paradigm of athletic competition, as defined by Simon.

Another strategy used to oppose the transition into a doping paradigm might resort to the fact that most athletes resist lifting the ban. So, after all, perhaps the argument on the current sport paradigm points out a problematic aspect of the liberal position; namely, that the majority of the sport community seems to be against doping. On the basis of this argument, some prohibitionists have attempted to meet the criticism that the ban unjustifiably constrains the freedom of athletes by suggesting that athletes themselves introduce the ban as a self-imposed restriction on their activity.

> What is now required is that athletes agree on the sort of practices they do not wish to engage in and then request the assistance of international sports governing bodies in assuring compliance. Against this proposal some might argue that all we require is better enforcement and then we will achieve the state we desire. The problem is that most efforts at better enforcement require more violations of privacy rights. We do require better enforcement, but the merit in such enforcement only comes if it is a result of the athlete's choice, thus mitigating the problem of the violation of privacy rights.
>
> (Schneider and Butcher 1993: 74)

Schneider and Butcher are optimistic about the likelihood of athletes reaching an agreement on the ban on doping. Their reasons are game-theoretical. Viewing the decision to dope as a form of prisoner's dilemma, they expect that athletes will realise that there is no reason to allow doping. If everyone dopes, all athletes have a fair chance of victory. If no one dopes, all athletes also have a fair chance of victory, but without risking their health. So, being rational agents who try to maximise their benefits (or minimise their risks), sports practitioners will concur in banning performance-enhancing methods. Schneider and Butcher formulate this argument in Chapter 13 in the following terms:

> If doping is irrelevant to sport, if it does not enhance one's skill, it is easy to see why athletes would prudently choose to avoid it ... provided one's competitors do not dope there is no reason for any athlete to dope. Because there is no game-productive reason for doping, athletes would be wise to avoid it as an unnecessary risk ... *Doping is only an advantage, in terms of 'winning', if you dope and your opponent does not.* That advantage is lost if everyone dopes.
>
> (this volume: 197, my italics)

Could that help prohibitionists to resist the attack of doping liberals? I cannot see that it could. First, we should not underestimate the degree to which athletes accept (and would continue to accept) doping. The IOC's statistics might be far too optimistic in denying the existence of dark figures concerning doping use. The supposed agreement Schneider and Butcher refer to might, then, in reality be no agreement at all. In that sense, we should be cautious not to equate explicit rejection of doping with actual compliance with anti-doping regulations.

Furthermore, we have reason to believe that the opinion on doping put forward by sports practitioners does not necessarily correlate with their actual stance on the issue. Those who dope obviously benefit from arguing for maintaining the ban: otherwise, their competitive advantage will disappear. Whatever their real opinion on doping is, those who do not dope also have an interest in opposing a liberalisation: with the ban, they still have the possibility of doing something about their disadvantaged position without being compelled to jeopardise their health by doping. And all athletes – doped as well as not doped – are naturally hindered from overtly advocating lifting the ban; that would amount to casting a shadow of doubt over their previous athletic successes. So, there seem to be good game-theoretical reasons not to give any consideration to athletes' statements on doping!

Another problem with Schneider and Butcher's argument is that, even if it were assumed that general consensus on the ban could be achieved, that consensus would be unstable. The reason for this is that, given the ban, it becomes rational not to abide by it. Even if a hypothetical agreement could be achieved among athletes on banning doping, this cannot secure that anti-doping regulations will actually be served. That brings us back to the present situation, with an escalating and expensive race between cheating athletes and controllers.

Finally, the picture presented by Schneider and Butcher of athletes concurring in banning performance-enhancing methods is not realistic. In that sense, they are simply wrong when they claim that 'Doping is only an advantage ... if you dope and your opponent does not'. Differences in genetic makeup turn using performance-enhancing methods into a more profitable strategy for some athletes than for others. If, due to my physiological characteristics, I can obtain a competitive advantage by doping that you are not able to obtain, I probably will oppose the acceptance of a ban by the athletic community. And even if – contrary to my will – a ban were adopted, this would only have the effect of adding a further reason for me to dope: I will now be clearly superior not only to those athletes who genetically cannot benefit as much as I do from doping, but even to those (equally able to profit from doping) who now decide not to dope simply because they want to abide by the rules. Therefore, the solution advanced by Schneider and Butcher fails to solve the practical problem presented by doping. Only lifting the ban does.

Schneider and Butcher's proposal does not solve the morally problematic aspects of the ban I have discussed, either. It is true that, according to their proposal, it is the athletes themselves, and no longer the IOC and other sports organisations, who would be imposing and enforcing doping regulations on the sport community. If I agree to a prohibition, then perhaps I might reasonably be said to be under an obligation to abide by it. But that obligation will not include new actors entering the sport arena. In most professional areas, it is often newcomers who contribute to develop and expand the skills required in the activity involved. If a sport practitioner wished to improve her results by resorting to a performance-enhancing method, denying her that right on grounds of a (supposedly) fully complied-with agreement made in the past by her senior colleagues, this strikes me indeed as a rather weak reason. Granted, we could make her acceptance of the agreement a condition for her present participation. Unless she does not enter the agreement, we – her fellow athletes – will not allow her to participate in competitions. Aside from being arbitrary, I cannot see how that strategy might avoid encouraging athletes to simulate acceptance, and then maximise benefits by ignoring regulations. In other words, we are back in the original situation. The ban on doping is unworkable because athletes, like other professionals, will always try to better themselves and their achievements. And the ban is also unwarranted: if society finds it unacceptable to limit development in other professions, then it is also unacceptable to place limits on sports.

Conclusion

In this chapter, the traditional arguments against doping have been submitted to scrutiny. I could summarise my conclusion by saying that the ban on performance-enhancing methods constrains the professional activities of athletes, and that the reasons often advanced to support that constraint do not stand criticism. The prohibition rests either on arbitrary delimitations or on ungrounded prejudices, or both.

But, it could then be asked, why does it enjoy so much support amongst the general public? In my opinion, different reasons could be advanced to account for such support.

One reason could be that the public still associates doping with a drug-liberal society. This is a misconception. I have already argued for the plausibility of being restrictive on recreational drugs, while at the same time advocating lifting the ban on doping. The amount of aggregated social harm originated by these two practices will probably differ.

From the assertion that 'sport has to be clean', another usual misconception consists in concluding that doping is against the 'nature' of sport. At least in one sense of the term 'clean', the above standpoint no doubt expresses a valuable insight. Whether we practise sport as a leisure activity or as a profession, our lifestyle should be a healthy one. Alcohol and drug intake are counterproductive to any kind of sport activity, no matter how intense it is. From this, however, it does not follow that doping also is incompatible with any kind of sport practices. To grasp this argument properly, we need to concentrate on the distinction (still unobserved by some people, and unduly neglected by most) between recreational and professional sports. This leads us into the next reason lying (in my opinion) behind public support for the ban on doping.

The primary goal of recreational sports is to promote health and enjoyment for its practitioners. To dope within such a context will no doubt be counterproductive. The athlete who dopes will probably ruin her health and will not experience any amusement. Professional sport, instead, is ruled by different goals. A professional athlete aims to become excellent in her discipline and to achieve the external goals – mainly prestige and money – that usually follow such victory. Given the hard competition that characterises professional sports, doping is not only rational, but even necessary, for securing those goals. Although they have a common origin, recreational and professional sports have evolved in different ways and today constitute two very distinct social practices. And different social practices should reasonably be guided by different rules.

Professional sport, then, goes free from the accusation of promoting unsound strategies to victory. If my arguments in this chapter are correct, all kinds of performance-enhancing methods should be allowed in professional sports. Certain doping damages will then be unavoidable. This is a regrettable effect of my proposal. These damages, however, are not essentially different from the injuries that affect other professional categories. We should do everything we can to minimise them, as we do in other professions, short of implementing paternalistic restraints in the activity. A condition for reducing doping injuries, I have argued, is lifting the ban. But we will not be able to prevent all doping injuries fully. We should not be surprised. Working always breaks down workers' health, so why should sports jobs be different?

Note

1   We could also distinguish an intermediate class, consisting of substances the consumption of which during most of the twentieth century has been illegal but which are at present used for medical purposes. Marijuana is such an example, prescribed by some physicians as an analgesic.

Chapter 15

Selected champions

Making winners in the age of genetic technology

Christian Munthe

Introduction

One of the most lively current controversies within sports concerns those interventions with the human body (and mind) that are acceptable in a 'fair competition' and those that are not so acceptable. On the philosophical level, this issue actualises the more basic query regarding the underlying criteria for demarcation between acceptable and unacceptable interventions. Traditionally, the controversies in this field have regarded intake of achievement-enhancing substances (some, like water, are allowed; others, like steroids, are prohibited; and yet others, like transfusion of one's own blood from a period of 'top shape', are controversial), but also peculiar forms of 'designed environment' in training (such as the 'low oxygen, low air pressure' house made so famous by the Norwegian cross-country skier Björn Dählie). In this chapter I will take the discussion at least one step beyond these issues and consider the prospect of using various forms of gene technology in the making of winners in elite sports.

The second section of the chapter describes various opportunities to use gene technology in sports. As will be evident, genetic interventions may proceed in very different ways, and it is not obvious that they can all be treated alike in the context of sports. In the third section, I discuss to what extent ideals and values within sports used to back up reasons for prohibiting doping may also be a basis for rejecting genetic interventions. My conclusion, summed up in the last section, is that this may be plausible regarding some interventions, but not by a long way is it plausible regarding them all. In fact, genetic interventions in order to enhance athletic achievement in many ways seem to *promote* important values within sports! Moreover, even for those interventions which in theory may be classified as analogous to doping, in practice it will often be impossible to check whether or not an athlete has made use of them or not.

Gene technology: present realities and future prospects

Every living organism is a product of environmental impact and genetic inheritance. For a long time, our way of coping with obstacles for the attainment of various ends (such as winning an athletic competition) has been manipulation of the environment (intake of substances, bodily exercise, change of climate, technical tools, etc.). However, up till now, it has seldom been possible to 'fine-tune' environmental interventions on the basis of *precise* knowledge about how they interplay with genetic factors. Either it has been impossible to detect the genetic factors, or the impact of these factors in different environmental settings has been not well enough known. Even less has it been possible to change or 'design' the genetic basis for an individual's potential for achievement in sports. However, as will be described, this is a situation that will most probably be radically changed during the course of just a couple of decades.

For many years, a huge international research project, popularly called the HUGO-project, has been working on mapping the entire human genome.[1] Already, it has given considerable input to the management of various genetic diseases. However, a good deal of the information obtained does not relate to health as we normally perceive it. The genes uncovered govern the function of the cells in our body (more precisely, the production of various proteins in these cells). When a gene is abnormal this may cause dysfunction, disease or death. However, another abnormality may instead cause the *enhancement* of bodily traits and/or functions, many of which are particularly relevant in sports. For example, a gene governing the propensity for muscular growth may in some variants (or *mutations*, as the geneticists say) have normal effects, but in other variants cause serious muscular diseases, and in yet other variants cause a higher than normal propensity for muscular growth. Of course, muscular growth may also be influenced by other factors (other genes or environmental influence). However, recent molecular biological research has indeed revealed a gene having tremendous impact on the volume of muscle mass (indeed, even the *number* of muscles!) in mammals (this gene explains the enormous muscle mass of the famous Belgian Blue bull).[2] Higher than normal propensity for muscular growth is, of course, of relevance for any sport where muscle mass to some extent influences achievement. An example of another trait with high relevance for many sports which is already known to be strongly genetically determined is capacity for oxygen uptake. In fact, there are even well-known *natural* mutations present in the human population that predispose for lower- or higher-than-average capacity for oxygen uptake significant enough to influence athletic achievement.[3]

There are at least four ways in which this kind of knowledge may be used in order to increase the likelihood of superior achievement in athletic competitions.[4]

Background for environmental interventions

In the medical field of genomics, genetic information is used to fine-tune normal types of medical interventions (such as the use of drugs).[5] In the ideal case, the chemical composition of a drug is fine-tuned in relation to a particular patient's genetic makeup (which in turn influences metabolism, sensitivity to various substances, etc.). Similarly, it is quite possible to perceive a peculiar 'genomics of sports', aimed at optimising the effect of training, nutrition, etc. in relation to the individual athlete's genetic makeup. The increased knowledge in such a field might also lead to discoveries of completely new nutritional and metabolic aspects of relevance for athletic achievement.

Somatic genetic modification

In the field of gene therapy, procedures are developed in order to modify the genome in very specific ways. Although already implemented within the industrial cultivation of crops (e.g. the well-known soya bean) and animal breeding, the use of such procedures in health care is still limited. However, there is aggressive development regarding the treatment of somatic cells − that is, the 'normal' cells making up our tissue, blood, various organs, etc. (but not our gametes). Interventions on such cells will always be 'local' and will not be inherited by the modified individual's offspring. However, with access to appropriate genetic knowledge such procedures may still be useful for athletes interested in improving their physical fitness in very specific ways; for example, 'blood-doping' with genetically modified red blood cells (which can be infinitely multiplied and stored in freezers, thus completely eliminating the need for excessive training in order to get enhanced red blood cells) or increased 'in-body' production of various hormones.

Germ-line genetic modification

Many basic structures of the human body (in turn determining the limits of various physical capabilities) are founded very early in life. In particular, this concerns the metabolic capabilities of cells and their basic chemical structures in other respects. For this reason, in order to achieve more drastic improvements built into the organism from the start, genetic modification has to be performed before the genome of the cells starts to become specialised (or *differentiates*) for various purposes. Simply put, interventions must be made on sperm, unfertilised eggs or, at the very latest, the newly fertilised egg (so-called germ-line cells). As a side effect, the modification has to be performed before the affected individual actually exists and will also be inheritable. Up till recently, this possibility has remained theoretical, since germ-line cells very soon begin to differentiate. However, the successful somatic cloning resulting in the famous sheep Dolly[6] (and the recent repetition of this experiment in USA on mice[7]) has radically changed the situation. The idea of genetically modifying 'ordinary' somatic cells (which are already fully developed and therefore do not differentiate further), the nucleus of which is inserted into an 'emptied' (or *enucleated*) unfertilised egg and then 'reprogrammed' to the germ-line stage with the 'Dolly-procedure', is now considered technically feasible among most experts in the field and may soon be applicable to human beings.[8]

Genetic selection of individuals

While reliable and specific gene therapy is still a vision for the future, selection of individuals on genetic grounds (without modifying their genome) is already quite feasible. Indeed, it has been a part of the routine management of genetic diseases for many years: techniques for testing (a very small cell sample is usually sufficient) are already in place and the only limit is set by the available genetic knowledge. Thus, forthcoming knowledge regarding genes influencing traits relevant for athletic achievement can be implemented in order to select among different people on such grounds. For example, when a national Olympic committee or commercial sponsor initiates support programmes for promising young athletes, those whose genome makes it unlikely that they will ever reach the elite (no matter what the amount and quality of training) can be sorted out from the very beginning, thereby ensuring that scarce resources are not 'wasted' on such 'hopeless cases'. In fact, the selection may actually be undertaken before the individuals to be selected among even exist. Genetic testing of potential parents, sperm or ova donors in assisted reproduction, early embryos in in vitro fertilisation (so-called pre-implantation genetic diagnosis, or PGD), or foetuses in already initiated pregnancies (regular prenatal diagnosis), are all examples of techniques already in use[9] which (assuming the availability of the appropriate knowledge) may be applied for the purpose of pre-selecting future children whose genetic makeup is particularly fitting for a successful career in (certain) sports.

Genetic interventions and arguments against doping

The extent to which arguments in favour of prohibiting the use of certain substances (such as steroids) within sports may be extended to various genetic interventions depends, of course, on what these arguments are. Generally, there seem to be four kinds of reasons advanced in order to motivate regulations within sports (such as bans on the use of certain substances) – reasons of safety, reasons of 'moral purity', pragmatic reasons and reasons of athletic tradition. I will consider these in turn, and apply them to the various forms of genetic intervention described above.

Reasons of safety

One argument for banning the use of substances such as steroids is simply that such use is dangerous – for the athlete, for others, or both. It may, of course, be debated whether or not this is a good reason for such bans.[10] But the fact remains that this reason is actually in use and, furthermore, that it connects to a widely recognised value, namely the avoidance of harm and the promotion of well-being. This is reason enough to investigate its range of applicability to the issue at hand.

Genetic interventions in sports may, of course, be objected to on this ground inasmuch as they are dangerous for athletes. This is easiest to imagine in the cases of genomics, somatic genetic modification and selection of existing individuals. Genetic modification may bring side effects that the athlete would have been significantly better off without. The 'fine-tuning' of nutrition in a genomics of sports may go wrong and endanger the health and well-being of the athlete. The genetic testing underlying the selection of individuals for athletic support programmes may be misleading, thereby causing individuals to be 'tricked' into believing that they are more/less promising candidates for success than they in fact are. And, since 'no athlete is an island', such effects will in turn mean that other parties are also harmed: family, trainers, supporters, sponsors, etc.

At the same time, however, it should be observed that all these interventions may equally well *increase* safety compared with presently used methods. Genetically *un*informed nutritional directions and selections of athletes, as well as excessive training in order to compensate for genetic 'shortcomings', may all be *more* dangerous than any genetic intervention. One reason for believing so is that present practices are based on a more crude and less nuanced collection of knowledge than any working genetic intervention would be. One real-life example of this is the detection of athletes with the genetic trait for the hereditary blood disease Sickle Cell Anemia, which may be life-threatening in combination with certain kinds of physical exercise.[11] But, of course, *new* methods are always *especially* sensitive to failure and that fact cannot be ignored when pondering whether or not to welcome their introduction.

When moving on to germ-line genetic modifications and genetic *pre-selection* of *future* individuals, the analogy to safety arguments against doping becomes more tricky to uphold. The reason for this is that these interventions influence not only the genome of future individuals, but also *which* individuals actually exist in the future.

This fact is most easily demonstrated in the case of pre-selection. Suppose that a couple is very interested in having children well suited for athletic achievement in sports requiring a high degree of physical strength (perhaps because they have themselves failed in this sport and want their children to secure the success they themselves failed to achieve). Evidently, if sports organisations, teams, sponsors, etc. use genetic tests for selecting which athletes to support, this will constitute a further reason for such a couple to use genetic pre-selection. Suppose further that genetic tests have established that both the man and the woman are carriers for a gene which leads to increased propensity for muscular growth in their offspring if inherited from both of the parents (who themselves only carry the gene in one copy each). According to the laws of heredity, there is a 75 per cent probability that normal procreation (through sexual intercourse) will not lead to this result. Therefore, the couple uses PGD in order to select one specific 'test-tube' embryo among many (available after a round of in vitro fertilisation) meeting their desires. As a result, a child is born with a good genetic basis for becoming physically very strong later on in life. Now, had this couple instead procreated in the normal way, it is extremely probable that *that* child would have resulted from the joining of a *different sperm and a different unfertilised egg* than the child they in fact have (through PGD). In consequence, the use of PGD secures not only that the child born has a certain genetic makeup, but also that this child is a *different individual* from the one who would have been born had the couple instead elected not to use PGD.

The implication of this phenomenon for the applicability of reasons of safety is the following. Suppose further that the child resulting from the PGD suffers some physical damage due to the impact of the PGD procedure.[12] At first glance, it is tempting to conclude that the child has therefore been harmed by the use of PGD. However, since *this* child would never have existed had PGD not been used (though *another* child might have existed in its place), this conclusion seems very hard to sustain unless the harm is of extreme severity, guaranteeing a short life dominated by the most dreadful agony, so that it is plausible to suggest that such a life is actually worse for the child than no life at all.[13] It does not seem unreasonable to suggest that such *grave* risks of PGD are in fact very small. The explanation is that such grave damage has to occur very early in physical development and that no child born after PGD (presently around 200) has been reported to be so damaged. In short, therefore, since existing with some physical damage or handicap may very well be preferable to not existing at all, it is hard to see how PGD could be harmful to resulting children even if it actually causes some damage to them. This does not exclude the claim that the damage may still be claimed to be *undesirable*, although unharmful. However, it is extremely controversial whether and how such a claim can be supported.[14]

The same reasoning partly repeats itself regarding germ-line genetic modifications, again powered by the fact that the peculiar technical procedures involved will most probably mean that a different individual results than if procreation had been achieved by sexual intercourse. This is not to suggest that one isolated modification of an individual's genome *in itself* makes it into another individual. Since two different persons can have the same genetic makeup (namely, genetically identical twins), our individuality cannot be that closely connected to our genome. All I am claiming is that, since germ-line genetic interventions will mean that procreation proceeds so differently (and at a different time) compared to procreation by sexual intercourse, chances are they will not result in the same sperm and egg joining to give rise to an embryo.[15]

In connection with germ-line genetic modifications, the fear of actual harm to resulting children is more warranted, since *nothing* is known about the severity of possible damages to the offspring due to genetic modifications (since such modification of human beings has never been accomplished). However, should risks for extremely severe damage prove to be very low, this reason will disappear.

Not even athletes are islands, as I said above, and this, of course, is relevant also regarding the presently considered interventions. Here, it seems obvious that all risks of damage to the resulting child will mean that its parents are harmed by being disappointed, feeling cheated, and having to cope with the child's special needs arising out of the damage done to it. Moreover, the reproductive technologies used may physically harm the woman. However, none of this will, of course, apply when the intervention is a success. And, therefore, when these procedures in the future are safe and reliable (which they undoubtedly will become, sooner or later) reasons of safety will no longer be applicable.

In conclusion, therefore, reasons of safety may at best support a strong requirement of precaution in the *introduction* of new procedures for genetic intervention in the context of sports. This requirement should, it seems reasonable to suggest, in general be stronger than in the context of health care, since enhancement in order to secure greater chance of superior athletic achievement is not an important human need in the same way as greater chance of preventing or curing diseases. However, when the risks are clarified and the methods are reliable and safe, the introductory phase is over and the reasons for precaution disappear.

Reasons of 'moral purity'

In some cases, bans within sports on the intake of certain substances mainly seem to be motivated from demands for a kind of 'moral purity' on the part of athletes. This, for example, seems to be the case with bans against marijuana or when soccer and ice-hockey players are expelled from a team or tournament because of excessive drinking. Can this kind of reason be extended to genetic interventions? In order to answer that question, we must first look closer into what is involved in these kinds of reasons.

Obviously, a ban within sports against marijuana-smoking or excessive drinking cannot be supported on the ground that these practices enhance athletic performance in an illegitimate way. On the contrary – the moral dislike within sports against such activities seems, rather, to arise from the fact that they *decrease* the chance of winning, thereby indicating that athletes engaging in such activities are not strongly committed to an aim of superior athletic achievement (victory, in other words). The underlying premise here, of course, is that it is a moral virtue of athletes to have such a strong commitment to 'a sound mind in a sound body'. One peculiar thing with this kind of argument is that it seems to point in the opposite direction compared with arguments against doping (steroids, hormones), which typically stress the desirability of athletes *tempering* their commitment to victory (such reasons will be discussed below).

From this it seems evident that reasons of 'moral purity' cannot be used against genetic interventions in sports, since their use will obviously be governed by strong desires for superior athletic achievement. The only possible exception I can see is in the case of genetic pre-selection, when the technical procedures used mean that embryos or foetuses are killed. It *might* be argued that, *if* such actions are generally immoral (as some indeed claim them to be), someone engaging in them does not have a 'sound mind' in the way that athletes should have (in virtue of their being athletes). I gladly confess that such a line of reasoning is questionable at best (not least because the pre-selection, for obvious reasons, is never decided on by the athlete). However, it does seem to be a *possible* extension of reasons of 'moral purity' covering at least *some* genetic interventions.

Pragmatic reasons

Some years ago, the track and field discipline of javelin got into problems because of the increased length of the throws – the standard field was simply not long enough any more. The simple solution to this problem was new regulations regarding the characteristics of the javelin, which made it much harder to make such long throws. This is one example of pragmatic reasons for regulations in sports. Another example is when the rules of soccer changed so that the goalkeeper was no longer allowed to catch the ball with his or her hands as much as before. The reasoning behind this was that the old rules tended to make the games boring to watch (since they made too much room for extremely defensive tactics). In this case the pragmatic reason clearly connected to the role of elite sports as a section of the contemporary entertainment industry.

Could there be similar objections to genetic interventions? For example, would an increased use of such interventions within sports constitute a threat to their entertainment value?

Torbjörn Tännsjö suggests that it would do so, and seriously so (see Chapter 7). In my view, however, this is mistaken. Genetic interventions could in many ways *contribute* to the entertainment value of sports! The simple reason is that they will (if they work as intended) increase the level of excellence of athletes. This might have the side effect of making some sports very impractical in the same way as the increased strength and skill of javelin throwers did. However, as we have seen, this may be handled by changes of rules regarding competitive procedures, materials, etc. If necessary, particular disciplines may be taken away altogether and replaced by other ones where the impractical effects do not occur.

I can see only one possible scenario where genetic interventions would seriously threaten the pragmatic value of sports. If all athletes were to be genetically identical clones and equally well skilled, trained, nurtured and prepared in other respects, then many sports would become extremely boring. However, it is hard to believe that any such 'perfection' would ever be actualised. Rather, small differences in relevant factors would determine who would win – so small that it is practically impossible to guarantee that all athletes are equal in all respects that influence results. One simple reason for this is that even genetically identical clones (twins, for instance) do not remain so identical for a very long time (as we all do, they already begin to mutate in the womb). Another reason is, of course, that it is practically impossible *perfectly* to control *all* environmental factors that may influence athletic results (such as the wind, the angle of the sunlight, the temperature, etc.).

This, I conjecture, is enough for most fans of sports to maintain their interest. Add to this the increased level of excellence and excitement (the latter due to the closeness in strength and skill of the competing athletes), and we may certainly look forward to even more engaging sports in the future.

Reasons of athletic tradition

Sports, it is often said, should be a fair competition between athletes (or teams of athletes). Such fairness in turn seems to be seen as a function of the athletes' competing under similar conditions. Now obviously this cannot be taken to imply a requirement of similarity in all respects (relevant to the outcome of the competition). Rather, it must be understood as a similarity in certain selected respects (traditionally these have not included the genetic makeup of athletes). Some of these conditions are included, everyone agrees, in the very definition of different sports (100m necessarily includes running no less than 100m, ice hockey cannot be executed without ice skates, etc.). However, many of the conditions are such that it seems perfectly possible to deviate from them but still be executing the sport in question, although not in a *proper* way. Such conditions are thus less semantic or ontological in nature than they are normative. This difference is, of course, one of degree, but nevertheless it seems clear to me that, for example, the game of soccer could very well continue to exist even if soccer players were to be allowed to use steroids, although they *should not* be so allowed.

What, then, determines whether or not some procedure or substance *is* improper as a means to winning in sports? One simple suggestion could be that nothing more can be said about this than 'look at the list of presently prohibited procedures'. Regarding forthcoming procedures we have to wait and see what the high-and-mighty ones in the world of sports will eventually decide, and then we will have the only answer we can get. Evidently, this suggestion is potentially compatible with *any* view regarding the appropriateness/inappropriateness of genetic interventions.

However, the majority of people would almost certainly feel rather discontent with such a bleak approach to normative issues. Surely, even the high and mighty of the world of sports may have *better or worse reasons* for deciding one way rather than the other. Normative issues are not only a question of 'Who's in charge?', but a question of whether or not those in charge make *well-founded* decisions. What, then, would characterise a well-founded decision regarding the issue at hand? What would constitute good reasons for deciding one way rather than another regarding genetic interventions in sports?

One possible way of approaching this question is to invoke traditional basic ideas from normative ethics, such as utilitarianism, ethics of rights, theories of justice, etc. However, it seems extremely clear to me that such basic ideas are miles away from the norms usually applied in order to resolve normative issues within sports. Take, for example, the celebrated idea of justice as fairness put forward by John Rawls.[16] Rawls suggests that we would rationally prefer a just social arrangement under conditions of ignorance regarding our own situation in this arrangement. We are then forced to reason from the assumption that we might as well be losers as winners and will, Rawls claims, therefore prefer arrangements that give large opportunities for the worse off to compensate for the shortcomings which make them worse off. Clearly, this is no basis whatsoever for arguing against the use of steroids or other achievement-enhancing substances in sports, since such substances are means of compensation for, say, economic shortcomings. Regarding other normative ethical theories, it is even harder to see how they could ever motivate bans on doping in any simple manner.[17] Even less, I claim, can they so motivate bans on genetic interventions in sports, unless they are used for arguments against the whole phenomenon of elite sports.

My suggestion, therefore, is the following. Decisions regarding which things are to be included in the 'competition on similar conditions' clause indeed *are* guided by a set of basic normative considerations. However, these considerations are hard to spell out in the form of some traditional basic ethical view – indeed, they are hard to spell out *at all*, since they have never been explicitly formulated. Rather, they are implicit in the actual practice of decision-making in sports management. And, I suggest, what we see in this practice is the expression of a peculiar and partly vague *conservative* ideal, aimed at preserving the athletic tradition shaped by practices of the past.

Not in such a way that radical changes of 'sports policy' are never made – on the contrary. Rather, the conservative attitude is directed at *patterns of reasoning* that have been employed in the past when making decisions. Moreover, this conservatism is not absolute in any way, but rather of the *precautionary* kind, requiring small steps and a slow pace when changing such patterns. In this way decisions will never involve a complete break with athletic tradition: even if a change of some rule is radical in comparison with how it was before the change, it is still motivated from a pattern of reasoning that connects it to past decisions.

What, then, is the pattern of reasoning underlying bans against the intake of various substances (besides reasons of safety, moral purity and pragmatics, that is)? This, of course, is hard to say for sure, but it seems to me that one important *part* of the answer is that intake of such substances directly influences the biochemistry of the body in a way *very different* from the influence of this kind one would have been exposed to *had one lived an average life rather than ventured into the athletic elite*. This pattern of reasoning is vague, of course, but nevertheless seems to capture an important part of what the sports community finds objectionable in the use of steroids, hormones, etc. The vagueness also explains why some procedures are controversial. It is not easy to answer either yes or no to questions regarding whether or not 'high-altitude houses' and blood-doping can be fitted into the pattern of reasoning just spelled out. However, this pattern is still *sufficiently* clear and intelligible in order to function as a basis for the further treatment of the specific case of genetic interventions – to which I now return.

May we object to genetic interventions using the above pattern of reasoning? I will claim, yes in some cases, but mostly not. *Somatic* genetic modifications may be described as just another way of messing with the biochemistry of the body. In this case we have an individual with certain initial bodily functions which are then changed by the use of gene technology. Say, for example, that the result of this is that the in-body production of some hormone is increased. From the point of view of the pattern of reasoning underlying bans against the *intake* of such hormones, it seems quite sensible to suggest that attaining a similar result (increasing the amount of such hormones in the body) by modifying the molecular structure of some cells is insignificantly different. The important thing is the upshot (the biochemistry of the body is much too different compared with the individual who had not been involved in elite sports), not the means of production.

However, when turning to the other brands of genetic intervention such analogies seem much harder to sustain. A genomics of sports seems no different in essence to the use of nutritional and other kinds of scientific knowledge already employed today in training and preparatory procedures. What has been added is only further background knowledge which enables even more fine-tuned procedures of preparation. Thus, as long as these procedures do not lead to biochemical changes in the athlete which are comparable to 'regular' doping, to undertake them against a background of precise genetic knowledge seems unobjectionable.[18]

Something similar is true regarding genetic *selection*. There is no ban on selecting individual athletes for training camps or support programmes on the basis of hypotheses about their potential for future success, in turn based on knowledge about their physiology, bodily biochemistry, etc. In fact, it is perfectly permitted to use the more crude genetic information one can get from knowledge about an athlete's family for this purpose. Thus, it is hard to see how the adding of more precise knowledge by the use of genetic testing could involve any break with athletic tradition. Moreover, procedures for selection can in no way be described as involving *changes* of the initial biochemistry of the body. All it means is that information about individuals (whose biochemistry has not been improperly changed) is used to decide which of these shall be the subject of support. The same reasoning applies with even greater force regarding *pre*-selection on the basis of genetic information, since, in this case, the selective decision can be taken even before the individual exists. Thus, here, there are no initial bodily functions to interfere with when the selection is undertaken. Rather, the selection determines *which* initial bodily functions *will* exist in the future (by determining which individual will exist).

How about germ-line genetic modifications, then? On the one hand, such interventions surely involve interference with the bodily biochemistry of some individual (through the modification of genes). But, on the other hand, it is not likely that the individual interfered with is the same individual as the one who may reap athletic profit from this interference. This is most easily seen in the case when the athlete is the child of parents who have undergone germ-line genetic modification. To be true, the *parent's* biochemistry has been interfered with, maybe even to an improper extent. However, this does not imply that the bodily biochemistry of their *child* has been changed, at least not in a way analogous to presently prohibited forms of doping. The child's bodily biochemistry is the same, no matter if he or she ventures on a career in elite sports or not.

This line of reasoning can be extended also to the case in which the intervention is performed on the embryo from which the athlete has sprung. First, it may be debated whether or not this embryo and the grown-up athlete really are the *same* individual. One basis for doubt regarding this is that it seems hard to sustain the claim that a grown-up is the same *person* as the embryo from which he or she once evolved.[19] Another basis is that it is debatable whether embryos in their early stages can be ascribed any *individuality* at all, since they may split into twins, triplets, etc.[20] Second, even if they *are* the same individual, it is hard to sustain the claim that this individual's biochemistry has been changed in a way that makes it different compared with if he or she had not ventured on an athletic career. Since the intervention is undertaken at such an early stage of the individual's existence, it will affect his or her biochemistry in the same way, no matter what paths he or she will follow in life. Third, it is even impossible to say that, because of the germ-line genetic modification, the resulting individual's biochemical bodily characteristics have been changed compared to if the modification had never been undertaken. This is due to the fact mentioned above that, due to the procedures used to attain the modification, *another* individual will exist compared with if no such procedures had been used. Therefore, the situation is very much similar to the case of genetic pre-selection.

The end of elite sports?

There are good reasons in terms of safety for being extra cautious when introducing procedures for genetic interventions in sports. However, when a sufficient degree of reliability and unharmfulness has been proven, it is hard to see any convincing way of arguing *generally* against the use of such interventions, no matter if the basis be reasons of safety, 'moral purity' or pragmatic concerns. Somatic genetic modifications *may* be analogous to more regular forms of doping (and objected to on the same ground as these are commonly objected to). However, other types of genetic interventions seem completely immune to such criticism. In all, therefore, I conclude that, with the possible exception of certain ways of performing genetic interventions and certain types of somatic genetic modifications, there are within sports no good reasons for objecting against the use of genetic technologies for increasing athletic excellence. Indeed, athletic virtues and pragmatic reasons even seem to support the *desirability* of such a development!

However, in practice, these differences between various types of genetic interventions do not matter very much. For, even if some athlete should use somatic genetic modification, for example, in order to increase the in-body production of some hormone, how are we to distinguish this person from one who has a *natural genetic mutation* with the same biochemical effect? The answer is that, as long as the modification has been skilfully done, we cannot make this distinction in practice. Moreover, we cannot plausibly exclude people from athletic competitions merely because they have exceptionally favourable genetic makeups, since that would most probably mean that we would have to expel the large majority of *today's* champions! In practice, therefore, it seems unavoidable that the sports community will eventually have to accept *all* genetic interventions for the purpose of selecting champions and making winners.

What, then, will this mean for the future of elite sports? Does the arrival of genetic technology signal the beginning of the end for this, the most successful entertainment project of the twentieth century? Much of what has been said above suggests that the answer to this question is negative, if safe, genetic interventions fit traditional athletic virtues like a glove and may even promote some important pragmatic values within sports.

Acknowledgments

For factual guidance, many thanks to Mikael Andäng and Lars Ährlund-Richter at the section for Mammalian Embryology and Genetics, Department of Bioscience, Karolinska Institutet/NOVUM in Stockholm and Jan Wahlström, Section of Clinical Genetics, Department of Selected Specialities, Sahlgrenska University Hospital/East in Göteborg.

Notes

1   See, for example, Grant (1994).
2   See Gollnick and Matoba (1984), Grobet, Martin *et al.* (1997), Grobet, Poncelet *et al.* (1998), Kambadur *et al.* (1997), McPherron and Lee (1997) and Szabo *et al.* (1998).
3   See, for example, Le-Gallais *et al.* (1994), Leitch *et al.* (1975), Salkie *et al.* (1982) and Williamson *et al.* (1992).
4   One possibility which will not be mentioned further is genetic modification of food (such as crops and meat) in such a way that it 'naturally' contains achievement-enhancing substances today only available as drugs.
5   See Marshall (1998a, b) for descriptions of two recently undertaken projects of genomics.
6   Wilmut *et al.* (1997), Ashworth *et al.* (1998) and Signer *et al.* (1998).
7   Wakayama *et al.* (1998).
8   Solter (1998) and 'Adult Cloning Marches On'.
9   For an overview, see 'Genetic Testing and Screening'.
10   For more about this, see Chapter 14.
11   See, for example, Browne and Gillespie (1993), Eichner (1993), Jones and Kleiner (1996), Kerle and Nishimura (1996); Monahan (1987) and Sedivy *et al.* (1997).
12   At the present state of knowledge, risks for such damage due to PGD cannot be ruled out (mainly because children born after PGD are still very young). See, for example, Handyside (1996), Verlinsky and Kuliev (1998) and Verlinsky *et al.* (1997).
13   This presupposes a certain idea regarding what makes a life better and worse for the individual living this life. I assume that this is determined mainly by the subjective well-being/suffering enjoyed/suffered by this individual. It should be noted, though, that other views are possible, so pre-selection in sports connects to deep philosophical issues. For more about this, see Munthe (1996: chapter 3, 1998, 1999a).
14   See Munthe (1996: chapter 3, 1998, 1999a: chapter 5), Robertson (1994) and Steinbock (1992). For a classic reference regarding the basic philosophical problems involved, see Parfit (1984).
15   This point is expanded in Munthe (1999b).
16   Rawls (1971).
17   See Chapter 14 for more on this.

18 It should be observed, though, that it is not unreasonable to expect that a genomics of sports will also give rise to a number of *new* ways for nutritional athletic preparation for some of which it may be very unclear whether they are 'like doping' or not.

19 See, for example, Parfit (1984: chapters 10, 11) and Tooley (1984: 120–146).

20 See, for example, Donceel (1970, 1984), Mahoney (1984: 82), McCormick (1991) and Ramsey (1970).

References

Aarnio, A. (1987) *The Rational as Reasonable: A Treatise of Legal Justification*, Dordrecht: Reidel.

'Adult Cloning Marches On' (1998) anonymous editorial, *Nature* 394: 303.

Appiah, K. (1996) 'Cosmopolitan Patriots', in *For Love of Country*, ed. J. Cohen, Boston: Beacon Press.

Archetti, E. (1992) 'Argentinian Football: A Ritual of Violence?', *International Journal of the History of Sport* 2: 209–236.

Aristotle (1941) *Ethica Nicomachea* (Nicomachean Ethics), in *The Basic Works of Aristotle*, ed. R. McKeon, New York: Random House, pp. 935–1127 .

—— (1976) *The Ethics of Aristotle – The Nicomachean Ethics*, trans. J.A.K. Thompson, London: Penguin.

Arneson, R. (1982) 'The Principle of Fairness and the Free Rider Problem', *Ethics* 92: 616–633.

Ashworth, D., Bishop, M., Campbell, K., Colman, A., Kind, A., Schnieke, A., Blott, S., Griffin, H., Haley, C., McWhir, J. and Wilmut, I. (1998) 'DNA Microsatellite Analysis of Dolly', *Nature* 394: 329.

Bairner, A. (1997) 'Civic and Ethnic Nationalism in Celtic and Nordic Versions of Sport', unpublished manuscript.

Baker, G. and Hacker, P. (1980) *Wittgenstein: Understanding and Meaning – An Analytical Commentary on the Philosophical Investigations*, Oxford: Blackwell.

—— (1985) *Wittgenstein: Rules Grammar and Necessity – Volume 2 of an Analytical Commentary on the Philosophical Investigations*, Oxford: Blackwell.

Baker, W. (1987) 'Political Games: The Meaning of International Sport for Independent Africa' in *Sport in Africa*, ed. W. Baker and J. Mangan, New York: Africana, pp. 272–294.

Bender, D. and Leone, B. (eds) (1995) *Male/Female Roles: Opposing Viewpoints*, Opposing Viewpoints Series, San Diego, CA: Greenhaven Press.

Ben-Ze'ev, A. (1993) 'The Virtue of Modesty', *American Philosophical Quarterly* 30: 235–246.

Birrell, S. and Cole, C.L. (eds) (1994) *Women, Sport and Culture*, Champaign, IL: Human Kinetics, pp. 207–237.

Blau, F.D. and Ferber, M.A. (1992) *The Economics of Women, Men and Work*, Englewood Cliffs, NJ: Prentice Hall.

Bluestone, N. (1987) *Women and the Ideal Society: Plato's Republic and Modern Myths of Gender*, Amherst, MA: University of Massachusetts Press.

Blum, L.A. (1980) *Friendship, Altruism and Morality*, London: Routledge & Kegan Paul.

Bordo, S. (1990) 'Reading the Slender Body', in *Body/Politics: Women and the Discourses of Science*, ed. M. Jacobus, E. Fox Keller and S. Shuttleworth, New York: Routledge, pp. 83–112.

Bouchard, C., Malina, R.M. and Perusse, L. (1997) *Genetics of Fitness and Physical Performance: Human Kinetics*, Champaign, IL.

Brohm, J.-M. (1978) *Sport – A Prison of Measured Time*, London: Links.

Broverman, I., Broverman, D., Clarkson, F., Rosenkrantz, P. and Vogel, S. (1981) 'Sex Role Stereotypes and Clinical Judgments of Mental Health', in *Women and Mental Health*, ed. E. Howell and M. Bayes, New York: Basic Books.

Brown, W. (1992) 'The Meaning of Baseball', *Public Culture* 4: 43–69.

Browne, R.J. and Gillespie, C.A. (1993) 'Sickle Cell Trait: A Risk Factor for Life-threatening Rhabdomyolysis?', *Physicians and Sports Medicine* 21: 80–82.

Butcher, R.B. and Schneider, A.J. (1993) 'The Ethical Rationale for Drug-Free Sport', Ottawa, ON: Canadian Centre for Drug-Free Sport.

Cahn, S. (1994) *Coming on Strong: Gender and Sexuality in Twentieth-Century Women's Sport*, New York: The Free Press.

Caillois, R. (1961) *Man, Play, and Games*, New York: Free Press of Glencoe.

Carlson, A. (1991) 'When is a Woman not a Woman?', *Women's Sport and Fitness* (March): 24–29.

Cavell, S. (1969) *Must We Mean What We Say?*, New York: Scribners.

Chossudovsky, M. (1998) 'Financial Warfare' (circulated on the internet; contact Chossudovsky at chossudovsky@sprint.ca.

Cohen, G. (1993) *Women in Sport: Issues and Controversies*, Newbury Park, CA: Sage Publications.

Corea, G. (1985) *The Hidden Malpractice: How American Medicine Mistreats Women*, revised edition, New York: Harper Colophon Books.

Coubertin, P. de (1912) 'Women in the Olympic Games', *Olympic Review*.

Creedon, P. (ed.) (1994) *Women, Media and Sport*, California: Sage Publications.

D'Agostino, F. (1981) 'The Ethos of Games', *Journal of the Philosophy of Sport* 8: 7–18.

Dancy, J. (1993) *Moral Reasons*, Oxford: Blackwell.

De Wachter, F. (1985) 'In Praise of Chance: A Philosophical Analysis of the Element of Chance in Sports', *Journal of the Philosophy of Sport* 12: 52–61.

Dingeon, B. (1994) 'Gene Biochemistry and Gender Testing', *Olympic Message* 40: 65–68.

Dingeon, B., Hamon., P., Robert, M., Schamasch, P. and Pugeat, M. (1992) 'Sex Testing at the Olympics', *Nature* 358: 447.

Dixon, N. (1995) 'The Friendship Model of Filial Obligations', *Journal of Applied Philosophy* 12: 77–87.

Donceel, J. (1970) 'Immediate Animation and Delayed Hominization', *Theological Studies* 31(1): 76–105.

—— (1984) 'A Liberal Catholic's View', in *The Problem of Abortion*, ed. Joel Feinberg, Belmont, CA: Wadsworth Publishing Company, pp. 15–20.

Dreifus, C. (ed.) (1977) *Seizing Our Bodies: The Politics of Women's Health*, New York: Vintage/Random House.

Dubin, Charles L. (1990) *Commission of Inquiry into the Use of Drugs and Banned Practices Intended to Increase Athletic Performance*, Canadian Government Publishing Centre, Canada.

Dworkin, R. (1978) *Taking Rights Seriously*, Cambridge, MA: Harvard University Press.

—— (1986) *Law's Empire*, Cambridge, MA: Harvard University Press.

Eckhoff, T. and Sundby, N.K. (1988) *Rechtssysteme: eine systemtheoretische Einführung in die Rechtstheorie*, Berlin: Grüter.

Ehrenreich, B. (1997) *Blood Rites: Origins and History of the Passions of War*, New York: Henry Holt.

Ehrenreich, B. and English, D. (1989) *For Her Own Good: 150 Years of the Experts' Advice to Women*, Garden City, NY: Anchor Books.

Eichner, E.R. (1993) 'Sickle Cell Trait, Heroic Exercise, and Fatal Collapse', *Physicians and Sports Medicine* 21: 51–61.

Elster, J. (1992) *Local Justice. How Institutions Allocate Scarce Goods and Necessary Burdens*, New York: Russell Sage.

Engels, F. (1976 [1894]) *Anti-Dühring*, English translation of the third German edition of *Herrn Eugen Dührings Umwälzung der Wissenschaft*, Peking: Foreign Languages Press.

English, J. (1979) 'What Do Grown Children Owe Their Parents?', in *Having Children: Philosophical and Legal Reflections on Parenthood*, ed. Onora O'Neill and William Ruddick, New York: Oxford University Press, pp. 351–356.

—— (1995) 'Sex Equality in Sports', first printed in *Philosophy and Public Affairs* 7 (1978), reprinted in *Philosophic Inquiry in Sport*, 2nd edition, Champaign, IL: Human Kinetics, pp. 284–288.

Fairchild, D. (1987) 'Prolegomena to and Expressive Function of Sport', *Journal of the Philosophy of Sport* 14: 21–33.

Fausto-Sterling, A. (1985) *Myths of Gender: Biological Theories About Women and Men*, New York: Basic Books.

Ferguson-Smith, M.A. and Ferris, E. (1991) 'Gender Verification in Sport: The Need for Change?', *British Journal of Sport Medicine* 25: 17–20.

Fox, J.S. (1993) 'Gender Verification – What Purpose? What Price?', *British Journal of Sport Medicine* 27(3): 148–149.

Fraleigh, W. (1984) *Right Actions in Sport: Ethics for Contestants*, Champaign, IL: Human Kinetics Publishers.

Frye, M. (1983) *The Politics of Reality: Essays in Feminist Theory*, Freedom, CA: Crossing Press.

'Genetic Testing and Screening' (1995) in *Encyclopedia of Bioethics*, revised edition, vol. 2 (London: Simon & Schuster/Prentice Hall International.

Gettier, E (1963) 'Is Justified True Belief Knowledge?', *Analysis* 23(6): 121–123.

Gibson, J.H. (1993) *Performance versus Results*, Albany, NY: SUNY Press.

Gilberg, R. (1996) *Gull, men ingen grønne skoger? En vurdering av idretten i økologisk perspektiv* (An Evaluation of Sports from the Perspective of Ecology), The Norwegian Confederation of Sports/The Norwegian University for Sports and Physical Education.

Goffman, E. (1967) *Interaction Ritual. Essays on Face-to-Face Behavior*, New York: Pantheon Books.

Goldman, A. (1967) 'A Causal Theory of Knowledge' *Journal of Philosophy* 64: 357–372.

Gollnick, P.D. and Matoba, H. (1984) 'The Muscle Fiber Composition of Skeletal Muscle as a Predictor of Athletic Success. An Overview', *American Journal of Sports Medicine* 12: 121–217.

Gomberg, P. (1989) 'Marxism and Rationality', *American Philosophical Quarterly* 26: 53–62.

—— (1990a) 'Can a Partisan be a Moralist?', *American Philosophical Quarterly* 27: 71–79.

—— (1990b) 'Patriotism is Like Racism', *Ethics* 101: 144–150.

—— (1994) 'Universalism and Optimism', *Ethics* 104: 536–557.

—— (1995) 'Against *Competitive* Equal Opportunity', *Journal of Social Philosophy* 26: 59–74.

—— (1997) 'How Morality Works and Why It Fails: On Political Philosophy and Moral Consensus', *Journal of Social Philosophy* 28: 43–70.

Grant, Cooper N. (ed.) (1994) *The Human Genome Project: Deciphering the Blueprint of Heredity*, Mill Valley: University Science Books.

Greider, W. (1997) *One World, Ready or Not: The Manic Logic of Global Capitalism*, New York: Simon and Schuster. .

Grobet, L., Martin L.J.R., Poncelet, D., Pirottin, D., Brouwers, B., Riquet, J., Schoeberlein, A., Dunner, S., Menissier, F., Massabanda, J., Fries, R., Hanset, R. and Georges, M. (1997) 'A Deletion in the Bovine Myostatin Gene Causes the Double-Muscled Phenotype in Cattle', *Nature Genetics* 17: 71–74.

Grobet, L., Poncelet, D., Royo, L.J., Brouwers, B., Pirottin, D., Michaux, C., Menissier, F., Zanotti, M., Dunners, S. and Georges, M. (1998) 'Molecular Definition of an Allelic Series of Mutations Disrupting the Myostatin Function and Causing Double-Muscling in Cattle', *Mammalian Genome* 9: 210–213.

Guttmann, Allen (1978): *From Ritual to Record – The Nature of Modern Sports*, New York: Columbia University Press.

—— (1994a) *Games and Empires*, New York: Columbia University Press.

—— (1994b) *The Olympics: A History of the Modern Games*, Urbana, Chicago: University of Illinois Press.

Gutmann, Amy (1993) 'The Challenge of Multiculturalism in Political Ethics', *Philosophy and Public Affairs* 22 (3): 171–206.

Handyside, A. (1996) 'Preimplantation Genetic Diagnosis Today', *Human Reproduction* vol. II, supplement 1: 139–151.

Hargreaves, J. (1995) 'A Historical Look at the Changing Symbolic Meanings of the Female Body in Western Sport', in *Sport as Symbol, Symbols in Sport*, ed. F. van der Merwe, ISHPES Studies/Germany: Academia Verlag, vol. 4, pp. 249–259.

Hart, H.L.A. (1994) *The Concept of Law*, 2nd edition, Oxford: Clarendon Press.

Haugeland, J. (1998) *Having Thought*, Cambridge, MA: Harvard University Press.

Hay, E. (1981) 'The Stella Walsh Case', *Olympic Review* 162 (April): 221–222.

Heinilä, Kalevi (1982) 'The Totalization Process in International Sport', *Sportwissenschaft* 2: 235–254.

Hoberman, J. (1996) *Mortal Engines. The Science of Performance and the Dehumanization of Modern Sports*, New York: The Free Press.

Hubbard, R. and Lowe, M. (eds) (1983) *Women's Nature: Rationalizations of Inequality*, New York: Pergamon Press, the Athene series.

Hughes, R. and Cloakley, J. (1991) 'Positive Deviance among Athletes: The Implications of Overconformity to the Sport Ethic, *Sociology of Sport Journal* 8: 307–325.

Huizinga, J. (1950) *Homo Ludens. A Study of the Play Element in Culture*, London, Routledge & Kegan Paul.

Humphreys, D. (1997) ' "Skinheads Go Mainstream"? Snowboarding and Alternative Youth', *International Review for the Sociology of Sport* 32: 2.

Inizan, Françoise (1994) 'Masters and Slaves of Time', *Olympic Review* (July/August): 306–310.

Jhally, S. (1998) ' "Free at Last" – Sponsorship, Fanship, and Fascism', *Journal of Sport & Social Issues* 22(2): 224–226.

Jones, J.D. and Kleiner, D.M. (1996) 'Awareness and Identification of Athletes with Sickle Cell Disorders at Historically Black Colleges and Universities', *Journal of Athletic Training* 31: 286–287.

Kambadur, R., Sharma, M., Smith, T.P.L and Bass, J.J. (1997) 'Mutations in Myostatin (GDF8) in Double-Muscled Belgian Blue and Piedmontese Cattle', *Genome Research* 7: 910–916.

Kerle, K.K. and Nishimura, K.D. (1996) 'Exertional Collapse and Sudden Death Associated with Sickle Cell Trait', *Military Medicine* 161: 766–767.

Kirby, S. and Brackenridge, C. (1997) 'Coming to Terms: Sexual Abuse in Sport', unpublished manuscript.

Lander, L. (1988) *Images of Bleeding: Menstruation as Ideology*, New York: Orlando Press.

Larmore, C. (1996) *The Morals of Modernity*, Cambridge: Cambridge University Press.

Lasch, C. (1979) *The Culture of Narcissism: American Life in an Age of Diminishing Expectations*, New York: Warner.

Lefkowitz, M. and Fant, M. (1985) *Women's Life in Greece and Rome: A Source Book in Translation*, Baltimore, MD: The Johns Hopkins University Press.

Le-Gallais, D., Prefaut, C., Mercier, J., Bile, A., Bogui, P. and Lonsdorfer, J. (1994) 'Sickle Cell Trait as a Limiting Factor for High-Level Performance in a Semi-Marathon', *International Journal of Sports Medicine* 15: 399–402.

Leitch, A.G., Clancy, L. and Flenley, D.C. (1975) 'Maximal Oxygen Uptake, Lung Volume and Ventilatory Response to Carbon Dioxide and Hypoxia in a Pair of Identical Twin Athletes', *Clinical Science and Molecular Medicine* 48: 235–238.

Lenin, V. (1970 [1916]) *Imperialism, the Highest Stage of Capitalism*, in *Selected Works*, vol. 1, Moscow: Progress Publishers.

Lenskyj, H. (1984) *Sport Integration or Separation*, Ottawa: Fitness and Amateur Sport.

—— (1986) *Out of Bounds: Women, Sport and Sexuality*, Toronto: The Women's Press.

Lindsey, L.L. (1990) *Gender Roles: A Sociological Perspective*, Englewood Cliffs, NJ: Prentice Hall.

Loland, Sigmund (1989) *Fair Play i idrettskonkurranser – et moralsk normsystem*, unpublished PhD dissertation, The Norwegian University College for Sport and Phys. Ed., Oslo.

—— (1995) 'Coubertin's Ideology of Olympism from the Perspective of the History of Ideas', *Olympika: International Journal of Olympic Studies* 4: 49–78.

—— (1998a) 'Fair Play – Historical Anachronism or a Topical Ideal?', in *Ethics and Sport*, ed. J. Parry and M. McNamee, London: Chapman and Hall, pp. 79–103.

—— (1998b) 'The Record Dilemma'. Paper presented at the 20th World Congress in Philosophy, Boston, 9–16 August.

Loland, S., Sandberg, P. and Skirstad, B (1995) 'Kjønnstester i idretten', mimeograph.

MacAloon, J. (1984a) *Rite, Drama, Festival, Spectacle: Rehearsals Toward a Theory of Cultural Performance*, Philadelphia: Institute for the Study of Human Issues.

—— (1984b) 'Olympic Games and the Theory of Spectacle in Modern Societies', *Rite, Drama, Festival, Spectacle: Rehearsals Toward a Theory of Cultural Performance*, Philadelphia: Institute for the Study of Human Issues.

—— (1991) 'The Turn of Two Centuries: Sport and the Politics of Intercultural Relations', in *Sport, The Third Millennium*, ed. F. Landry, M. Landry and M. Yerles, Saint-Foy: Les Presses de l'Université Laval.

MacIntyre, A. (1984) 'Is Patriotism a Virtue?', Lindley Lecture, Philosophy Department, University of Kansas.

MacKinnon, C. (1987) 'Women, Self-Possession and Sport', *Feminism Unmodified: Discourses on Life and Law*, Cambridge, MA: Harvard University Press, pp. 117–126.

Mahoney, J. (1984) *Bioethics and Belief*, London: Sheed & Ward.

Mandell, R.D. (1984) *Sport – A Cultural History*, New York: Columbia University Press.

Marshall, E. (1998a) 'GENOMICS: A Second Private Genome Project', *Science* 281: 1121.

—— (1998b) 'Hubris and the Human Genome', *Science* 280: 994–995.

Martin, D., Carl, K. and Lehnertz, K. (1991) *Handbuch Trainingslehre*, Schorndorf: Hofman.

McCormick, R.A. (1991) 'Who or What is a Pre-Embryo?', *Kennedy Institute of Ethics Journal* 1(1): 1–15.

McDowell, J. (1998) *Mind, Value, and Reality*, Cambridge, MA: Harvard University Press. .

McNamee, M. (1995) 'Theoretical Limitations in Codes of Ethical Conduct', in *Leisure Cultures: Values, Genders, Lifestyles*, ed. Graham McFee, Wilf Murphy and Garry Whannel, Eastbourne: Leisure Studies Associaton, pp. 145–157.

McPherron, A.C. and Lee, S.J. (1997) 'Double Muscling in Cattle Due to Mutations in the Myostatin Gene', *Proceedings of the National Academy of Sciences of the United States of America* 94: 12457–12461.

Messner, M. and Sabo, D. (eds) (1990) *Sport, Men and the Gender Order: Critical Feminist Perspectives*, Champaign, IL: Human Kinetics.

—— (1994) *Sex, Violence and Power in Sports: Rethinking Masculinity*, Freedom, CA: Crossing Press.

Mill, J. (1972) *Utilitarianism, On Liberty, and Considerations on Representative Government*, ed. H. Acton, New York: E.P. Dutton & Co.

Miller, D. (1995) *On Nationality*, Oxford: Clarendon Press.

Monahan, T. (1987) 'Sickle Cell Trait: A Risk for Sudden Death During Physical Activity?', *Physicians and Sports Medicine* 15: 143–145.

Morgan, W.J. (1994) *Leftist Theories of Sport. A Critique and Reconstruction*, Urbana, IL: University of Illinois Press,

Morgan, W.J. and Meier, K. (eds) (1995) *Philosophic Inquiry in Sport*, Champaign, IL: Human Kinetic Publishers.

Munthe, C. (1996) *The Moral Roots of Prenatal Diagnosis*, Gothenburg: Centre for Research Ethics.

—— (1998) 'On Choosing Children', in *Applied Ethics*, vol. 2, ed. P. Kampits, K. Kokai and A. Weiberg, Kirchberg am Wechsel: Austrian Ludwig Wittgenstein Society.

—— (1999a) *Pure Selection. The Ethics of Preimplantation Genetic Diagnosis and Choosing Children without Abortion*, Gothenburg: Acta Universitatis Gothenburgensis.

—— (1999b) 'Genetic Treatment and Pre-selection. Ethical Similarities and Differences', in *Gene Therapy: Ethical Legal and Social Perspectives*, ed. A. Nordgren, Uppsala: Centre for Research Ethics.

Nagel, T. (1995) *Other Minds: Critical Essays 1969–1994*, Oxford: Clarendon Press.

Nathanson, S. (1989) 'In Defense of Moderate Patriotism', *Ethics* 99: :535–552.

Nisbet, R. (1994) *History of The Idea of Progress*, London: Transaction Publications.

Noddings, N. (1984) *Caring: A Feminine Approach to Ethics and Moral Education*, Berkeley: University of California Press.

Nozick, R. (1981) *Philosophical Explanations*, Cambridge, MA: Harvard University Press.

Ofstad, H. (1989) *Our Contempt for Weakness: Nazi Norms and Values – and Our Own*, Stockholm: Almqvist & Wiksell International.

Okruhlik, K. (1995) 'Gender and the Biological Sciences', *Canadian Journal of Philosophy* 20: 21–42.

Olsen, E. 'Drillo', Larsen, Y. and Semb, N.J. (1994) *Effektiv Fotball* (Effective Soccer), Oslo: Gyldendal.

Parfit, D. (1984) *Reasons and Persons*, Oxford: Clarendon Press.

Perelman, C (1980) *Justice, Law, and Argument: Essays on Moral and Legal Justification*, Dordrecht: D. Reidel.

Perkins, H. (1989) 'Teaching the Nations How to Play: Sport and Society in the British Empire and Commonwealth', *International Journal of the History of Sport* 6: 145–155.

Plato (1961) *Republic*, in *Plato: The Collected Dialogues*, ed. E. Hamilton and H. Cairns, Princeton, NJ: Princeton University Press, pp. 575–844.

—— (1969) 'Phaedo', in *The Collected Dialogues of Plato*, ed. E. Hamilton and H. Cairns, Princeton, NJ: Princeton University Press.

Postow, B. (ed.) (1995) 'Women and Masculine Sports', in *Philosophic Inquiry in Sport*, ed. William J. Morgan and Klaus V. Meier, Champaign, IL: Human Kinetics, pp. 323–328.

Ramsay, P. (1970) 'Reference Points in deciding About Abortion', in *The Morality of Abortion: Legal and Historical Perspectives*, ed. J.T. Noonan Jr, Cambridge, MA.

Rawls, J. (1971) *A Theory of Justice*, Cambridge MA: Harvard University Press.

Rescher, N. (1995) *Luck. The Brilliant Randomness of Everyday Life*, New York: Farrar, Straus, Giroux..

Rigauer, B. (1969) *Sport und Arbeit*, Frankfurt am Main: Suhrkamp.

Roberts, G.C., Treasure, D.C. and Kavussanu, M. (1997): 'Motivation in Physical Activity Contexts: An Achievement Goal Perspective', *Advances in Motivation and Achievement* 10: 413–447.

Robertson, J.A. (1994) *Children of Choice. Freedom and the New Reproductive Technologies*, Princeton, NJ: Princeton University Press.

Roden, D. (1980) 'Baseball and the Quest for National Dignity in Meiji Japan.' *American Historical Review* 85: 511–534.

Salkie, M.L., Gordon, P.A., Rigal, W.M., Lam, H., Wilson, J.B., Headlee, M.E. and Huisman, T.H.J. (1982) 'Hb A2-Canada or Alpha 2 Delta 2 99 (G1) Asp Replaced by Asn, a Newly Discovered Delta Chain Variant with Increased Oxygen Affinity Occurring in Cis to Beta-Thalassemia', *Hemoglobin* 6: 223–231.

Schiebinger, L. (1989) *The Mind Has No Sex? Women in the Origins of Modern Science*, Cambridge, MA: Harvard University Press.

—— (1993) *Nature's Body: Gender in the Making of Modern Science*, Boston: Beacon Press.

Schneider, A.J. (1992) 'Harm, Athletes' Rights and Doping Control', in *First International Symposium for Olympic Research*, ed. R.K. Barney and K.V. Meier, London, ON: University of Western Ontario, Centre for Olympic Studies, pp. 164–172.

—— (1993) 'Doping in Sport and the Perversion Argument', in *The Relevance of the Philosophy of Sport*, ed. G. Gebauer, Berlin, Germany: Academia Verlag, pp. 117–128.

—— (1995) 'Gender, Sexuality and Sport in America', *Journal of the Philosophy of Sport* 22: 136–143.

Schneider, A. J. and Butcher, R. B. (1993) 'For the Love of the Game: A Philosophical Defense of Amateurism', *Quest* 45(4): 460–469.

—— (1994) 'Why Olympic Athletes Should Avoid the Use and Seek the Elimination of Performance-Enhancing Substances and Practices in the Olympic Games', *Journal of the Philosophy of Sport* 20, 21: 64–81. .

—— (1997) 'Fair Play as Respect for the Game', *Journal of the Philosophy of Sport* 24: 1–22.

Schreiber, C.T. (1979) *Changing Places: Men and Women in Transitional Occupations*, Cambridge, MA: MIT Press.

Searle, J. (1979) *Speech Acts. An Essay in the Philosophy of Language*, Cambridge, MA: Harvard University Press.

Sedivy, R., Bankl, H.C., Stimpfl, T., Bankl, H. and Kurkciyan, I. (1997) 'Sudden Unexpected Death of a Young Marathon Runner as a Result of Bronchial Malformation', *Modern Pathology* 10: 247–251.

Serrat, A. and de Herreros, A.G. (1996) 'Gender Verification in Sports by PCR Amplification of SRY and DYZ1 Y Chromosome-Specific Sequences; Presence of DYZ1 Repeat in Female Athletes', *British Journal of Sport Medicine* 30: 310–312.

Sherif, M. *et al.* (1988) *The Robbers' Cave Experiment: Intergroup Conflict and Co-operation*, Middletown, CT: Wesleyan University Press.

Sherwin, S. (1992) *No Longer Patient: Feminist Ethics and Health Care*, Philadelphia: Temple University Press.

Signer, E.N., Dubrova, Y.E., Jeffreys, A.J., Wilde, C., Finch, L.M.P., Wells, M. and Peaker, M. (1998) 'DNA Fingerprinting Dolly', *Nature* 394: 329.

Simon, R. (1995) 'Good Competition and Drug-Enhanced Performance', in *Philosophic Inquiry in Sport*, ed. W.J. Morgan and K. Meier, Champaign, IL: Human Kinetics, pp. 209–214.

Singer, P. (1993) *Practical Ethics*, 2nd edition, Cambridge: Cambridge University Press.

Skillen, T. (1998) 'Sport is for Losers', in *Ethics and Sport*, ed. M.J. McNamee and S.J. Parry, London: Routledge, pp. 169–181.

Skirstad, B. (1996) 'Kjönnstesting av kvinnelige idrettsutövere. Etikk på mannes premisser', mimeograph.

Solter, D. (1998) 'Dolly *is* a Clone – and No Longer Alone', *Nature* 394: 315.

Spaulding, A. (1911) *America's National Game*, New York: American Sports Publishing.

Spears, B. (1988) 'Tryphosa, Melpomene, Nadia, and Joan: The IOC and Women's Sport', in *The Olympic Games in Transition*, ed. J. Segrave and D. Chu, Champaign, IL: Human Kinetics Publishers, pp. 365–374. .

Steinbock, B. (1992) *Life before Birth. The Moral Status of Embryos and Fetuses*, Oxford: Oxford University Press.

Suits, B. (1978) *The Grasshopper: Games, Life and Utopia*, Toronto: Toronto University Press.

—— (1988) 'Tricky Triad: Games, Play and Sport', *Journal of Philosophy of Sport* 13: 1–9.

—— (1995) 'The Elements of Sport', in *Philosophic Inquiry in Sport*, ed. W.J. Morgan and K. Meier, Champaign, IL: Human Kinetics, pp. 8–15.

Sutton-Smith, B. (1974) 'Towards an Anthropology of Play', *The Association for the Anthropological Study of Play Newsletter* 1(2): 8–15.

Szabo, G., Dallmann, G., Muller, G., Patthy, L., Soller, M. and Varga, L. (1998) 'A Deletion in the Myostatin Gene Causes the Compact (CMPT) Hypermuscular Mutation in Mice', *Mammalian Genome* 9: 671–672.

Szekely, E. (1988) *Never Too Thin*, Toronto: The Women's Press.

Tajfel, H. (1981) *Human Groups and Social Categories*, Cambridge: Cambridge University Press.

Tangen, J.O. (1997) 'Samfunnets idrett: En sosiologisk analyse av idrett som sosialt system, dets evolusjon og funksjon fra arkaisk til moderne tid', PhD dissertation, University of Oslo.

Tännsjö, T. (1998) *Hedonistic Utilitarianism*, Edinburgh: Edinburgh University Press.

—— (1999) *Coercive Care: The Ethics of Choice in Health and Medicine*, London and New York: Routledge.

Tavris, C. (1977) *The Longest War: Sex Differences in Perspective*, New York: Harcourt Brace Jovanovich.

Taylor, C. (1985) *Philosophy and the Human Sciences*, Philosophical Papers 2, Cambridge: Cambridge University Press.

—— (1989) *Sources of the Self: The Making of the Modern Identity*, Cambridge: Cambridge University Press.

—— (1992a) *Ethics of Authenticity*, Cambridge, MA: Harvard University Press.

—— (1992b) *The Politics of Recognition*, Princeton, NJ: Princeton University Press.

Taylor, G. (1985) *Pride, Shame, and Guilt*, Oxford: Oxford University Press.

Tolstoy, L. (1968) *Tolstoy's Writings on Civil Disobedience and Non-Violence*, New York: New American Library.

Tong, R. (1995) 'What's Distinctive About Feminist Bioethics?' ed. F. Baylis, J. Downie, B. Freedman, B. Hoffmaster, S.

Tooley, M. (1984) *Abortion and Infanticide*, Oxford: Oxford University Press.

Trⱥnøy, K.-E. (1986) *Vitenskapen – samfunnsmakt og livsform*, Oslo: Universitetsforlaget.

Travis, C. (1996) 'Meaning's Role in Truth', *Mind* 105: 451–566.

Tuttle, L. (1986) *Encyclopaedia of Feminism*, Essex: Longman.

van der Hagen, B. (1995) 'Medisinske problemer omkring bruk av kjønnstester av idrettsjenter', mimeograph.

Verlinsky, Y. and Kuliev, A. (1998) 'Progress in Preimplantation Genetics', *Journal of Assisted Reproduction and Genetics* 15(1): 9–11.

Verlinsky, Y., Munné, S., Simpson, J.L., Kuliev, A.A.A., Ray, P., Sermon, K., Martin, R., Strom, C., Van Stairteghem, A., Veiga, A., Drury, K., Williams, S., Ginsberg, N. and Wilton, L. (1997) 'Current Status of Preimplantation Diagnosis', *Journal of Assisted Reproduction and Genetics* 14(2): 72–75.

Vold, R. (1995) 'Juridisk utredning om kjønnstesting', mimeograph.

Wakayama, T., Perry, A.C.F., Zuccotti, M., Johnson, K.R. and Yanagimachi, R. (1998) 'Full-Term Development of Mice from Enucleated Oocytes Injected with Cumulus Cell Nuclei', *Nature* 394: 369–374.

Weiss, P. (1969) *Sport: A Philosophical Inquiry*, Carbondale, IL: Southern Illinois University Press.

Williams, B. (1973) 'Ethical Consistency', *Problems of the Self*, Cambridge: Cambridge University Press, pp. 166–186.

Williamson, D., Langdown, J.V., Myles, T., Mason, C., Henthorn, J.S. and Davies, S.C. (1992) 'Polycythaemia and Microcytosis Arising from the Combination of a New High Oxygen Affinity Haemoglobin (Hb Luton Alpha 89 His->Leu) and Alpha Thalassemia Trait', *British Journal of Haematology* 82: 621–622.

Wilmut, I., Schnieke, A.E., McWhir, J., Kind, A.J. and Campbell, K.H. (1997) 'Viable Offspring Derived from Fetal and Adult Mammalian Cells', *Nature* 385: 810–813.

Wittgenstein, L. (1953) *Philosophical Investigations*, trans. G.E.M. Anscombe, Oxford: Blackwell.

Wolfe, M.L. (1989) 'Correlates of Adaptive and Maladaptive Musical Performance Anxiety', *Medical Problems of Reforming Artists*, March: 49–56.

Wright, Georg Henrik von (1991) *Vitenskapen og fornuften*, Oslo: Cappelen.

Young, I.M. (1995) 'The Exclusion of Women From Sport: Conceptual and Existential Dimensions', first published in *Philosophy in Context* (1979) 9: 44–53, reprinted in *Philosophic Inquiry in Sport*, 2nd edition (1995), ed. W.J. Morgan and K. Meier, Champaign, IL: Human Kinetic Publishers, pp. 262–266.

Zita, J. (1988) 'The Premenstrual Syndrome: Dis-Easing the Female Cycle', *Hypatia* 3(1): 77–99.

Index

Aarnio, A. 39
aesthetic quality of sport 1, 68, 17, 22,
   168, 169
Albright, M. 96
Ali, M. 94
alienation 91, 130
altruism 72, 77, 79
amateur ethos 52
amennorrhea 127, 128
amphetamine 200
anabolic steroids 47, 120, 188, 194,
   200
Appiah, K. 59, 60
Archetti, E. 53
Aristotle 15, 36, 111, 125, 132, 158,
   179
Arneson, R. 170 n. 5
Aryan race 12
Ashworth, D. 230 n. 6

Bach, J.S. 106
Bailey, D. 51
Bairner, A. 61
Baker, G. 177, 180, 182 n. 7
Baker, W. 67
Barr test (or, buccal smear test) 117,
   131
Ben-Ze'ev, A. 86 n. 8
beta-blockers 192, 200
Birrell, S. 131
Blau, F.D. 130
blood doping 121, 190, 206, 207, 220,
   227
Bluestone, N. 124
Blum, L. 86 n. 3
Bohr, N. 155 n. 4
Bordo, S. 127
Bouchard, C. 43

Brackenridge, C. 129
Breivik, G. 4, 141, 157, 170 n. 1
Brohm, J.M. 42
Broverman, I. 128
Brown, W. 62, 64, 189
Browne, R.J. 230 n. 11
buccal smear test (or, Barr test) 117,
   131
Butcher, R.B. 123, 137 n. 1, 185, 196,
   213, 214, 215

Cahn, S. 126
Caillois, R. 171 n. 19
Camus, A. 157
capitalism 42, 91, 92, 95
Carlson, A. 116, 121, 122
Caucasian 107, 114
Cavell, S. 182 n. 8
cheating 113, 116, 119, 186, 187, 193,
   195, 214
Chossudovsky, M. 95
Clarke, R. (Renée Richards) 131
Cloakley, H. 199 n. 3
cocaine 200
Cole, C.L. 131
Comaneci, N. 33
commercialisation 12, 25, 30, 36, 37,
   53, 205
concentration camp 63
contempt for weakness 2, 10, 12, 13,
   16, 18, 19, 20, 21, 22, 25, 30, 31,
   36, 43
Corea, G. 131
correspondence theory of truth 141
Creedon, P. 124, 127
Croke, Archbishop 61
Cruyff, J. 85